A GENEALOGY OF
MARION'S PHILOSOPHY OF RELIGION

Indiana Series in the Philosophy of Religion

Merold Westphal, editor

A Genealogy
of Marion's Philosophy
# of Religion

Apparent Darkness

Tamsin Jones

Indiana University Press
Bloomington & Indianapolis

This book is a publication of

Indiana University Press
601 North Morton Street
Bloomington, Indiana 47404-3797 USA

www.iupress.indiana.edu

Telephone orders 800-842-6796
Fax orders   812-855-7931
Orders by e-mail iuporder@indiana.edu

∞ The paper used in this publication
meets the minimum requirements of
the American National Standard for
Information Sciences—Permanence of
Paper for Printed Library Materials,
ANSI Z39.48-1992.

Manufactured in the United States of
America

Library of Congress Cataloging-in-
Publication Data

Jones, Tamsin, [date]
  A genealogy of Marion's philosophy of
religion : apparent darkness / Tamsin
Jones.
      p. cm.—(Indiana series in the
philosophy of religion)
  Includes bibliographical references
(p.   ) and index.
  ISBN 978-0-253-35594-2 (cloth : alk.
paper) — ISBN 978-0-253-22286-2
(pbk. : alk. paper) 1. Marion,
Jean-Luc, 1946–   2. Phenomenological
theology. 3. Negative theology.
4. Gregory, of Nyssa, Saint, ca. 335–ca.
394. 5. Dionysius, the Areopagite,
Saint, 1st cent. I. Title.
  BT40.J66 2011
  210.92—dc22

                              2010030729

      1 2 3 4 5 16 15 14 13 12 11

CONTENTS

CONTENTS

ACKNOWLEDGMENTS

This work would not have been possible without advice, support, and guidance from several quarters. First of all, the communities of Harvard University and Harvard Divinity School provided a fertile environment in which this project could grow in its original incarnation as a doctoral dissertation. I am very grateful to my advisor, Sarah Coakley (now at Cambridge), for her counsel and support throughout. She has been a vital influence in my intellectual formation, and her rigor has always challenged me to think more systematically. Truly, any achievement of conciseness of expression is due to her efforts. I owe my thanks to Amy Hollywood, whose sharp and insightful readings of several drafts invariably improved later versions. Other faculty at Harvard influenced my research and helped me to think through aspects of the book at various stages, especially David Lamberth, Thomas A. Lewis, Robert Orsi, Parimal Patil, Francis Schüssler Fiorenza, and Ronald Thiemann. I am especially grateful to Nicholas Constas, who not only led me deeper into the intricate beauty of the writings of the Cappadocians and of Dionysius the Areopagite but was also very formative in the initial moments of proposing this research.

Many of my colleagues at Harvard, past and present, provided a resource not only for tremendous cooperative learning but also for editing, advice, and feedback on various aspects of this work as well as support through the occasional battlefields of graduate studies. I would mention, especially, Mary Anderson, Niki Clements, Carly Daniel-Hughes, Sutopa Dasgupta, Ben Dunning, Paul Dafydd Jones, Piotr Malysz, Mark McInroy, Brenna Moore, Cameron Partridge, Rachel Smith, Charles Stang, Robert St. Hilaire, and Mara Willard.

I have also benefited from interactions with various scholars in other academic institutions. Above all, Richard Kearney (Boston College) has been a wonderful teacher and conversation partner, as well as an acute reader of the work. I am immensely grateful for the clarity of his own writing, his enthusiasm, and his intellectual generosity. I have also profited by advice from Khaled Anatolios (Weston Jesuit School of

Theology), John Behr (Saint Vladimir's Theological Seminary), Philip Clayton (Claremont), Kathryn Tanner (University of Chicago), Scot Douglass (University of Colorado), and Morwenna Ludlow (Exeter University). I am especially grateful to Christina Gschwandtner (University of Scranton) and Kevin Hart (University of Virginia) for their supportive and insightful suggestions and to Merold Westphal (Fordham), my general editor, and Dee Mortensen, my sponsoring editor, at Indiana University Press.

And, of course, I am grateful to Jean-Luc Marion who, very early on when I pressed him about his intellectual inheritance of Gregory of Nyssa, encouraged me with an enigmatic smile to explore the general line of this research. His thought captured my attention from the very first pages of *God Without Being*. Wrestling with his ideas has been, and will continue to be, a profoundly rewarding endeavor.

I wish to acknowledge Harvard Divinity School and the Social Science and Humanities Research Council of Canada, which provided me with financial support throughout my doctoral studies, and the Committee on the Study of Religion, which employed me to teach and advise undergraduates in Harvard College.

It remains to thank my family and friends without whom this would have been a profoundly lonely project. Thank you to Elizabeth, Leeanna, Melanie, Hilary, Jonathan, Michele, Jim, Rachael, Benjamin, Daniel, Jessica, Emily, Catherine, Matthew, Terry, Leslie, and Mandy. A special thank-you goes to those whose presence, support, and love proves the defining example of a phenomenon that "saturates": to Devlin, Sascha, and Simone.

A GENEALOGY OF
MARION'S PHILOSOPHY OF RELIGION

Introduction

Jean-Luc Marion's dense and provocative writings have ignited both devotees and vehement critics. A member of l'Académie française, he has enlivened debates within and also between phenomenological and theological discourses.[1] As a historian of philosophy, he is admired as one of the leading interpreters of Descartes writing today.[2] Yet as a theologically oriented phenomenologist, he is often identified as the *bête noire* of the "new phenomenology."

Much scholarship on Marion has engaged in a debate over his ideological allegiances: theological versus phenomenological. I contend that this particular line of commentary occludes rather than illuminates Marion's intellectual enterprise. In particular, it distracts from a more critical analysis of the internal coherence of Marion's thought, an analysis that would parse the tension, not between philosophy and theology, but rather between two philosophical methods and the two (apophatic) theologies with which they intersect.

For this reason, in this study I intend to read Marion *cohesively* (at times distinguishing between the "theological" and the "phenomenological" without rendering them necessarily disjunctive), in order, precisely, to probe the *coherence* of his corpus. His entire philosophical enterprise is dominated by a positive and a negative motivation: positively, he seeks to return to all things (the "things themselves"); and negatively, he resists the objectification or idolatrous conceptualization of any thing. Holding the opposing forces of these motivations together produces the paradoxical juxtaposition of "givenness" and "saturation," the radical manifestation as well as the endless hiddenness of phenomena, the universality of a rigorous method and the contextuality of infinite interpretation. It is the way in which Marion holds these two elements together that yields such a fecund and original phenomenology. Nevertheless, these tensions may also usher in his undoing. My task is to explore whether there is a point where the brilliant paradoxical balance can no longer be maintained and the various tensions dissolve into incoherence.

I propose a novel approach to examining Marion's philosophy, namely, the analysis of his use of patristic sources, specifically, the Greek Fathers. This analysis functions as an illuminating lens through which I evaluate the tension central to Marion's philosophical project in itself. In order to explain the approach of my argument, I first need to introduce certain basic themes in Marion's thought and survey trends in the reception of it.

Marion has written widely on topics ranging from aesthetics to late medieval and early modern history of philosophy, from biblical exegesis to the discourse of *eros*. As a result, his intellectual identity and disciplinary location is a contentious question. His thought is usually separated into distinct categories that follow a loose chronology. First, there is his research in the history of philosophy, which centers on Descartes: *Sur l'ontologie grise de Descartes. Science cartésienne et savoir aristotélicien dans les 'Regulae'* (1975), *Sur la théologie blanche de Descartes. Analogie, creation, des vérités éternelle et fondment* (1981), and *Sur le prisme métaphysique de Descartes. Constitution et limites de l'onto-théologie dans la pensée cartésienne* (1986). Secondly, there are his theological writings: *L'idole et la distance: cinq etudes* (1977), *Dieu sans l'être. Hors-texte* (1982), and *Prolégomènes à la charité* (1986). Thirdly, Marion's need to ground his ideas more phenomenologically in the face of many criticisms issued in a final category of writings: *Réduction et donation: Recherches sur Husserl, Heidegger et la phénoménologie* (1989); *Étant donné: Essai d'une phénoménologie de la donation* (1997); and *De surcroît: Études sur les phénomènes saturés* (2001). More recently, both *Le phénomènes érotiques: Six meditations* (2003) and *Au lieu de soi: L'approche de Saint Augustin* (2008) have shifted his entire discourse into the key signature of love.[3]

Despite the dominance of this model for mapping the periods and categories of Marion's thought, it remains unsatisfactory. First of all, it encourages a potentially pejorative meta-narrative on the progression of his thought. Marion is cast as a rigorous historian of early modern philosophy who subsequently experiments in conservative, confessional theology and who seeks, finally, to shore up his theological interests via the resources of phenomenology. This narrative allows for Marion's critics to separate his Cartesian research from the rest of his thought and leave it, for the most part, respected but unexamined. At the same time, it enables an obsessive focus on the question of the relationship between Marion's phenomenology and his theology. Christina M. Gschwandtner has challenged both the lack of attention to the Cartesian writings and the excessive fixation with defining Marion either as a phenomenologist who has no business intruding into the theological domain or as a theologian who masquerades as a phenomenologist. Her detailed and thorough study of Marion persuasively argues that the roots of his ideas can be found within his work on Descartes.[4]

In agreement with Gschwandtner, I assume the basic *cohesiveness* of Marion's corpus to date. Behind his work on Descartes, his theological writings, and his meditations on *eros,* on givenness, and on saturation, there is one thinker who is motivated by the same set of questions and concerns. Part of the problem with the disjunctive approach is that the narrow focus on the question of Marion's theological versus his phenomenological identity distorts the analysis and interpretation. Marion is read according to one polarity or another. He is seen as too theological,[5] not theological enough,[6] or not theological in the right way.[7] He is read, on the one hand, as having destroyed the "subject" and forbidden entrance to the role that interpretation plays,[8] and, on the other, as remaining too "egological."[9] He is too much of a hermeneut and not hermeneutical enough.[10] How can these conflicting interpretations be drawn from one and the same thinker? I argue that reading Marion with only these polemics in view distracts readers from a different and more significant set of oppositional forces in his thought. In other words, these polemics draw attention away from the presence of real tension within his thought, a tension that makes possible the contradictory readings in the first place. In this study I read against the grain, paying little attention to making distinctions between phenomenological and theological arguments in order, precisely, to step back and look at how more fundamental tensions arise in Marion's work.

The oppositional forces emerge out of the twofold motivation of all of Marion's writing. First, following Husserlian phenomenology, there is a commitment to return to the "things themselves." (This return to the "things themselves" already implies an attempted correction of the Kantian emphasis on the "thing-in-itself," which, because of the epistemological gap between the *noumena* and *phenomena,* one can never actually reach.) Marion radicalizes this principle even further than Husserl by insisting that the return to the "things themselves" must be construed as a return to *all* phenomena and a refusal to forbid, a priori, the appearance of any phenomenon.

The second overarching motivation propelling Marion's thought is the attempt to free those phenomena to which one returns from all constraints, especially from metaphysical constraints (e.g., the horizons of being—spatiality and temporality—and the horizon of the transcendental ego). In other words, Marion wants to secure the possibility of phenomena to "show themselves" freely and fully, without any subjective influence affecting that showing:

> I have but one theme: if the phenomenon is defined as what *shows itself* in and from itself (Heidegger), instead of as what admits constitution (Husserl), this *self* can be attested only inasmuch as the phenomenon first *gives itself*... the thought that does not do justice to the given remains most of the time and first of all powerless to receive a number of phenomena for what they are—givens that show themselves. Also, it excludes from the field of manifestation not only many phenomena, but above all those most endowed with meaning and those that are most powerful. Only a phenomenology of givenness can return to the things themselves because, in order to return to them, it is necessary first to see them, therefore to see them as they come and, in the end, to bear their unpredictable landing.[11]

Marion's concern is that if we *predetermine* the limits of what can and cannot appear as a phenomenon, restricting the field of possible phenomena to those things that can be objectified or adequately conceptualized, then we exclude those phenomena whose very significant impact on our lives often exceeds that which we can conceptually control or manage. These excessive phenomena "saturate" or overwhelm our cognitive capacities such that we cannot properly understand or define the phenomena. The two sides of Marion's philosophical project might be put together succinctly: Marion is, above all, a thinker of "givenness," but also of the potentially "saturating" quality of givenness.

Tensions emerge from this twofold motivation.[12] On the one hand, we find that the attempt to justify the inclusion of all phenomena, even "excessive" phenomena once refused a place at the philosophical table, compels Marion to secure his phenomenological method as a "rigorous science" and claim the status of "first philosophy"[13] for his phenomenology of givenness. This attempt to secure the foundations of his phenomenology arises in the face of criticisms that his thought "smuggles in" theological claims and "abandons" the strict neutrality of Husserl's method. I contend that this aspect of Marion's thought is too quickly glossed over in much scholarship. Indeed, it could be suggested that an obsessive need to excavate and expel any signs of *theological dogmatism* in the corpus, while expected, given Marion's intellectual context within a post-1968 Paris, has nonetheless distracted readers from potential *philosophical dogmatisms.*

On the other hand, the strong anti-idolatry impulse in Marion compels him to guard against the cognitive containment of phenomena. In fact, Marion will argue boldly that this resistance comes from the phenomena themselves. Certain phenomena can never be adequately defined, but only endlessly interpreted. The resultant tension between these two impulses—to justify the inclusion of all phenomena in philosophical discourse and to refuse to constrain said phenomena by any single interpretation—has not been sufficiently explored. This tension underlies what is most creative and provocative in Marion's enterprise, but its final coherence must be tested.

Another reason that Marion is such an exciting yet difficult thinker to read is his intense engagement with a broad range of Western thought from Augustine and Aquinas to Kant, Husserl, and Derrida. One of the significant tasks of interpreting Marion has been an analysis of the various influences on him and the intellectual debates in which he is (or should be) engaged.[14] Much work has already been accomplished in this realm. I have already referred to Gschwandtner's work on Marion and Descartes, but the work of Morrow and Alweiss also deserves mention.[15] There was a loud outcry in response to Marion's treatment of Aquinas in *God Without Being,*[16] a critique that Marion took seriously enough to modify his interpretation of Aquinas substantially.[17] There have also been sustained critiques of his indebtedness to Husserl[18] and to Heidegger[19] as well as the relationship between Marion and Levinas,[20] and Marion and Derrida.[21]

Another formative source of Marion's thought during his years at university has gained less attention. Although it may have been outside of the lecture halls, Marion enjoyed a no less influential discipleship at the tail end of the movement within French Catholicism known as "*la nouvelle théologie,*" a movement that (amongst other aims) sought to renew interest in the significance of the church fathers for the twentieth century (*ressourcement*). Marion studied privately with some of the central figures in this movement: Louis Bouyer, Jean Daniélou, Henri de Lubac, and Hans Urs von Balthasar.[22] Marion's first publications reflect this influence. In particular, Marion wrote many articles examining various doctrines central to Christianity as well as many exegeses of, and engagements with, the early Christian writers.[23] These articles are untranslated and are, for the most part, ignored in scholarship on Marion. However, in his early engagement with the church fathers, one already finds the concepts and the terminology of "givenness," "saturation," and "idolatry." From this evidence, and from the fact that these fathers of the church continue to be a common reference throughout his corpus, one must assume a vital influence on his thought. And yet very little scholarship has been done thus far on Marion's retrieval of patristic writings.[24] This study aims to begin to fill this void in a very specific way.

Rather than comprehensively chart each and every patristic influence and citation in Marion's corpus, I engage his retrieval of two figures in particular: Gregory of Nyssa and Dionysius the Areopagite. These two thinkers are particularly helpful because they evidence the need for a more sophisticated classification of discourses than simply the "philosophical" or the "theological." A comparison between these two theologians demonstrates that significant distinctions can be drawn even *within* the tradition of Christian *apophasis*. These distinctions trouble Marion's even retrieval of the Fathers and, moreover, reverberate distinctly in different locations of Marion's corpus.

Given Marion's most recent work,[25] one might expect more weight to be given here to his retrieval of Augustine. While this work on Augustine will certainly be discussed, it is not the primary focus of this book for the following reasons. First, as I shall argue, Marion's attention on Augustine represents something of a late turn in his thought in which he shifts his focus and emphasis decidedly from *apophasis* to *confession*, and from invisibility to beatitude. I will return to more evaluative remarks concerning this decision in later chapters—suffice it to say for now that I believe something of the creative friction within his thought is lost in the shift. More to the point, however, this book will not focus primarily on Marion's recent Augustinian meditations because they do not fit within the primary analytic approach of my argument—an approach that hypothesizes that (paradoxically to be sure) an examination of Marion's univocal retrieval of two Greek Fathers, who are much more proximate within the traditions of Christian apophasis than is Augustine, is particularly helpful at illumining the tensions inherent in Marion's phenomenological project as a whole (in a way that his retrieval of Augustine is not).

The following questions structure my study. First and most basically, I ask about the patristic citations throughout Marion's corpus. Whom does he cite, when, for what purpose, and in what way (chapter 1)? Secondly, I question the legitimacy of his univocal retrieval of the Eastern Fathers by comparing the apophatic visions of Gregory of Nyssa and Dionysius the Areopagite (chapter 2). I then examine Marion's methodological allegiances to see how they influence his reading of Dionysius (chapter 3). Fourthly, I explore the difficult question of the relation of the "pure givenness" to the "endless interpretation" of saturated phenomena in Marion and ask whether Gregory of Nyssa might be employed in such a way that some of the tension between these central elements in Marion's thought is eased (chapter 4). And finally, I evaluate the coherence and insightfulness of Marion's apophatic phenomenology and ask how Gregory might become a more explicit resource for Marion's thought (chapter 5).

Jettisoning the need to establish his phenomenology of givenness as "first philosophy" and the attendant methodological universality, I suggest that Marion can hold the remaining tensions in his thought together in a generative balance: the "pure givenness" of the saturated phenomenon is balanced by the *subsequently* endless interpretation of it. This balancing act is accomplished, however, only through my own extension of Marion's (thus far) limited use of Gregory. In this way, my study demonstrates the risk of contemporary retrievals of patristic thought (that one imports more than was bargained for) but also the rich potential of such a retrieval that offers a way of thinking outside of the particularly antimetaphysical paradigms regnant in Continental thought today.

A Note on Terminology

The characterization of Marion's phenomenology as "apophatic" requires some justification. For instance, why do I use "*apophatic* phenomenology" rather than "*negative* phenomenology"? One reason is that, having suggested the term "negative phenomenology" for himself in a published response to reviews of his work *Reduction and Givenness*,[26] Marion later finds it inappropriate "because the phenomena that I mentioned (boredom, the call, etc.) in fact have nothing negative about them . . . in this sense, it was an issue of the most positive of phenomenologies, and some prejudice is necessary not to recognise it as such."[27]

Negativity is an insufficient descriptor of Marion's phenomenology primarily because Marion is interested in the excessive plenitude of intuition rather than its poverty. Thus, the inability to arrive at adequate concepts is driven by an *excess* rather than a *lack*.

Another reason is my own dissatisfaction with the limited resonances "negation" tends to have in contemporary discourse. As mentioned above, Marion's thought takes place within a movement in Continental philosophy that has been variously identified with a "turn to religion" or even a "theological turn." Frequently this "turn" has been aligned with a sort of "negative theology." This negative discourse, however, often merely connotes a linguistic or epistemological strategy employed in the face of lack or deficiency. The contemporary discourse also usually retrieves "negative theology" as a single undeviating tradition to either identify with or be distinguished from. Indeed, the dominant debate around negative theology has been in confrontation with the writings of Jacques Derrida. On the one side are those who seek to call Derrida a "negative theologian,"[28] and on the other, those who want to disavow any connection.[29] In any case, this debate circles endlessly around whether or not the linguistic strategy is negative *enough*. This frustration with the limitations of "negativity" in current philosophical discourse causes Marion to reject the use of the term "negative theology" in favor of "mystical theology" or "apophasis."[30] How, then, ought one decide between these terms?

I believe the term "mystical" is misleading for a couple of reasons. Marion correctly uses it only in a specific connection to the Dionysian corpus (whence the term originates) in order to denote a mode of discourse appropriate in theology, whereas I am looking for a term that encompasses the anti-idolatry orientation of Marion's work as a whole and not limited to his explicitly theological writing. Secondly, the term "mystical theology" is often elided with a discussion of the modern word *mysticism,* which carries with it the implication of individual union with or "experience" of the divine that cannot be applied unproblematically to any of the three main figures of this study.

This brings us to the term "apophatic." Lampe's *Patristic-Greek Lexicon* supplies two derivations for the Greek word *apophasis* (ἀποφάσις): it derives from ἀπόφημι (to deny or negate) and from ἀποφαίνω (to decree or declare plainly).[31] There is, in other words, an ambiguity embedded within the Greek word that moves one away from limiting its meaning to mere linguistic negation. As we have already seen, Marion's use of the term implies more than mere negation. Similarly, in chapter 2 I demonstrate the way in which, for Dionysius and Gregory, a theory of *apophasis* brings with it a whole way of being, an existential condition, in the face of certain ontological conditions. One's particular understanding of *apophasis* is shaped by basic presuppositions about the world and one's place in it: a certain excess or plenitude dominates this vision to overwhelm the individual inside it. Assumptions regarding the constitution or formation of a particular selfhood arise from his or her response to this reality. By using the term "apophatic phenomenology" in connection to Marion, I refer, in the fullest manner possible, to both an ontology[32] of plenitude and an anthropology of response.

I propose an analysis of Marion's phenomenology that I characterize as driven primarily by an anti-idolatry motivation. Idolatry here is not confined to religious idolatry but refers primarily to the constraining of any phenomenon within limits alien to the way it gives itself, or shows itself. Defining the phenomenon according to one's own subjective conceptual limitations is, for instance, idolatrous. In agreement with others such as Thomas Carlson, Merold Westphal, and Robyn Horner, I argue that Marion's entire corpus—the Cartesian studies, works on aesthetics, theological writings, as well as his "pure" phenomenological work—should be understood as an attempt to think outside of these idolatrous binds. Characterizing his thought as "apophatic" is a shorthand way of signifying his fundamentally critical stance toward the subjectivist hold on modern philosophy and his attempt to escape conceptual idolatries in both theology and phenomenology. Idolatry refuses to recognize excess or plenitude, but an appropriately apophatic stance begins in response to this excess.[33] This excessive apophatic dimension marks Marion's thought as one of the most interesting and sustainable responses to the critique of modernity and its concurrent return to premodern writings as a source of argument and inspiration at the "end of metaphysics."

A few other terms need clarification. The importance of locating Marion's thought at the "end of metaphysics," for instance, requires an explanation of what precisely has come to an "end." What is meant by the terms "metaphysics" or "metaphysical," which are slung around with such derogatory force in late-twentieth-century Continental philosophy? And why, exactly, is "onto-theology" such a bugbear?

These terms have a particular meaning within the Heideggerian context from which they arise. Heidegger's definition of metaphysics is inherently negative or polemical: it is a way of philosophizing that Heidegger wants to "overcome."[34] The fundamental problem with metaphysics "during its long history from Anaximander to Nietzsche" is a forgetting of the "ontological difference" resulting in the concealment of the "truth of Being."[35] Metaphysics is characterized by this impotence to think Being as such (*esse, Sein, être,* to be), but only in terms of "beings," namely, as *a* being (*ens, Seiende, étant,* entity).

"Metaphysics is onto-theology" when it asks the question of Being in terms of the Being of beings, rather than Being as such. Asking after the Being of beings is a twofold question: it asks about being in general (*ontology*), and at the same time it questions which of the particular beings is the highest (*theology*).

> Metaphysics thinks of the Being of beings both in the ground-giving unity of what is most general, what is indifferently valued everywhere, and also in the unity of the all that accounts for the ground, that is, of the All-Highest. The Being of beings is thus thought of in advance as the grounding ground. Therefore all metaphysics is at bottom, and from the ground up, what grounds, what gives account of the ground, what is called to account by the ground, and finally what calls the ground to account.[36]

This is problematic not least because of the reciprocal "groundings" of Being and beings: "Being grounds beings, and beings, as what *is* most of all, account for Being."[37] Metaphysics is doomed to "end" because the definition that makes metaphysics intelligible also makes it impossible: something (Being) cannot be grounded by that which it, in turn, grounds (beings). The twofoldness of the question of Being, as well as its tenuousness, lies in its foundational reciprocity.

A concurrent effect of metaphysical thinking is the fact that "God" is inscribed within the metaphysical domain, that is, thought as "a being." God establishes a causal foundation of all entities for which it is the reason. Thus God must assume the function, if not the name, of *causa sui,* the supreme founding entity because it founded itself.[38] The problem with the onto-theological deity is that "God" is determined "starting from and to the profit of that which metaphysics is capable, that which it can admit and support";[39] such a God can only be, to use Marion's terminology, an idol, a measure of what we can intend or aim at. Thus, "metaphysics infallibly leads, by way of blasphemy (proof), to the twilight of the idols (conceptual atheism)."[40]

In Marion's own corpus metaphysics takes on an even more precise meaning. He adds two following characteristics. First, it determines the conditions for the possibility of phenomenality: the horizons of temporality and spatiality and the constituting function of the "I." Secondly, and relatedly, metaphysics upholds the subjective starting point of philosophy and privileges the question of Being.[41] Bringing these various strands together, Robyn Horner provides the most concise and straightforward definition of the term *metaphysics* in Marion's thought: metaphysics is "a conception in terms of beings as presence, with a claim to some kind of absoluteness, on the foundation of a transcendental I, whose existence and certainty is guaranteed by a term posited beyond the conceptual system."[42] Following Marion's own usage,[43] I use "metaphysics" or "metaphysical" intending this precise meaning. (As my argument unfolds, it will become clear just how alien such a notion of metaphysics would be to the patristic writers who are retrieved into this discussion.)

In contrast to this technical and narrow employment of the term *metaphysics,* I propose to use the term *ontology* quite broadly. Taking it in its most common sense signification, ontology simply points to what I will refer to in chapter 2 as "the world language inhabits," that is to say, a thinker's assumptions about the "subject" (however configured or called), her reality (world), and the relation between the two. It includes assumptions about the cause of that reality—a cause that may or may not be identified as divine—as well as implications regarding the origins and ends of the subject. In other words, I am intentionally using "ontology" and "ontological" in the broadest and least-technical, least-philosophical sense to signify the assumptions and the implications of a thinker's concepts vis-à-vis the world, or reality in its entirety. Such a broad usage permits me to consider, with due caution, the "ontology" of a thinker like Marion without suggesting that his philosophy remains within the horizon of Being, where "Being" suggests the unavoidable horizons of temporality and spatiality. I will argue that, despite his allergy to the "ontological" language of Being/being, even Marion cannot avoid implying certain ontological options—certain understandings of reality and one's place within it—over others.

One of the curious ironies in Marion's thought is that the patristic sources he retrieves into a contemporary conversation have no hesitation whatsoever in making ontological claims; they would not even understand the concern. Marion is not alone in this return to premodern sources in an attempt to rebut a particular modern inheritance. Counter-intuitively, both metaphysics and ontology are common parlance in the sources being retrieved to surpass and "overcome" metaphysics and ontology. One might question the possibility of success with such a strategy. Denys Turner has stated the challenge accusingly:

> A recycling today of the classical, late antique and medieval *vocabularies* of the apophatic but uprooted from their soil in a metaphysics, leaves that vocabulary suspended in a vacuum of *rhetorics,* a displaced, residually Christian semiotics, retaining the illusion of force from the metaphysics it has abandoned as no longer possible.[44]

I intend to argue that Marion does not, finally, fall prey to this accusation. However, his avoidance of the charge is not neat. He avoids it by involving himself in that which he seeks to avoid, if not metaphysics in the narrow and technical post-Heideggerian sense, then at least ontology in its broadest sense. Indeed, the richness and depth with which Marion does retrieve these sources, beyond a simple transference of vocabulary, is precisely what makes his thought so fertile but also what renders it problematic. At the center of the "current apophatic rage"[45] in Continental philosophy, with its concurrent retrieval of early Christian writings, Jean-Luc Marion is both the most successful interpreter of apophaticism in the Greek Fathers and, ironically, the most dazzled within his own phenomenological project by a univocal use of them.

ONE

Sightings: The Location and Function of Patristic Citation in Jean-Luc Marion's Writing

The purpose of this first chapter is to ascertain the places and the ways in which Jean-Luc Marion cites the church fathers, particularly with an eye to the Greek apophatic tradition and, most specifically, to Dionysius[1] and Gregory of Nyssa. The task is quite discrete: Whom does Marion cite? How frequently? In what works? And most importantly, why? What work do these citations and retrievals accomplish for Marion? The chapter will begin with some general comments and then will proceed chronologically through the various stages of Marion's writing: from his earliest articles, to the groundbreaking theological works, *The Idol and Distance: Five Studies* and *God Without Being*, to his debate with Derrida concerning the status of "negative theology," and finally to his most recent meditations on Augustine in *Au lieu de soi*.

The chapter puts forth both a stronger and a "softer" thesis. The latter, easier to prove, is simply that Marion retrieves these "orthodox"[2] patristic sources univocally and shows little interest in parsing differences between individual thinkers. In this vein, it becomes clear how "orthodoxy" functions as a validating source for the contemporary debates in which Marion is engaged. Within this strategy of a retrieval of "orthodoxy," it is no surprise that Gregory and Dionysius are retrieved univocally. However, the second, stronger claim is more specific— Marion actually allows Gregory to "speak" in the place of Dionysius in crucial moments of exposition of the latter.

In this chapter, I will chart patristic citation practices in Marion diachronically in order to demonstrate that, while the substance of Marion's central insights remains the same, there is a shift in rhetorical emphases. Such a sweep will show how Marion initially retrieves the Fathers broadly as a homogeneous and authoritative unit. Nevertheless, fairly early on in his writings, Dionysius gets singled out as particularly helpful to Marion for articulating and conceptualizing certain themes: the play of visibility and invisibility, manifestation and concealment; the notion of "distance"; and the "hymnic" mode of discourse. Indeed, Dionysius proves so crucial to Marion's thought in his formative writings that, I will argue, he turns Dionysius into a kind of "shorthand" for many of the apophatic strains of his phenomenology without recognizing when Dionysius is of less use within a changed rhetorical landscape. Specifically, as Marion begins to emphasize the "pragmatic" quality of discourse, he still calls this a "Dionysian" discourse without recognizing that he no longer cites Dionysius, but must instead turn to other more suitable patristic sources such as Gregory of Nyssa.

General Comments

Given Marion's primary intellectual interests in phenomenology and the modern history of philosophy, one may be surprised by the prevalence and frequency of patristic citation in his writings. While most of these citations are found in his earlier theological works and again, more recently, in his writing on "negative" and "mystical" theology, even his works on Descartes and his phenomenological writing still contain some references to the Fathers. In other words, almost without exception, every major work of Marion's has some reference to the church fathers.[3]

He cites some of the earliest Christian figures and apologists— Ignatius of Antioch, Clement of Rome, and Justin Martyr—as well as the Alexandrians—Clement, Origen, and Athanasius. He is clearly familiar with all three of the Cappadocians, and they appear throughout his writings. He cites Ambrose and Augustine, the formative ecumenical councils of the fourth and fifth centuries, John of Damascus, Theodore the Studite, and Maximus the Confessor. However, the influence most frequently present to Marion's thought is found in the writings collected under the name of Dionysius the Areopagite. Gregory of Nyssa, on the other hand, appears (in name, at least) less frequently.

Thus, while the reasons for choosing to look at Dionysius are obvious, the case is not so clear with Gregory. Nevertheless, that Gregory wields a significant influence on Marion can be seen in the *way* he cites him in those few places. Gregory's words occupy crucial positions within Marion's arguments, even when those arguments concern Dionysius explicitly. Gregory's words often provide the proof text for the most foundational of Marion's concepts.

Furthermore, tracking Marion's use of Gregory and Dionysius nicely demonstrates a broader trend in his retrieval: his approach to the Fathers is characterized by a lack of discrimination. Marion is not interested in discerning differences or parsing out the discrete positions of these writings. Instead, they are treated almost monolithically as a source of "truth" or "orthodoxy" with which to bolster Marion's own contemporary theses.[4] The Fathers, then, offer a homogeneous unit of authoritative source material for Marion to mine—a continuous tradition of an orthodoxy in which Marion would also like to be placed.

Such a retrieval of the Fathers for apologetic purposes is not a unique or even infrequent approach to these writings. Nevertheless, Marion is equipped for a more discerning retrieval. Marion's knowledge of the early Christian tradition in general, and more specifically its *apophatic* strand, is tremendously impressive. He is fluent in broad swathes of patristic thought, reads these texts in the original language, and is knowledgeable of the broader philosophical schools of thought, terms, and issues contemporaneous to the Fathers. He is perfectly capable, then, of determining difference amongst the various sources he cites. In other words, Marion knows the Fathers in a more nuanced way than he allows them to function in his writing. This is clearest in his earliest writings, many of which are straight expositions or meditations on debates occurring in the early church. It is to these writings that we now turn.

Earliest Publications

"I don't understand myself as a theologian. I'm not theologically trained," Marion said in an interview.[5] While this may be true, there is no question that theology (of a particular stripe) imbues Marion's world from the earliest stages of his intellectual development. Indeed, his little-known earliest essays are astonishingly pietistic. They are either preoccupied with fairly straightforward theological themes (Christology, the contemplation of the Eucharist, the incarnation, and the resurrection), or they are expositions of a particular early Christian figure (Dionysius, Augustine, Maximus the Confessor). Furthermore, it is in these writings that Marion's theological influences are most apparent.

Many of Marion's teachers were propagators of "*la nouvelle théolo-gie*," so to understand Marion's earliest work their influence needs to be recognized. One of the primary characteristics of this movement was a renewed interest in intensive study of patristic theologians as sources with which one might combat the dominance of Neo-Scholasticism in Catholicism. Despite Neo-Scholasticism's fight against the central tenets of modernity and the Enlightenment, the very character of its reaction resulted in the unconscious acquisition of those very same tenets. Thus, a critique of Neo-Scholasticism by "*la nouvelle théologie*" was bolstered by a return to *premodern* sources, specifically the retrieval of the church fathers as resources against the curiously "modern" anti-modernism of Neo-Scholasticism.

In an article intending to situate Marion's writing in its "field of cultural production,"[6] Graham Ward firmly places Marion within the "conservative" movement of French Catholicism in the latter half of the twentieth century.[7] Ward contrasts the influence of Catholicism on Marion to its influence on other French postmodern figures such as Jacques Lacan, Michel Foucault, Julia Kristeva, and Luce Irigaray for whom Catholicism exercises a less "profound and conservative" impact.[8] Though I will problematize the straightforward application of the label "conservative," it is not difficult to understand the initial designation upon reading these early articles.

Certain characteristics of Marion's early writing can be noted: first, they are products of extensive work in the original language of these patristic writings, and secondly, there is an apologetic tenor in which the categories of "orthodoxy" and "heresy" arising out of debates in Late Antiquity are treated as illuminative for contemporary discussions. With this latter characteristic one already can see Marion's interest in the proper "starting place" of all thought, something that, according to him, the Fathers repeatedly insisted upon and the "heretics" repeatedly misunderstood, ignored, or countered.

The first characteristic requires little elucidation. Marion cites the critical editions of the patristic texts almost exclusively. If upon occasion he does reference a French translation, this is never the case with either Dionysius or Gregory of Nyssa. Marion's translations of patristic pericopes appear to be fairly independent of any prior French transla-tion and provide evidence of a high degree of familiarity and depth of study in the Fathers. Marion does not rely on secondary sources primarily—as he himself acknowledges[9]—but works through the primary sources himself.[10] The second characteristic requires a little more attention.

Marion's earliest essays are shot through with patristic references, so much so that rather than *refer* to the Fathers, they are *about* them. For instance, the following articles published in the journal *Résurrection* rehearse the fundamental tenets of Catholic faith as they are articulated by their primary patristic progenitors: *"Penser juste ou trahir le mystère: Notes sur l'elaboration patristique du dogme de l'Incarnation"* surveys and defends the "orthodox" doctrine of Christ against both the Arian and Monophysite "heresies"; *"Les deux volontés du Christ selon saint Maxime le Confesseur"* continues this orthodox articulation of Christ's nature, specifically as it is expounded by Maximus; *"Presence et distance: Remarque sur l'implication reciproque de la contemplation eucharistique et de la presence reelle"*[11] and *"Le splendeur de la contemplation eucharistique"*[12] both frame a "realist" approach to liturgy, contemplation of the sacraments, and the possibility of worship, at least in part, through a retrieval of Dionysius. One can observe the influence of Louis Bouyer in these articles.[13] Significantly, we might note that Marion's first retrieval of Dionysius was not in the service of apophasis primarily, but was intended as an apologetics for the possibility and necessity of "real presence" in the sacraments in a post–Vatican II liturgical context.

In all of these articles the "orthodoxy" Marion is defending has a specific identity: it begins with the acceptance of the gift of revelation, precisely as a gift, something received rather than possessed. One can already identify a central methodological tenet of Marion's thought: treatment (including judgment, analysis, description) of something must not begin from our own preconceptions of it, but rather as the thing in question presents itself. For instance, in *"Ce mystère qui Juge celui qui le juge"* Marion argues that one can judge the appearances of the resurrected Christ only properly in faith, which he glosses as what happens when one lets go of the need for a certain type of "judgment" and rather receives as gift "the unthinkable fact of the Resurrection." Only then does one learn "not to judge the resurrection but to be judged by the One who 'will come in glory to judge the living and the dead.'"[14] With this stance, Marion draws a distinction between "natural" and "revealed" theology and locates himself, along with Barth and Balthasar, in the latter category.[15]

In these early essays, Marion less argues this point than stridently insists upon its necessity. The Fathers are trotted out in defense of his thesis; he cites the Nicene Creed, Augustine, Origen, Irenaeus, and Gregory of Nyssa amongst others. According to Marion, all agree: "The Fathers, from Athenagoras to Gregory of Nyssa, are not deceived on this point, which grounds their good right to believe in the Resurrection only on the sovereign right of God, as creator, to fashion men and to transform their history."[16] The Fathers are "not deceived" *ensemble*. Throughout these articles, all of which have an explicitly apologetic tone, the Fathers are cited as proof texts in one voice. They all agree and, especially in contradistinction from the "heretics," they see things from the right perspective, that is, they wait to receive properly what is to be received from God instead of starting from human reason. This methodological orientation guarantees their "rightness"—their orthodoxy. It is worth noting that Marion has a particularly apophatic notion of orthodoxy: it is this patristic displacement from the human to the only appropriate theological authority that separates the Fathers from the "heretics."

The "heretics," conversely, do not begin from the right place. Rather, they begin with a need for "accounting," a "logic" or "an explication which begins by submission to arithmetic" rather than the gift of the event and the logic proper to, in this particular case, the incarnation.[17] Thus, in the same way that the Fathers are retrieved in one voice for a contemporary apologetic purpose, so too the "heretics" inevitably function as a foil against which Marion's present questions and concerns are sharpened.

Before I discuss Marion's more familiar works, one other article among Marion's earliest writings ought to be mentioned as pertinent to this discussion. *"Distance et louange: Du concept de Réquisit (aitia) au statut trinitaire de langage théologique selon Denys le mystique"* marks the beginning of Marion's interest in Dionysius and different sorts of discourse or language. In this article Marion already identifies the basic principle that will hold true for all of his "theological" writing (and by extension, and with different formulation, also to his phenomenological writings): "God cannot be named starting from any language other than [God's], not as a referent among others; but [as] an absolute referent, He holds language to the interiority of the distance of Goodness."[18] From this, various consequences follow, not least of which is the fact that language is understood as "given." We shall return to Marion's understanding of language in Dionysius in chapter 3.

In this article we can also observe one citation practice that establishes a pattern that Marion will continue throughout his retrieval of Gregory and Dionysius. Specifically, when Marion is tracing the contours of his notion of the "icon of the invisible" or the "icon without resemblance," he conflates the two writers. In this context, Marion writes that "of God no investigation is possible because no vestige is left, nor any part of the trace." This sentence is supported with a reference to Dionysius' *Divine Names* I, 2, 588c, but the only direct quotation he supplies is from Gregory's commentary *On the Beatitudes* 6 (PG 44, 1268 b): ". . . the way of the essence of God cannot be followed and its route is 'practicable' to no one."[19] Briefly, then, already we see an instance where a crucial point in an article about Dionysius is backed up with a quotation of Gregory rather than Dionysius.

From this brief glance over these neglected early essays we have discovered several trends. First, we can find incipient versions of major themes of Marion's thought borrowed from the corpus of Dionysius: givenness as a methodological starting point, and the shifting play between visibility and invisibility. Secondly, we have seen how the category of "orthodoxy" functions both authoritatively and at the same time, ironically, apophatically. Finally, Marion's univocal retrieval of the Fathers extends to his citation of Gregory as a proof text for Dionysius.

The Idol and Distance and *God Without Being*

Two major works of Marion, *The Idol and Distance: Five Studies* (*ID*) and *God Without Being* (*GWB*), lend themselves to simultaneous treatment. Although we shall need to examine *The Idol and Distance* in greater detail (since it contains a sustained conversation with the Dionysian corpus), both works stem from a similar context—Marion's initial response to Heidegger, his critique of onto-theology, and the so-called "death of God." This response to Heidegger, part critique and part expansion (because it still leaves the basic Heideggerian critique of onto-theology uninterrogated), in many ways dictates Marion's reasoning. Most notably it leads him to find in Dionysius a counterpart in the Christian tradition to Thomas Aquinas (who, at this point in his writing, is understood by Marion to be the *bête noire* of onto-theological thinking). Thus, in both works Marion attempts to uproot "the question of God not only from metaphysics (and the fate of the 'Death of God'), but also from what made possible an investigation that had become as obsessive as imprecise into the 'existence of God,' namely, the unquestioned horizon of Being as supposedly the sole frame of his presence."[20] These two works were written within a single period of Marion's intellectual development (*ID* was published in France in 1977, and *GWB* in 1982) when he was still primarily known as a scholar of Descartes.[21] These were his first book-length forays dealing directly with Heidegger's critique of onto-theology, specifically with a theological response.[22]

The Idol and Distance

The project of *The Idol and Distance* is to follow where the "death of God" leads in order to discover a different sort of discourse, one in which "distance" is preserved rather than eradicated by the "marches of metaphysics." Marion summarizes the goal of the book to establish his central concept of "distance": "a distance outside of onto-theology for Nietzsche, a filially received distance of the presence of God who is paternally in withdrawal from Hölderlin, and a distance traversed liturgically toward the Requisite by the discourse of requestants for Denys." In other words, in this book Marion brings together a number of studies on Nietzsche, Hölderlin and, finally, Dionysius in order to fill out a sketch of the idea of "distance" and the only discourse proper to it, "praise."[23]

"Distance" is as multivalent in, as it is central to, Marion's thought. In its various usages it commonly refers to the space or separation that both makes relationship possible and prevents relationship from becoming an identification with, or absorption of, the other. It refers to the space existent in multiple relationships: interpersonal, inter-Trinitarian, and between God and the human. In its strongest sense, *distance* stands in for the term *God*. It signifies that graciousness or givenness of the divine which enables relation.[24] I will have more to say about the genesis of this term below.

Dionysius performs a crucial role in this intellectual narrative: the culminating vision is his. Nietzsche functions propaedeutically to liberate us, negatively, by announcing the death of all idols or "gods." Hölderlin then intimates in his poetry a "withdrawal of the Divine" and the necessary response of a poetic discourse that can preserve distance while "deliver(ing) the thing and man to an intimately and silently harmonized dialogue."[25] However, it remains the task of Dionysius to supply a "nonpredicative theory of discourse" that, although it has been called "negative theology," in fact, "has nothing negative about it, but ensures a discourse in the modality of praise."[26]

In the four sections of *The Idol and Distance* that treat Dionysius directly (§13–§16, pp. 139–96), Marion extracts from the Dionysian corpus a notion of discourse suitable to, and preserving of, distance. This is accomplished through (a) an analysis of *apophasis* (or more specifically, the relation between *apophasis* and *cataphasis*) (§13. "Unthinkable Eminence"); (b) a significant reinterpretation and translation of the term αἰτία as the "Requisite" instead of as ontological "cause" (§14. "The Request of the Requisite"); (c) an analysis of divine "mediation" though the hierarchies that demonstrates the Trinitarian foundation of distance (§15. "Immediate Mediation"); and finally, (d) a scriptural basis for a discourse of praise that is non-predicative (§16. "The Discourse of Praise"). Each of these steps in the argument involves significant interpretative readings of Dionysius, which I will examine in turn.

Marion's primary intent is to find a language or discourse that is "suitable to distance."[27] His most fundamental principle is stated through the voice of Dionysius: "It is necessary to understand the divine things divinely."[28] Marion, then, reminds his readers (and here he has in mind, especially, those who want to identify Dionysian *apophasis* with Derridean *différance*) that Dionysius does not use the term "negative theology," though he speaks of "negative theologies" inseparable from "affirmative theologies."[29] Negation is helpful in avoiding the most obvious idolatry. Nevertheless, it is not the last theological word because, although inverted, it still remains predicative, and thus idolatrous: to say S is "not P" is still to predicate something (−P) of S.[30] For Marion, anything that fixes the divine as "x" or as "not-x" remains idolatrous because it attempts to stabilize our understanding of God as "x" or as "not-x."[31] Instead, according to Marion, Dionysius seeks a "third way," which is the characteristic of distance, "namely that it is up to distance itself to speak the discourse."[32] Marion concludes that revelation is given as a gift that withdraws itself just as it presents itself.[33]

Marion proceeds in the next section (§14) to produce one of his more consequential translations, not only of a word but also of a concept of Dionysius: αἰτία as "Requisite."[34] The basic significance of this translation is summarized by Thomas Carlson: "The 'cause' or 'Requisite' (αἰτία) of all things caused (αἰτιάτα) is that which all things require, and hence that which all things petition, that to which all things make request (αἰτέω, *requérir*) in prayer."[35] On first glance this would seem to be a somewhat quixotic translation by Marion. The primary sense of ἡ αἰτία is "cause, origin, ground or occasion."[36] Secondary meanings involve a sense of responsibility, blame, or fault, which carry a litigious connotation—thus, αἰτίαν ἔχειν means "to be accused" and αἰτίαν ὑπέχειν means "to lie under a charge." In translating αἰτία as the "Requisite," Marion has departed from the literal translation of "cause" or "blame." Is this rendering of αἰτία legitimate, or is it a sleight of hand, even if an evocative and creative one?

Marion justifies the translation by arguing that there is an etymological relation between αἰτία and αἰτέω, "to ask, beg, or demand." According to Marion, αἰτία has nothing to do with "Greek" (including Neoplatonic) thought and is not one of Aristotle's four causes. Rather, it "is necessary here to understand this relation in all its lively rigor and simplicity, as the praying request in which requestants appeal, by hurling accusations or by making an appeal, to a Requisite."[37] In a footnote following this sentence, Marion explicitly draws a connection to the legalistic and juridical connotations of αἰτία, citing classical references for the connection (Plato and Homer) and, more importantly, early scholia on Dionysius (that of Pachymere):

> It is known that Αἰτία signifies the accusation, the grief, the charge brought against the one toward whom one makes a request. It is a matter, then, of that which is aimed at by the action of *accusing on a point that concerns me*, αἰτιάομαι . . . In this context, I would underline that αἰτιάτον depends on a middle, αἰτιάομαι, *to accuse in that which concerns me*; one therefore cannot translate it as 'effect,' but one must converse the nuance of the middle: *that which the requestant requests/requires for itself*. On this conceptual constellation, see the *Commentary* of Pachymere on CH, III, 3, 2: Called requestants, αἰτιάτα, are the terms that, in order to be in whatever way one might want, need an exterior requisite (αἰτία). Requisites (αἰτίαι), the completed terms, in view of which, in tending toward them, we complete the requestants and those of which they are the terms. (PG, 3, 456c)[38]

I will challenge this translation as well as Marion's justification of it in chapter 3. However, let us accept the translation for the moment in order to examine how it functions in his argument. What does Marion gain toward the achievement of his goal (establishing a discourse of praise appropriate to "distance") with this translation of αἰτία?

The designation of αἰτία as a divine name affirms little positively about God. Αἰτία, precisely as "cause" of all beings, marks itself off from all being just as much (or more, as Marion would have it) as it marks a relation between cause and caused beings: "'Αἰτία/cause of Being for all things, itself non-being inasmuch as beyond essence' (οὐσία)."[39] Marion will also cite many other appropriate examples to support this thesis.[40] Nevertheless, he insists that one cannot simply replace "Being" or "Good" with αἰτία as the singularly proper divine name within what remains a predicative discourse.

Marion claims that Dionysius shifts away from predicative discourse by locating a "precise co-occurrence" and "privileged relation" between αἰτία and praise in which praise intentionally substitutes for predication: "It is as cause/αἰτία of all things that God is praised; for Denys does not say: 'these things are predicated (κατηγορεῖται) of God,' but properly that he is praised for them (ὑμνεῖται)."[41] However, it should be noted that Marion must draw upon scholia of Dionysius by Maximus the Confessor in order to make this particular connection between αἰτία and praise. It is not an explicit connection in Dionysius' corpus. Αἰτία "announces itself as the operative concept within the critique of all idols of the divine, including the conceptual: representing nothing, it signals the very operation through which the mind exposes itself to the unthinkable as unthinkable . . . not only does it not proceed idolatrously, but it proceeds to the disqualification of idols."[42] Thus, in a dizzying reversal of its straightforward ontological meaning, Marion has constructed a place of crucial importance for the term αἰτία within his fortress that guards against idolatry.

Given the burden placed on this term, it must be asked whether Marion's translation and reconceptualization of it is warranted. His bold claim that Dionysius' use of the term has no reliance on Platonic or Neoplatonic thought is unsupported. While it may be true that αἰτία ought not to be simply identified with either Aristotle's "efficient" or "final" cause, nevertheless, an indebtedness to Neoplatonic ontology is necessary to understand Dionysius' use of the term.[43] Marion's explicit interest in the concept has less to do with ontology than with language and discourse, but its ontological resonances must be addressed. This is one of the "uneasy borrowings" from Dionysius that I will discuss more fully in chapter 3. Yet even within the linguistic realm, Marion's use of this term still raises questions.

Marion's primary concern is that αἰτία not act as another "name" that functions to predicate something of God. Instead, "the cause [aitia] intervenes here in order to mark precisely the reverse, namely, that we have no naming suitable to God, not even in negation."[44] While this argument may be seen plausibly as a complement or expansion of Dionysius' position, nowhere in the corpus does he actually state such a teaching specifically with regard to the term αἰτία. In fact, one of the interesting aspects of Dionysius' treatment and use of αἰτία is that, despite its frequent usage in the corpus, and especially in *Divinis Nominibus*,[45] Dionysius nowhere treats it specifically as one of the divine names, or even as *the* divine name. This indicates that Marion may be making this term do a little more work than is justified by the *corpus Dionysiacum*.[46]

In the next section Marion treats the Dionysian notion of "hierarchy." He begins with an aporia: How can one conceive of a discourse of praise that addresses the divine without "reduc[ing] distance to a space that is possessed because well known, and known because travelled at length," while simultaneously having a notion of distance that enables relation instead of forbidding it?[47] Marion thinks that Dionysius responds to this double-sided question with his neologism, "hierarchy."

Marion argues that "hierarchy" is only crudely understood as a nonreciprocal relation of power.[48] Hierarchy has a different goal than the exercise of power in Dionysius: "the goal of every hierarchy is a conforming and a union with God, as far as possible; . . . *completion* [τελείωσις][49] for each being in the hierarchy, consists in ascending, according to their proper capacity, toward the semblance of God."[50] Hierarchy "aims, therefore, to produce relation with God"—not to hide, but rather to manifest God.[51]

Hierarchy has an ecstatic origin in the excessive love that goes out of itself to create.[52] Marion is quick, however, to distance this creation from a Plotinian[53] view of "emanation in loss":

in multiplying itself, the One undoubtedly loses and dissolves itself; but charity in giving itself manifests itself all the more authentically. Each redundancy of the gift, where it abandons itself without return, attests its unique and permanent cohesion. Thus Denys can define hierarchy by "ascent" as well as by "emanation" . . . The essential perhaps is this: each member receives the gift only in order to give it, such that this gift, in the same gesture, regives the gift in redundancy ("emanation") and, giving, sends the original gift back to its foundation ("ascent").[54]

Marion emphasizes that the nature of hierarchy functions to provide the basis for mutuality rather than different "levels of being": "The gift passes from one end to the other without loss, and necessarily, since reception provokes propagation within an unfailing redundancy."[55] He acknowledges that expressions such as "inasmuch as it is possible," or "according to their analogies" would seem to indicate a "diminishing transmission of the gift."[56] However, he argues that this is not a result of "divine jealousy" but rather of "the relative and variable impotence of each among the givers/recipients to carry out the redundancy themselves also 'without envy.'"[57]

While Marion is right that the "diminishing transmission of the gift" is not a result of divine jealousy, this does not precisely solve his problem. One either grants that the hierarchies entail various levels or "scales" of being, or one does not.[58] It is insufficient simply to place responsibility for this into the hands of the individual beings (recipients of the gift of being), for this ignores the fact that the "relative and variable impotence" of beings is a result of their place in the hierarchies—their created possibilities, in other words. There is room for movement within the hierarchies but not between them. The point is, for Dionysius, that there is nothing wrong with this; it allows for cosmological harmony, order, and, thus, beauty. Despite questions about Marion's treatment of the hierarchies within the *Corpus Dionysiacum,* he at least recognizes that there is an issue. Marion's willingness to engage in speculation of the relationship between a non-predicative discourse of praise and the hierarchically structured cosmos is dropped entirely in his later writings.

In the final section of *Idol and Distance* in which Marion discusses Dionysius, his argument culminates in the arrival at a type of discourse that is not subject to metaphysical constraints or critique: the biblical discourse of praise.[59] Marion assumes, following Balthasar's reading, that the verb "to say" (φημί), which can be only predicative, is replaced by the verb "to praise" or, more precisely, "to hymn" (ὑμνεῖν) in Dionysius.[60] Furthermore, Marion suggests that praise elicits a multiplication of names that operates equally as does "silence" as a strategy to guard against idolatry: "The same distance that masks the excess of signification (anonymity) provokes the excess of meanings and the multiplication of names: 'he who is praised by multiple praises and named by multiple names, the unspeakable and the anonymous' (DN, VII, 1, 865c)."[61]

This shift to praise does not entail a performative view of language—its success does not stand or fall with the utterance of the speakers: "One can see that the request, in order to be performed, here depends on more than the requestant, who cannot and must not make request except in that which commands and precedes it, in the anterior distance, the Requisite."[62] With this statement, he returns to his primary point, the place from which we begin makes all the difference: in *Idol and Distance* the starting place always must be God. As a result, "the language of praise plays its own game," one that can be understood only on its own basis. Marion acknowledges, in conclusion, that this is a structure of discourse that he has only begun to sketch through the exercise of "rereading Denys."[63]

How successful is this early rereading of "Denys"? In general, Marion is an astute and highly nuanced reader of much of Dionysius' writings. Yet I have also isolated instances in which Marion seems to be manipulating Dionysius a little too much. An important aspect of Marion's reading of Dionysius is the identity of his primary guide into this material, Hans Urs von Balthasar. Balthasar is cited throughout *Idol and Distance*[64] and is, furthermore, the primary person to whom Marion gives thanks in the foreword.[65] He also reveals the extent of his indebtedness in a footnote on the crucial concept of distance: "I here use this concept of *distance,* which commands all of the present work, with reference to that which H. Urs von Balthasar named 'the areopagite feeling of distance,' and which he comments on by seeing in it a 'distance which preserves, *wahrende*' (*Kosmiche Liturgie* [Fribourg, 1941, 177 and 248])."[66]

This reliance on Balthasar points to one of the most intriguing instances of the uncited references to Gregory of Nyssa in this work. There are distinct echoes of Gregory in the central concept of the entire work, a concept Marion tells us is borrowed from Balthasar: *distance.* "Distance" has four dimensions in Balthasar, two divine and two human. The divine distance refers to inter-Trinitarian distance as well as that between Father and Son on the cross. From the human perspective, however, "distance" refers to both the natural difference between God and the human, and the difference that results from human sinfulness.[67] While Marion clearly takes on all four of these dimensions of the meaning of distance, it is the natural distance between God and humanity that interests us here. Balthasar uses the term *diastasis* in this context. Where does this term come from? Balthasar himself traces the idea back to Gregory of Nyssa. Indeed, Balthasar argues that *diastasis* or *diastema* (διάστημα) is the positive foundation upon which Nyssen's theology rests; Gregory's theology *starts* with διάστημα, which Balthasar translates as "spacing" or "distance."[68] I will have more to say about this crucial term later. For the moment, however, it is important to note that "distance," the central concept of *Idol and Distance*, can be traced back to Gregory via Balthasar. Gregory is heard in this term, even if his name is not visible in the main text.

Two further references to Gregory are made outside the main body of the work, in two epigraphs—one for the entire book, and the other at the beginning of the final section of the book. The first epigraph, "Every concept formed in order to reach and encompass the divine nature succeeds only in fashioning an idol of God and not at all in making him known,"[69] encapsulates the critical project of the work in one pithy sentence. The second epigraph, "The icon, which is the same as the prototype, nevertheless differs from it,"[70] already anticipates a major theme of Marion's next theological work, *God Without Being*. Gregory will have a more explicit imprint in this later work.

God Without Being

Marion's most well-known work in English translation remains *God Without Being* (*GWB*), in which he argues that "God gives Himself to be known insofar as He gives himself—according to the horizon of the gift itself."[71] Like *Idol and Distance*, underlying the entire work is an acceptance of Nietzsche's pronouncement of the "death of God" and Heidegger's critique of onto-theology.[72]

Within an onto-theological metaphysics, according to Heidegger (via Marion), "God" is determined "starting from and to the profit of that which metaphysics is capable, that which it can admit and support";[73] that is, it is an idol. The metaphysical "God" culminates in the *causa sui*, "under the figures of efficiency, of the cause, and of the foundation."[74] Yet such a god is limited, as Heidegger argues, for "before the *causa sui*, man can neither fall to his knees in awe nor can he play music and dance before this god."[75] This path of thought inevitably leads to the challenges made by Nietzsche: why do we need a cause to explain what

is? God, as cause, is optional, a concession that leads to the "death of 'God,'"
according to Marion. Marion wants to contrast such a dead "God" with
the God of the Christian religion, which thinks God, starting not from
the need for a "cause," but "starting from God alone, grasped to the
extent that he inaugurates by himself the knowledge in which he yields
himself–reveals himself."[76] Thus Marion ventures to ask whether it is
self-evident that God should have to be, hence to be as a being, in order
to give himself as God?

This question leads Marion to attempt to locate the major turning
point in the thinking of God, the historical moment when God was first
thought primarily in terms of Being. He pins this turning point on
Thomas Aquinas and his application of *Esse* as the highest and most
proper name of God. In order to show that this marks a change from
previous Christian thought, Marion seeks not simply to show that "Being" was not the primary name for God before Aquinas but also to show
that Aquinas need not have made this move—that he made an unnecessary mistake. For this reason he returns to one of Thomas's most cited
sources, Dionysius. If he can show that Dionysius does not favor "being"
as a divine name, then he can show that Aquinas did not merely depart
from previous tradition, but he also misread one of his favorite sources.
Thus Marion's citation of Dionysius performs an important rhetorical
and polemical function in *God Without Being*. He relies on Dionysius to
provide a doctrine of divine names that insists on a radical distance
between the nominator and that which is nominated, a distance to be
traversed rather than filled.[77]

Marion argues that Aquinas represents a rupture or break from
"the tradition of Denys' treatise *On Divine Names*" by substituting *esse*
for *bonum*, or *summum bonum*."[78] Thomas justifies this "turn," according to Marion, by an assumption of the relation between Good and
cause in Dionysius. Cause is given both an efficient and a final sense in
Aquinas: God is efficient cause as the creator of all beings, and God is
final cause "as desirable also by what is not at all." The term "Good,"
rather than being the primary name of God, is "limited to 'adding' the
consideration of the final cause to that of efficient cause" in a definition
of God that still rests most properly on "being."[79] Marion finds this reasoning faulty, not only because αἰτία cannot be reduced to "final cause"
but also because, in his opinion, Thomas never justified the application
of Aristotelian categories to Dionysian thought in the first place.

Borrowing from his translation of the term αἰτία in *Idol and Distance,* Marion explicitly pits Dionysius against Thomas. He cites *DN* 5.7. 821b—"for the divine denomination of the good manifests all the processions of the Requisite [*aitia*] of all things, and extends as much to beings as to nonbeings"—as the "text that Saint Thomas had to confront and bypass" when he attempted to establish *Esse* as the most proper name of God.[80] Unlike Thomas, argues Marion, Dionysius refuses both the necessity and the possibility of establishing any such "most proper name of God." Even Goodness is not a "proper" or defining name. The point is not to define God but to praise God. In this way Dionysius "decidedly abolishes every conceptual idol of 'God' in favor of the luminous darkness where Gød manifests (and not masks) himself, in short, where he gives himself to be envisaged by us."[81]

Marion also uses Dionysius as an authoritative source of *theo*-logy (as opposed to theo-*logy*), citing *DN* 2.9. 648b: Hierotheus "did not learn things of God other than through what he suffered, and by this mystical compassion toward them, he was led to the perfection of mystical union and faith, which, if one might say, are not taught."[82] In his corresponding footnote, Marion glosses this citation thus: "We could not put it better than to say that the love of Love constitutes an epistemological condition of theology as *theo*logy."[83]

Dionysius has provided a historical instance where "Good" seems to be prior to "Being" as a divine name at the same time as he disavows the identification of any one name as proper to God, a reminder that calling God by name is a question of praise, not predication, as well as holding up love as the best way of approach in *theo*-logy. At the same time, Dionysius provides Marion with the conceptual framework within which he can establish the primacy of givenness. Thus we see how a retrieval of Dionysius functions rhetorically and polemically to provide a vision capable not only of withstanding a broad Heideggerian critique of all Western metaphysics but also of correcting a trend within Christian theology toward the prevalence of Being as a theological category.

Gregory of Nyssa is also cited in support of some key points in Marion's argument. First, in the context of a discussion of "conceptual idols"—a crucial move that Marion makes in order to extend the notion of an aesthetic or material idol to that of a conceptual idol[84]—Gregory is offered as a justification:

> There is nothing surprising in the transition from an "aesthetic" to a conceptual idol, since in one and the other case it is only a question of apprehension. Hence the famous sequence from Gregory of Nyssa: "Every concept (*noema*), as it is produced according to an apprehension of the imagination in a conception that circumscribes and in an aim that pretends to attain the divine nature, models only an idol of God (*eidolon theou*), without at all declaring God himself." (*Vita Moysis,* II, par. 166, PG 44, 337b)[85]

Notably, this citation of Gregory's not only supports the broadening of the notion of idolatry to include "concepts," but it also significantly echoes Marion's desire to free God from any attempt at conceptual capture.

Secondly, in the context of talking about "vanity" and its reverse, Marion again quotes Gregory:

> As to Gregory of Nyssa, he first defines the vain/*mataion* as *anupostaton,* "that which does not reside, and only has being in the sole utterance of the word," in short, that which flies away, like words. From this, other, more current meanings are obtained: "Another vanity is applied to the uselessness of things produced through an effort that attains no goal, like children's structures in the sand, and firing arrows toward the stars, the pursuit of winds, or the race to catch up with one's shadow." (*Commentarius in Ecclesiasten* I, PG 44, 620c–d)[86]

As I will discuss in the next chapter, this appraisal of the vanity of earthly desires is juxtaposed by Gregory with the eternal fecundity of a desire "rightly oriented" toward the divine. In addition, I will discuss significant overlaps between the infinite nature and eschatological function of desire in Gregory and Marion in chapter 5.

The most interesting reference to Gregory in *God Without Being,* however, does not cite his name explicitly: Marion has a section in chapter 6 entitled "*Epektasis,*" or "*L'épectase.*"[87] This section is imbedded within a chapter that discusses the unique temporality and attributes of the Eucharist. His aim is to describe a concept of time, particularly of the present, which is not subject to a "metaphysics of presence" but which is still governed by past and future. Such a rethinking of time involves reconstruing it within the framework of "gift" and "givenness": "The initial demand—to think presence as a present, and the present as a gift—now finds an infinitely more concrete content. Presence must be received as the present, namely, as the gift that is governed by the memorial and *epektasis*. Each instant of the present must befall us as a gift: the day, the hour, the instant, are imparted by charity."[88]

If the Eucharist, Marion's locus for the contemplation of the present moment, is always also memorial, something done "in memory of me," that memorial also always aims ahead to a future. This future is not simply a historical "end time" for which the Christian waits, but in reality already interrupts the present and governs it:

> The presence to come does not define the horizon of a simple possibility, tangential utopia or historical term as if it were a question of a simple nonpresence that it would remain to bring, finally, to presence. On the contrary, the future determines the reality of the present in the very mode of the advent. The eucharistic gift relies, so to speak, on the tension that raises it since and for the future. The future *as future*, governs, runs through, and polarizes the eucharistic gift, thus "straining (*epekteinomenos*) toward that which is coming to it" (Phil. 3:13). The pledge, which the memorial sets into operation, now anticipates the future, so that the presence itself occurs entirely as this anticipation concretely lived.[89]

Furthermore, as the Eucharist simultaneously reveals and conceals the Christic presence it contains, it "surpasses our attention, dazzles our gaze, and discourages our lucidity."[90]

Marion refers to Philippians 3 in explanation of the section title. While a participle form of the verb is found in Philippians (ἐπεκτεινόμενος), the term *epectasis* was coined and popularized by Jean Daniélou, who applies it uniquely to Gregory as a sort of shorthand to describe Gregory's eschatological vision of the "perpetual progress" of the soul. I will discuss this aspect of Gregory's thought in the next chapter, but for the moment it is sufficient to understand that the concept of perpetual progress has to do with an infinite desire for God that is nourished without ever being sated. The fact that Daniélou is one of Marion's foremost teachers prevents this use of the term from being anything but a reference to Gregory (conscious or not). Furthermore, the description of the present which is governed by a desire for something that is already being given while remaining elusive in its fullness is more than an oblique allusion to Gregory's notion of what Daniélou called *epectasis;* it is a meditation on Gregory's eschatology transported onto a eucharistic present. Marion cites other church fathers throughout this section (John of Damascus, Ambrose, Ignatius, and Cyril of Jerusalem, for instance), but does not once cite Gregory. This is a very curious omission.

Further examination of common elements in Gregory's notion of *epectasis* and Marion's "saturated phenomenon" will occupy a major portion of chapter 4. The above discussion of Marion's earliest writings and theological works has demonstrated that Gregory, although appearing infrequently in comparison to Dionysius, is cited with surgical precision when he does appear explicitly and also that Gregory is present in allusion even where he is not explicitly cited. It remains to be seen how this early use of Dionysius and Gregory compares with Marion's more recent writings.

"In the Name: How to Avoid Speaking of It"

A short but important essay, "In the Name: How to Avoid Speaking of It," marks the second location of Marion's extended and direct explication of Dionysius—this time in debate with Jacques Derrida instead of Heidegger (or Aquinas). It is also significant in what it reveals about Marion's reliance upon Gregory in crucial moments of the argument. This essay was originally written and given in the context of a conference at Villanova in 1997. Following Marion's paper a discussion, "On the Gift," occurred between Marion and Derrida, moderated by Richard Kearney. Both the paper and the ensuing discussion were later published in *God, the Gift, and Postmodernism*.[91] Marion then revised the piece and published it in French as *"Au nom ou comment le taire"*—the sixth chapter of his work *De Surcroît: Études sur les phénomènes saturés*.[92] The primary difference between the original and the final versions of this essay is that in the latter Marion places even greater emphasis on the radical incomprehensibility of God. Furthermore, he makes a greater emphasis on the "pragmatic" quality and function of mystical and liturgical theology. This pragmatic emphasis carries over into later writings and becomes a significant point vis-à-vis his retrieval of Gregory and Dionysius.

"In the Name" can only be understood against an ongoing debate between Marion and Derrida, not only about the nature and function of the "gift" and "givenness," but also about the legitimate scope of Derrida's critique of any "metaphysics of presence." At stake in this argument is the question of whether or not theology ought to be subject to such a critique: "In short, can Christian theology as a theology provoked by a Revelation remove itself in principle, if not in what it really accomplishes, from the 'metaphysics of presence'—or is it, in the final analysis, reducible to metaphysics? Which amounts to asking: is Christian theology subject to deconstruction, or not?"[93] Before evaluating Marion's response, one must first understand Derrida's critique.[94]

According to Marion, Derrida's critique is fourfold: First, Derrida argues that negative theology's claim to make no positive statement concerning the divine is a pretence. Negative statements are still predicative: in not saying, it says "not x."[95] Secondly, by predicating of God, negative theology reinscribes God in a "metaphysics of presence." Thirdly, Derrida denies that his own notion of *différance* falls into the same trap. Finally, prayer as a mode of addressing God must also be disqualified by Derrida as a "disguised form of predication." With this rehearsal of the main points of Derrida's critique, Marion pinpoints that what is at stake for Derrida is not simply "negative theology" but "rather deconstruction itself, its originality and its final preeminence."[96]

To this rehearsal of Marion's, a couple of accusations against negative theology are raised by Derrida to which Marion is less equipped to respond. Derrida believes that negative theology, as it is especially exemplified in Dionysius, retains an "ontological wager" insofar as it posits, in the end, a guarantor of the system outside of it—a "transcendental signified."[97] Secondly, Derrida accuses negative theology of holding out a *promise* for the presence of God through a vision or union.[98] Finally, Derrida argues that "negative theology" is more concerned with secrecy and elitism than with the ineffability of God. Derrida admits that deconstruction also has been accused of "forming a sect, a brotherhood, an esoteric corporation, or more vulgarly, a clique, a gang, or (I quote) a 'mafia'" to hide the secret of meaning.[99] Yet he suggests that this is a case of mistaken identity. It is negative theology, not deconstruction, that should stand against such charges. Such a demand for secrecy, notes Derrida, is no secret in Dionysius' theology: "Since the promise is also an order, the allegorical veil becomes a political shield, the solid barrier of a social division; or, if you prefer, a *shibboleth*. One invents it to protect against access to a knowledge which remains in *itself* inaccessible, untransmissible, unteachable."[100]

Derrida's critique is not simply about "negative theology" in general but focuses on the theology of Dionysius. For this reason, Marion structures his response as a defense and explication of Dionysius. Nevertheless, in this response Marion vacillates between, on the one hand, a conversation about Dionysius and, on the other, a defense of the entirety of the Christian tradition of apophatic or mystical theology. In other words, Marion both allows Dionysius to speak for the entire tradition and, just as importantly, when Dionysius does not say exactly what Marion would like, allows others to speak for him. In this particular essay, Marion begins with a fairly concentrated explication of Dionysius and gradually broadens his scope to include others, especially Gregory. This results in the anomaly that Gregory, and not Dionysius, proves to be a central source for the most decisive points in Marion's argument.

Marion begins by articulating the profound and frustrating inadequacy of both terms, "metaphysics of presence" and "negative theology," saying that neither has "precise definition nor clear-cut historical legitimacy."[101] Regarding a "metaphysics of presence," Marion asks whether "presence" is simply identical to metaphysics. Can one envisage a metaphysics that treats on par, or even privileges, absence?[102] Regarding "negative theology," Marion reminds us that Dionysius uses "negative theology" only once and then in the plural (ἀποφατικαί θελογίαι) and hand in hand with the term "affirmative theologies" (καταφατιαί θελογίαι)—where theology "always designates the expressions Scripture uses to say (or not to say) God, at a great distance from metaphysics."

Marion argues that Dionysius offers a "third way" beyond the false antinomy between positive and negative theology,[103] something Marion calls "de-nomination." *Dénomination,* in the original French, has the dual connotation of simultaneously naming and un-naming:

> It is no longer a question of naming [*de le nommer*] nor by contrast of not naming [*de ne pas le nommer*], but of de-nominating God [*de le dénommer*]—in the twofold sense that this term can have: to name (to name in view of . . . , to nominate), but with something close to negation, and consequently also to undo [*le défaire*] from all nomination, to release and deliver God from it [*l'en dégager et délivrer*], thwarting it [*la déjouer pour Lui*]. In its ambiguity, de-nomination bears the twofold function of saying (affirming negatively) and undoing this saying of the name. It concerns a form of speech that no longer says something about something (or a name of someone) but which denies all relevance to predication, rejects the nominative function of names, and suspends the rule of truth's two values.[104]

Marion has recourse at this juncture to the translation he provided in *Idol and Distance* for the term αἰτία ("cause," or as Marion would have it, "Requisite").[105] In giving God (who surpasses all nomination) the title αἰτία, Dionysius does not speak of God as "metaphysical cause" but as "what all those who demand [αἰτιάτα, *aitiata*] demand [αἰτέω, *aiteo*] when they aim at the One from whom they come and to whom they return." In other words αἰτία has no claim either to name God or to deny the name of God; it has no predicative function, but only the pragmatic one of enabling a speaker to address that which remains beyond all designation:

> The αἰτία in no way names God; it de-nominates [*le dé-nomme*] by suggesting the strictly pragmatic function of language—namely, to refer names and their speaker to the unattainable yet inescapable interlocutor beyond every name and every denegation of names. With αἰτία, speech does not say any more than it denies—its acts by transporting itself in the direction of the One whom it de-nominates.[106]

It is in precisely in this way that Dionysius indicates a "new pragmatic function of language" that, according to Marion, will always escape any onto-theological trappings.[107]

Furthermore, with the introduction of his phrase "strictly pragmatic function of language," Marion confronts Derrida's objection that any prayer which praises (ὑμνεῖν) is always predicative insofar as it addresses someone; it "praises as . . . , therefore by naming" as opposed to a prayer, "pure and simple" (εὐχή).[108] In order to object to this false dichotomy, Marion employs a Cappadocian theory of language (without describing it thus). He accuses Derrida of assuming that naming one implies equating that name with an essence. Instead, argues Marion, "what is proper to the proper name consists precisely in the fact that it never belongs properly—by and as essence—to the one who receives it. *Never* is the proper name a name for the essence."[109] Marion goes on to conclude that names only have a pragmatic (or conventional) function, again in a way that echoes Gregory rather than Dionysius: "Consequently, the common/proper name implies that others beside me use it to intend me and designate me, in short, call me by it."[110] The way in which the proper name is experienced, therefore, is as that which marks a presence exceeding any essential definition. To attribute a name to God in praise "does not name God properly or essentially, nor in presence, but that it marks God's absence, anonymity and withdrawal—exactly as every name dissimulates every individual, which it merely indicates without ever manifesting."[111]

There is an incongruity to this aspect of Marion's defense of "hymnic discourse" in Dionysius; namely, it does not come out of the Dionysian corpus. Instead, this is precisely the argument in Gregory's *Contra Eunomium*, a text that Marion goes on to quote a few pages later. He is thus fully aware of the argument in this text. It is in his mind as he writes, even though he does not reference Gregory. In fact, Dionysius does not write about language and naming in this particular way. He employs other strategies to protect the inviolability and transcendence of God in language. For example, his notion of "dissimilar similarity," abundant metaphoric plurality, and silence are all ways of linguistically signaling divine incomprehensibility. Rather than drawing on these, Marion turns to the apophatic strategies of Gregory in *Contra Eunomium*.

Marion's next argument broadens the scope of the defense. No longer simply recuperating Dionysius, Marion is now pursuing the redemption of the entire Christian tradition (at least when it is "properly" understood). He argues that theology has the "means, the intention, and also every reason to ignore any invitation into a 'metaphysics of presence.'"[112] Instead, theology relies on the "privilege of the unknowable as the guarantor that God may remain God and not become an idol."[113] Marion's primary concern is to prove the way in which, within Christianity, one can already find a consistent desire to guard against the danger of idolatry, against the claim to know God, which would be tantamount to the claim to fix and circumscribe, determine, or limit God in any way. He provides a litany of theologians from the tradition to prove his point: Justin Martyr, Clement of Alexandria, Origen, Athanasius, Basil, Gregory of Nyssa, John Chrysostom, John of Damascus, Augustine, Bernard of Clairvaux, and Thomas Aquinas.[114]

Thus Marion establishes a pattern in the Fathers in which "theology does not consist in naming God properly, but well and truly in knowing God precisely as what cannot be known properly—what must not be known, if one wants to know it as such."[115] Furthermore, Marion goes on to say that it is not "theologians" who seek to confine God within presence, but "the heretics." It is in the context of the debate between the Cappadocians and Eunomius, according to Marion, that this strong privileging of the incomprehensibility of God gets its most robust development. Eunomius is raised as the sacrificial lamb upon which Marion lays his wrath: "Here deconstruction and theology can be in agreement, for the sake of contesting the same adversary—not the orthodox theologian, but the Arian, the sole metaphysician of presence, if there ever was such a thing."[116] Again, the categories of "orthodoxy" and "heresy" function as a helpful rhetorical device for his contemporary debates.

Having provided this litany of orthodox thinking, Marion arrives at what is arguably the primary thesis of the entire argument: Christian theology at its best (i.e., "orthodoxy") does not culminate in a "metaphysics of presence," whether masked behind the veil of negativity or not; instead, in Dionysius (and elsewhere), one finds a proponent of a *"pragmatic theology of absence*—where the name is given as having no name, as not giving the essence, and having nothing but this absence to make manifest; a theology where hearing happens, as Paul remarks, '... not only in my presence but also in my absence' (Phil. 2:12)."[117] It is in this context that he cites Gregory for a full page—a point to which we will shortly return. Here it is sufficient to note that Marion locates the seeds of this notion within the corpus of Dionysius.[118]

Having glossed Marion's use of Dionysius in order to establish a "pragmatic" and non-predicative philosophy of language, we now turn to look at how Gregory is employed in the same argument. The first time Gregory appears he is only one of many theologians cited as evidence of the Christian "privileging of divine unknowability." Gregory, as one might expect, states it forcefully: "This is the true knowledge of what is sought [that is to say, seeing the invisible and incomprehensible God—ἀκατάληπτὸν]; this is the seeing that consists in not seeing [τὸ ἰδεῖν ἐν τῷ μή ἰδεῖν], because that which is sought transcends all knowledge, being separated on all sides by incomprehensibility as by a kind of darkness."[119]

Interestingly, the French version of Marion's translation of this text mentions the "cloud of incomprehensibility (*nuée d'incompréhensibilité*)."[120] This differs from the standard French translation of Gregory by Daniélou, who speaks of a seeing that is "separated on all sides by an incomprehensibility as by a darkness [*une ténèbre*],"[121] a translation that follows the Greek more closely (οἷον τινι γνόφῳ τῇ ἀκαταληψία πανταχόθεν διειλημμέον). This means that in the English translation of Marion's article the translator, Robyn Horner, relies on the Paulist Press translation of *The Life of Moses*,[122] and in so doing, corrects Marion. Gregory does use the phrase "cloud [ἡ νεφέλη] of incomprehensibility," but not in this particular passage. While this is a minor mistake and no substantial change in meaning occurs as a result, it nevertheless actually demonstrates Marion's broad knowledge of

Gregory. First, it shows that Marion is working with the original texts and translating independently of prior French translations even if, as in this case, he is occasionally mistaken in so doing. Secondly, it is evidence of a deep familiarity with Nyssen's corpus such that he is aware that Gregory often uses the phrase "cloud of incomprehensibility" in similar contexts and (consciously or not) switches the one phrase for the other.

The other place in which Marion quotes Gregory is, I argue, the most significant. Here Marion turns to Gregory at a crucial point in his argument simply because he could not find the same argument in Dionysius. This citation marks the arrival at one of the primary goals of the entire essay—to establish "a *pragmatic theology of absence.*" This phrase signifies "not the non-presence of God but the fact that the name that God is given, the name that gives God, which is given as God (each of these going hand-in-hand, without being confused), serves *to shield God from presence.*"[123] Marion states that "Gregory of Nyssa saw and described this perfectly" and goes on to quote Gregory for almost a full page (the longest single citation in the essay). What follows is a condensed version:

> What is the significance of the unnameable name of which the Father speaks [when he says] "Baptize them in my name," without adding the signification uttered by this name? On this matter here is our opinion: we grasp all beings in creation through the signification of their names. Thus, he who says "sky" conveys to the mind of the one who is listening the creature shown by this name; and if one mentions "man" or one of the living things by his name, his form [*eidos*] is at once impressed upon the one who is listening . . . In contrast, only the uncreated nature, which we believe [to be] the Father, Son, and the Holy Spirit, surpasses all signification that a name can convey. This is why the Word, in saying this name, did not add to the tradition of faith what it is (how could he have found a name for a thing above all names?). But he gave our understanding the power to set about piously to find, according to its capacity, a name which indicates the supereminent nature and which is equally fitting to the Father, the Son and the Holy Spirit . . . And this, it seems to me, is what the Word decreed by this formula [that is to say, to say "the name" without saying which one]—in order to convince us that the name of the divine essence is unsayable and incomprehensible.[124]

This is a very clear and precise description of the idea that Marion is after. He finds it, in this instance, in Gregory instead of Dionysius.

Gregory is here called in to clinch an argument that has primarily been concerned with interpretations of Dionysius.

One might also note the baptismal and liturgical context of this citation, which Marion takes as a further element in such a pragmatic theory of discourse. He argues that what Gregory here describes—the fact that the Name does not function by inscribing God within our horizon of predication but "by inscribing us, according to a radically new praxis, in the very horizon of God"—can only occur within the context of baptism. When one is baptized, that person does not name God but receives one's name from God, thus entering into the "Name above all names."[125] Marion concludes: "In this way, mystical theology no longer has as its goal to find a name for God but rather to make us receive our own from the unsayable Name. Concerning God, this shift from the theoretical use of language to its pragmatic use is achieved in the finally liturgical function of all *theo*-logical discourse."[126] As I have shown, this argument is accomplished by a citation of Gregory as much as of Dionysius.

The Turn to Augustine: *Au lieu de soi*

Marion's most recent consideration of patristic thought is somewhat anomalous, not only because he shifts his attention from the Greek writers to the Latin giant Augustine, but also because in *Au lieu de soi* he is no longer merely citing a patristic source but devoting an entire monograph (and a lengthy one at that) to a sustained reading of Augustine's *Confessions*. It is impossible, therefore, to examine each citation; nonetheless, some general features of his interpretation of Augustine and its function within the primary argument of the work can be outlined here.

Au lieu de soi continues Marion's exploration of subjectivity—or, more precisely, what is found "in place of the self"—begun in *Being Given*. In this work, the self is something discovered or decided upon primarily (perhaps solely) in the face-to-face encounter with God. Thus a return to Augustine allows Marion to advance beyond both Levinas and Ricoeur: the self does not access or experience itself "*for* an other (Levinas) or *as* an other (Ricoeur)—but it becomes itself only *by* [*par*] an other." More explicitly, by "a gift" (*un don*) that comes ultimately from God.[127] In other words, in this work, Marion makes his own decision; the whence of the "giftedness" of the self (*l'adonné*) is made absolutely explicit—the self is a gift from God—discovered or decided upon only *coram Deo*. The theological trump card is unashamedly played. (Whether this is a necessary or advised move is another question.) Before discussing this shift, let me broadly rehearse the steps of Marion's argument.

Marion begins where he left off in *The Erotic Phenomenon*, namely, with the close entanglement of knowledge and truth with love. On the one hand, "one can only love that which one knows," and yet truth, as the goal of knowledge, is dependent upon a prior condition or disposition of love. In his critical review of *Au lieu de soi*, Joeri Schrijvers aptly communicates what is at stake with this entangled relationship between love and truth: "Truth therefore becomes dependent upon a certain practice and perhaps a decision: the question whether I will be able to live truthfully boils down to the question whether I decide for love and decide not to shy away from it—if and only if I may finally know what, who and even how to love—the world, myself, or God."[128]

The consequence of this entanglement of what (and how) we know with what (and how) we love is not only that truth requires a decision, and hence the involvement of the will, but therefore also that our statements shift to *confessions*. The function of our words is no longer predication, but orientation; they direct us toward that which we confess. With confession one speaks *to* God (*à Dieu*) rather than speaking *about* God (*sur Dieu*).[129] With confession one is aware of the experience of being placed before God (*coram Deo*). This experience reveals a truth made manifest "with perfect evidence," and thus which forces me

> to take a decision with regards to it, for or against its evidence; and according to my decision—to accept or refuse the evidence—the truth reflects on myself and my judgment, which is in principle theoretical, is turned against me ... Paradoxically, more essentially than a judgment over things (true or false), more essentially also than the manifestation of the phenomenon from itself, the truth produces a verdict over myself, according to which I can accept it or can challenge it only—love it or hate it.[130]

Confession, then, becomes the place where one's subjectivity is decided upon. Marion articulates this decision in a blunt dichotomy: the decision is for love or for hate.

Truth, the truth of the confrontation with God, according to Marion, "dismisses neutrality" for the reason that "it always imposes a choice upon the one who receives it and tests it."[131] One can refuse the truth, but one cannot avoid the confrontation with it that demands a decision. One has the freedom *not to choose* the truth, but he or she does not have the freedom to avoid the choice that is presented to one "with perfect evidence." Thus two basic options constitute the self: either one accepts it, or one "lies." These two—acceptance/love and lying/hate—are the only two options. Marion thus places the entire question of truth into the moral sphere. Truth is not neutral; it requires decision, commitment, orientation—even, in the end, obedience. To turn against the truth is to "lie," which Marion defines as "the possession of the self by self, without God."[132]

Any encounter with God immediately shows us all we cannot give to ourselves, for at its heart the confrontation reveals that any decision with regard to the self must be received as a gift. To attempt to achieve subjectivity oneself is to lie—to deny that the self is constituted, not merely *for* an other (Levinas) or *as* an other (Ricoeur), but only *by* (*par*) an other, namely, by God as a gift: "I will not love, therefore, because I decided to; I will not decide, therefore, because I wanted to, but because I will receive it as a gift . . . The temptation becomes, then, the trial of the self where the self learns whether it loves that which it receives as a gift, and whether it loves this gift more than any other thing."[133]

The question is, is one free to hate, or at least refuse, God? On the one hand, it would seem to be possible because Marion talks of the decision made in this confrontation in terms of sin, temptation, the lie, and even the "deformity of the sinner."[134] Marion's attachment to a moral judgment would seem to necessitate a sense of subjective agency and freedom. And yet he is also clear that God's grace is required to aid or give to the "will in danger" sufficient strength to love: "That which *my will absolutely cannot will*, God can authorize to will, provided that God gives him [power] to will it."[135] In so doing, Marion entrenches himself within the paradigmatic Augustinian conundrum: how to understand the relationship between free will and grace. Whence the capacity to decide for love or hate? Either it is solely from God, in which case I cannot be held responsible for the decision that is to decide my fate (and cannot be accused of yielding to temptation, or lying), or the decision rests, at least in part, on me, in which case my subjectivity is determined, at least in part, by myself. Marion cannot have it both ways. The discussion of the relationship between free will and grace in Augustine has dominated centuries of theological debate. Marion does not advance this debate in this work; he merely repeats the problem.

As mentioned above, *Au lieu de soi* is somewhat anomalous in our survey of Marion's patristic citation practices insofar as it is his first sustained monograph on a single church father. Moreover, it represents a shift in his retrieval from, predominately, the Greek patristic sources to the Latin behemoth Augustine, who had heretofore been relatively absent from Marion's writing. The work also represents a subtle yet significant philosophical shift in Marion: a turn to emphasize confession rather than apophasis as well as a shift from invisibility to beatific vision.[136] This shift, in turn, marks a movement to explore the moral implications of his thought (begun in *The Erotic Phenomenon*) in which Marion no longer contents himself with contemplating the paradox of an unlimited givenness and infinite hermeneutic, but seeks further to consider the culpability of the self in the reception of that givenness (and in a connected move, a willingness to identify the origin of that givenness). The philosophical consequences of these shifts in emphasis will be discussed in chapter 5. For now it is sufficient to remark that the general pattern in Marion's patristic citation is not here contradicted.

Univocity in the Service of Apologetics

In the introductory pages of *Idol and Distance,* Marion imagines possible objections about the way he "uses" other thinkers' writings:

> The cavalier alacrity of certain "interpretations" (the quotation marks indicating, by understatement, the mistranslations or the misinterpretations) shall seem violent, and even not very serious or objective, to the specialists. . . . One might even be surprised by the little attention paid to the very important secondary literature dedicated to these authors.[137]

Despite this caveat, Marion is no "dabbler" in patristics; his reading demonstrates extensive scholarship in the original language of these texts. As we have seen, although Marion is not interested in providing a history of patristic thought, he remains a comprehensive reader of Dionysius and the thought-worlds of Late Antiquity. Similarly, although he is not interested in locating himself explicitly within Dionysian scholarship, this does not mean he is not influenced by other readings of Dionysius—thinking especially here of Balthasar. Furthermore, he interprets and cites his sources selectively, with an eye to their rhetorical value for contemporary debates.

The Fathers serve an apologetic function for Marion. They are re-trieved as a source of authority, explicitly of "orthodoxy" in his earliest writings, and implicitly in his phenomenological work. As a result, pa-tristic citations tend to function univocally in Marion's writings, from his earliest essays in *Résurrection* to his debate with Derrida at Villa-nova. As we have seen, this is especially the case with Gregory of Nyssa and Dionysius. I have argued that Dionysius, who initially provides Marion with a generative framework within which to develop his ideas about givenness and visibility/invisibility, becomes shorthand for an enterprise that, in Marion's later writings, owes less to Dionysius than to other patristic sources. In a similar vein, I have argued that Gregory is a hidden presence in this same enterprise. We can identify Gregory be-hind the notions of "distance" and of "*epectasis*" as well as the achieve-ment of a "pragmatic theology of absence." Gregory can be enlisted to support a discussion that is explicitly about Dionysius because Marion nowhere acknowledges any real difference between the two patristic writers. This lack of a discrimination available to, but under-utilized by, Marion will be evaluated in the following chapter.

TWO

How to Avoid Idolatry: A Comparison of "Apophasis" in Gregory of Nyssa and Dionysius the Areopagite

This truly is the vision of God: never to be satisfied in the desire to see him.

—GREGORY OF NYSSA, *V. Mos.* 2.239

I am convinced in my mind that one may not disregard the received knowledge of divine things. I believe this not merely because one's spirit naturally yearns for and seeks whatever contemplation of the supernatural may be attainable but also because the splendid arrangement of divine laws commands it. We are told not to busy ourselves with what is beyond us, since they are beyond what we deserve and are unattainable. But the law tells us to learn everything granted to us and to share these treasures generously with others.

—DIONYSIUS THE AREOPAGITE, *DN* 3.3

While for Gregory of Nyssa *eros* overthrows all limits as it hastens after the ever-greater God, with Denys the self-same *eros* is contained in its striving after infinity within two limits: the possible (*hos ephikton*) and the permitted (*themiton,* strictly speaking: what can be attained without sacrilege).

—HANS URS VON BALTHASAR, "Denys" in *Glory of the Lord*

In the previous chapter I illustrated how Marion retrieves Gregory of Nyssa and Dionysius in one register, employing Gregory's words in the service of an exposition of Dionysius and allowing one to speak in place of the other. The purpose of this chapter is to call into question a univocal retrieval of this sort and to examine the significant *differences* between the apophaticisms of Gregory and Dionysius as encoded in the quotations above and summarized by Balthasar.

The organization of this argument is complicated by the difficulty, even the impossibility, of neatly separating out "apophaticism" from either author's vision. For both, apophasis is inherently and inseparably part of a cosmological and, even more specifically, a soteriological belief.[1] Apophasis is understood incorrectly when it is thought to be a mere linguistic method of correcting proper speech about God; rather, apophasis involves the basic presupposition of how God and creation are essentially related and also the soteriological horizon of this relation, the end, or *telos* of it. Apophasis is only, in the beginning, of epistemological significance. A more comprehensive view, however, reveals both its ontological necessity and its anthropological consequences.

For this reason, a comparative treatment of the diverse understandings of *apophasis* in Gregory and Dionysius will require not merely a discussion of language and naming but also of different notions of creation and of desire and how it is consummated. These themes, in turn, imply particular understandings of "participation," "union," "perfection," and "revelation" that must also be explored. This chapter compares the two writers following these categories. This undertaking does not constitute a comprehensive comparative analysis of Gregory and Dionysius;[2] although the study may draw broadly from different elements of the thought of each, it does so only with a view toward their significance for different apophaticisms.[3] Subsequent chapters will take up various elements introduced in this chapter's comparison and discuss them with greater specificity.

The argument will proceed thus: I will begin with (1) a survey of the comparative scholarship thus far and (2) a close reading of the depiction of Moses' ascent into darkness as a crystallized image of *apophasis* found in Gregory's *Life of Moses* and in Dionysius' *Mystical Theology* 1:3. From there I will turn to (3) a direct comparison of each thinker's philosophy of language. Already within the domain of language, its function and foundation, a sharp difference emerges between Gregory and Dionysius. These differences deepen when (4) the philosophy of language is situated within a robust vision of world, God, and the human being. These differences further imply (5) divergent understandings of human perfection and desire's consummation. Finally, (6) we return to the linguistic domain in order to compare the characteristics of divine revelation. Here the full divergence between Gregory's interruptive and transgressive view of revelation and Dionysius' originary and productive view is more visible. Throughout this comparison, my aim is not to demonstrate a *disjunction* or contradiction between the apophatic thought of Gregory and Dionysius, but to insist on the significant *distinctiveness* of each thinker.

Before I begin this analysis, a brief comment on the notions of "idolatry" and "radicality" will situate the significance of *apophasis* in relation to Marion's thought. For both Gregory and Dionysius apophaticism encompasses more than a mode of speech; it is a fundamental way of being in proper relation to God. The "way of being in right relation" can also be expressed negatively as a problem: how to avoid "idolatry." In other words, how is one to worship God without grasping at God? How is one to be in relation with God without turning God into an idol, literally an object that can be named, known, and assimilated? Apophaticism, for both thinkers, acknowledges that limits or boundaries of permissibility must be properly delineated in order to guarantee God's inviolability—limits of desire as well as limits of speech. What are the limits to which one's language about and desire for God can attain?

I argue that Gregory and Dionysius both draw these boundaries, and situate the human person vis-à-vis these boundaries differently. For Gregory, there is one principle boundary between God and the created world. Toward that boundary, which is impossible to traverse even with an eternal effort, one nevertheless finds oneself eternally moving. For Dionysius, however, within the one ultimate distinction between God and God's creation, there remain multiple levels of being beyond which one is not permitted to go and within which one achieves the measure of perfection attainable to each individual. For both, there remains movement. But for Gregory, it is an infinite thrusting of the "fullness" (πλήρωμα) of all created being at the "ontological" divide; whereas for Dionysius, it is an eternal "approximation" into God from one's proper location and participation.

Comparisons between Gregory and Dionysius often employ the category of "radicality" to assess the difference: who has the more "radical" apophaticism? The qualifier "radical" refers to the strength of the negative guarantee of God's otherness, ungraspability, or inviolability. Usually, Dionysius' apophaticism is claimed to be the more radical of the two. I differ in this assessment. I will argue that both writers achieve a certain "radicality" in their apophaticism, but they do so in very different ways and with very different linguistic and ontological consequences. They are not compared adequately by looking only at their philosophy of language and turning a blind eye to its ontological context.

I believe that insufficient attention has been given to Gregory in contemporary conversations of "negative theology" precisely because his apophaticism emerges, unavoidably, out of an ontology of the radical disjunction between God and creation. The contemporary distaste for ontological (or metaphysical) speculation forgets that theories of language are always embedded within particular understandings of the relationship between world and word, and by extension between God and word. Linguistic theories always already have some ontological presuppositions, or at the very least, implications.[4] This conjecture would also suggest an explanation for Marion's blindness to the difference between Gregory and Dionysius in his problematically univocal retrieval of them. Furthermore, drawing out the differences between the two patristic thinkers underscores the problems with treating "negative theology" as a single, monolithic tradition to be either associated with or dissociated from.

Survey of Literature

There is surprisingly little direct comparative scholarship on Gregory and Dionysius. Mostly, one must rely on broad overview texts on the history of "mysticism," the "mystical tradition," or "apophasis" (Louth, McGinn, Williams, Carabine[5]), or on writings about Dionysius that have sections on his relation to Gregory (Golitzin,[6] Balthasar,[7] Fisher,[8] Puech[9]). The only article that contains both names in its title compares Christian and Neoplatonic notions of "solitude" and simply assumes that Gregory and Dionysius are identical as two representative Christians (Corrigan[10]).

Some general classifications can be made within this comparative scholarship. In the first group is situated those for whom a relation of complementarity or linear progression between Gregory and Dionysius is either assumed or argued. Corrigan would fit into this category as would, in a more sophisticated way, McGinn, Carabine, and Golitzin.[11] The second group consists of those who reflect more on the difference between Gregory and Dionysius in the service of illustrating how Dionysius is the more "radical" of the two. In this category one could place Fisher, Williams, and, in a way unlike the others, Louth.[12] What is at stake here is something more than a purely historical comment. Often the discussion is laden with overtones from contemporary philosophical discussions.[13] Finally, we can form a third category made up of those who resist categorization. For instance, Puech argues that, in fact, Gregory has a more intensely experiential mysticism than Dionysius.[14] Balthasar's privileging of notions of divine presence in Dionysius in order to demonstrate his rich theological aesthetic will shade his comparative treatment of Dionysius and Gregory such that a greater emphasis is placed on "darkness" or "negativity" in Gregory. Despite this point, Dionysius remains the culminating figure in the apophatic tradition for Balthasar. In other words, he thinks Gregory is more "radically negative" but in a finally incoherent and baffling way, which makes Dionysius the greater progenitor of ancient Christian apophaticism.[15]

Despite this dismissal of Gregory, Balthasar stresses the same differences between Gregory and Dionysius that I will develop below. These differences center around the themes of limits and the possibility of perfection: "While for Gregory of Nyssa *eros* overthrows all limits as it hastens after the ever-greater God, with Denys the self-same *eros* is contained in its striving after infinity within two limits: the possible (*hos ephikton*) and the permitted (*themiton,* strictly speaking: what can be attained without sacrilege)."[16] The difference here is real and significant: for Dionysius the danger to be avoided is striving outside the bounds of permissibility, whereas for Gregory the danger lies in the idolatry of settling or stopping. (Of what does idolatry consist, in Marion's view? Subsequent chapters will demonstrate Marion's proximity to Gregory on this central point.)

Balthasar discusses Dionysius' emphasis on notions of "harmony" and "order" in revelation and soteriology:

> This methodical *harmonia* is an *analogia,* an appropriate relation, a proportion between revelation and the capacity for receiving it, set by the one who reveals himself with regard to a particular nature and comprehension of the subject. Providence itself, both as creating and as communicating salvation to the creature, is analogous, in that it guarantees to each being a primordial "worthiness" (*axia*) to receive God in accordance with its rank and imparts its divine self-expression in accordance with this "worthiness."[17]

Balthasar admits that this discrepancy between Gregory and Dionysius is precisely that—a discrepancy, something unexpected, in Dionysius:

The first thing that strikes one if one comes to Denys from Alexandria, from Origen and Evagrius and Gregory of Nyssa, and the more so as Denys is seen as the theologian of the divine limitlessness, is the emphasis he places on limits. Limit (*peras*), holy law of being (*thesmos*), rank (*taxis*), ordering (*diacosmesis*), measure (*metron*), symmetry (*symmetria*), analogy (*analogia*), holy graduation (*hierarchia*) are the perpetually recurring categories. Because God is beyond rest and movement, beyond finitude and infinity, there is no direct opposition between him and anything created.[18]

There is a genuinely "positive significance to finitude and limits"[19] in Dionysius that is not found in Gregory. In the latter we encounter a fear of, even a prohibition against, limits. Keeping this divergent impulse in mind, I now turn to an examination of the textual evidence in the writings of both patristic thinkers.

Moses' Ascent of Mount Sinai

The description of Moses' ascent of Mount Sinai is not the only trope Gregory and Dionysius use to discuss *apophasis*. However, it is the image in which their two descriptions most closely echo each other. I am starting, in other words, from where Gregory and Dionysius are closest.[20] For both, the ascent is marked by increasing purification, contemplation or illumination, and perfection. Most significantly, both follow Philo insofar as this is a movement from "light" into "darkness." Dionysius describes this as the "darkness of unknowing" (τὸν γνόφον τῆς ἀγνωσιάς) or the "darkness beyond light" (ὑπέρφωτων γνόφον),[21] while Gregory speaks of journeying into a "luminous darkness" (λαμπρω γνόφω) where true knowledge is identified as "the seeing that consists in not seeing" (τὸ ἰδεῖν ἐν τῷ μή ἰδεῖν).[22] For both, the darkness into which one moves is a direct result, not of human ignorance or lack, but of divine excess.[23] Furthermore, for both Dionysius and Gregory this is discussed within the framework of the liturgy.

In *The Life of Moses* Gregory uses Moses as a model of a person's eternal progression toward the Divine, that movement for which Jean Daniélou has coined the word *epectasis*.[24] Gregory describes the journey: "If nothing comes from above to hinder its upward thrust . . . the soul rises ever higher and will always make its flight yet higher—by its desire of the heavenly things *straining ahead for what is still to come* [ἐπεκτεινομένη], as the Apostle says [Phil. 3:13]."[25] Moses' life presents three moments of this "approach"[26] to God: from *light,* into the *cloud,* and ending in *darkness.* First, the movement from the shadow of ignorance to the *light* of right knowing is accomplished through asceticism, or *praktike.*[27] It is a purification of both the body and the soul, both moral and intellectual. The movement into the *cloud* is that of contemplation, or *theoria;* in this moment one knows that one is "enlightened" by the understanding that one is in the dark and does not, nor will ever be able to, understand or comprehend God.[28] In the exodus narrative, when Moses asks to see God's face, he has not yet fully understood this. God instructs Moses to enter a rock. God covers the entrance of the rock with the divine hand when passing before it. Moses is summoned to look. He is then granted a vision of God's "back," and he sees all that he will ever be capable of seeing.[29] And yet this vision of God's "back" does not satisfy one's desire to see God. One "follows" God eternally, hoping to gaze more and more lovingly at God. This is the third moment into deeper darkness, which is experienced, not as an ontological union, but as an ever-increasing movement of desire for God. Paradoxically, the eternal movement is the stasis.[30] The final "rest," Gregory's picture of the *eschaton,* is when all of creation is joined in this neverending movement toward God. There is, in other words, no final consummating union between God and the human, no beatific vision in which we see or know God perfectly.

Dionysius' explicit discussion of Moses' ascent occurs in the first chapter of the short but nonetheless monumentally influential *Mystical Theology.* The chapter opens with an encomium to the Trinity:

> Lead us up beyond unknowing and light,/ up to the farthest, highest peak/ of mystic scripture,/ where the mysteries of God's Word/ lie simple, absolute and unchangeable/ in the brilliant darkness [ὑπέρφωτων γνόφον] of a hidden silence./ Amid the deepest shadow/ they pour overwhelming light [ὑπερλάμποντα]/ on what is most manifest./ Amid the wholly unsensed and unseen/ they completely fill our sightless minds/ with treasures beyond all beauty.[31]

One notices many of Marion's core themes encapsulated in this brief passage: the elements of saturation—"our sightless minds" (τοὺς ἀνομμάτους νοάς) are "completely filled" (ὑπερπληοῦντα)—as well as the passivity of the one who is led "beyond unknowing and light" (ὑπεράγνωστον καὶ ὑπερφαῆ). Furthermore, the theme of eternal progress or *epectasis* is also implied; it is this passage that almost seems to be lifted directly from Gregory's corpus: ". . . my advice to you as you look for a sight of the mysterious things, is to leave behind you every-thing perceived and understood, everything perceptible and under-standable, all that is not and all that is, and, with your understanding laid aside, to strive upward as much as you can toward union with him who is beyond all being and knowledge."[32] A little further on, where Dionysius is describing Moses' ascent, echoes of Gregory again resound. The Word of God is said to be manifest only to those "who pass beyond the summit of every holy ascent, who leave behind them every divine light, every voice, every word from heaven, and who plunge into the darkness where, as scripture proclaims, there dwells the One who is beyond all things." Here, as with Gregory, Moses "does not meet God himself, but contemplates, not him who is invisible, but rather where he dwells."[33]

Gregory's interpretation of this moment for Moses is shaded in a slightly different way. Direct contemplation of God is impossible for both Gregory and Dionysius. Yet they have a different response to this impossibility. Dionysius speaks of contemplating "where God dwells," whereas Gregory suggests contemplation of the divine absence itself: "But as the mind progresses and, through an ever greater and more per-fect diligence, comes to apprehend reality, as it approaches more nearly to contemplation, it sees more clearly what of the divine nature is un-contemplated."[34] The darkness, for Gregory, results in an unflinching awareness of the inescapability of divine incomprehensibility. This un-derstanding that God is unknowable is, paradoxically, the truest, most perfect knowledge humans can possess.[35]

> For leaving behind everything that is observed, not only what sense com-prehends but also what the intelligence thinks it sees, it keeps on pene-trating deeper until by the intelligence's yearning for understanding it gains access to the invisible and the incomprehensible, and there it sees God. This is the true knowledge of what is sought; this is the seeing that consists in not seeing [τὸ ἰδεῖν ἐν τῷ μή ἰδεῖν], because that which is sought transcends all knowledge, being separated on all dark sides by incomprehensibility as by a kind of darkness.[36]

This teaching of divine incomprehensibility has the status of a divine commandment for both Nyssen and Dionysius. Nonetheless, its practi-cal implications are quite different for each thinker. For Gregory, divine incomprehensibility forbids any analogy or created representation of divinity as idolatrous: "The divine word at the beginning forbids that the Divine be likened to any of the things known by men, since every concept which comes from some comprehensible image by an approximate understanding and by guessing at the divine nature constitutes an idol of God and does not proclaim God."[37] This is quite different from Dionysius' redaction, which concludes from the fact of God's unknowability that the only remaining pathway open is to glean the knowledge of God left in the traces of creation, of perceptible images and symbols, as inadequate as they will always be.

Whereas for both Gregory and Dionysius it is idolatrous to mistake a created being for God, for Gregory even to contemplate such a being or intelligible concept as a means *through which* one seeks to contemplate the divine creator is also, in this passage, forbidden as idolatrous. Thus, despite the close parallels between Gregory and Dionysius in the depiction of the mystical ascent as a journey into ever-deepening darkness, already we have begun to see significant differences. These differences become more pronounced with a comparison of each thinker's understanding of religious language.

Philosophy of Language

Both Gregory and Dionysius argue that no language, in particular no one word, is *adequate* to the divine. Thus, insofar as it gestures toward God, language can also conceal God, or even corrupt our understanding of God. Apart from these likenesses, a different emphasis emerges. Gregory, in the context of his debate with the "proto-positivist" Eunomius, insists on the conventionality of language. It is a tool formed and wielded by human communities for instrumental purposes and has no ontological relationship to objects or beings signified. In a different context and without this polemical constraint, Dionysius is free to develop a whole treatise on the "divine names" that are given by God in creation and that point back toward, or signify, their Giver without ever capturing or being adequate to it.

If, in Gregory, one finds a conventional, although still "trustworthy" view of language, and if, in Dionysius, one discovers language to be essentially revealing, although simultaneously concealing, the question becomes whether, from these two very different starting points, Gregory and Dionysius do not meet somewhere in the middle. Are these positions simply flip sides of the same coin, one which, on whichever side it lands, possesses the same value? Or are the differences significant enough to yield different currencies? What difference, in other words, do the different emphases make? I will examine the position of each thinker in greater detail in order to respond to this question.

Gregory's philosophy of language can be understood properly only in the context of his debate with Eunomius out of which it emerges. Briefly stated, for Eunomius, names reveal essences because they are divinely given (i.e., natural) and not based on human convention. Consequently, if one knows the name, one knows the essence. God (the Father) is the only ungenerated or unbegotten essence (ἀγέννητος οὐσία). This essence can be named and thus known.

Eunomius contrasts divinely given names to those that are κατ᾽ ἐπίνοιαν, which for him means to be mere "invention" or "fancy."[38] As a result, the Cappadocian understanding of language as conventional, or as κατ᾽ ἐπίνοιαν, will cause Eunomius to accuse them of blasphemy, of producing a human conception of God that has no connection to reality but is purely a cultural artifact produced from linguistic convention. The danger of the Cappadocian understanding of language, according to their opponents, is that it undermines the certainty of any knowledge. Thus the debate over the Son is equally a debate about the status of religious language and knowledge.[39]

The Cappadocian response is exemplified in Gregory of Nyssa's rebuttal to Eunomius, *Contra Eunomium*. Against Eunomius, Gregory argues that language cannot give knowledge of essence, not even of the essence of created beings, let alone that of God. Language is not God-given, but rather it is developed through human conventions. Thus, there is no divinely ordained language; Greek is no better than Hebrew. The controversy with Eunomius has the effect of sharpening Gregory's understanding of the fundamental ontological divide or gap (*diastema*) between the created world and its creator. As I will discuss more fully in chapter 5, language resides on the created side and is governed by the *diastema*. From this understanding of language as conventional, certain dilemmas arise.

Scot Douglass describes Gregory's aporia thus: "More simply put, on what 'ground' can a creature speak from within a *diastemic episteme* about a transcendent creator?"[40] (The "diastemic episteme," to use Douglass's words, results from the situation of creation on one side of the infinite and non-traversable gap [*diastema*] between God and creation.) The problem of religious language is sharpened when it comes to the possibility and status of making creedal pronouncements about God such as that Christ is ὁμοούσιος τῷ πατρί. Furthermore, how might one continue to talk, as Gregory does, of scripture as the uniquely authoritative Word of God?[41] Douglass offers an interesting interpretative key out of this dilemma with what he calls "metadiastemic intrusions" into the "diastemic episteme."[42]

Douglass first establishes that diastemic discourse is occupied only and always with a "translation" that is "full of yearning to transgress" the *diastema*.[43] In other words, language is born out of, and constitutive of, a desire for transgression. The impossibility of accomplishing this transgression and of attaining the object of language's desire leads foremost to silence. Gregory writes: "By what name can I describe the incomprehensible? By what speech can I declare the unspeakable? Accordingly, since the Deity is too excellent and lofty to be expressed in words, we have learnt to honor with silence what transcends speech and thought."[44] The aporia still remains.

A differently oriented transgression, however, does succeed in opening up a possibility for human speech about God. In this transgressive movement, God traverses the gap between Godself and creation, primarily in the incarnation but also in the divine accommodation to our needs in scripture. Both occur through an act of divine *kenosis* in which the divine *energeia* fills and overflows the finite vessel of the human being, Jesus of Nazareth, and of human language in scripture. While this will be discussed in detail in subsequent chapters in relation to Marion's notion of "saturation," what is important to observe for the moment is that language is not ontologically related to the divine essence, or indeed to any essence. It is a result of human convention. As such, language can only act as a medium of divine revelation that always comes *subsequently* to fill it. This view of language is remarkably distinct from Dionysius' understanding, to which we now turn.

One of the strongest contributing factors to the recent surge of interest in Dionysius' "negative theology," or apophaticism, is his paradoxical understanding of language. A theory of language, signs, and representation saturates the entirety of Dionysius' theological system. This theory is summarized in *The Divine Names*:

> Hence, with regard to the supra-essential being of God—transcendent
> Goodness transcendently there—no lover of the truth which is above all
> truth will seek to praise it as word or power or mind or life or being. . . .
> And yet, since it is the underpinning of goodness, and by merely being
> there is the cause of everything, to praise this divinely beneficent Provi-
> dence you must turn to all of creation. . . . *Realizing all this, the theolo-*
> *gians praise it by every name—and as the Nameless One.*[45]

Epistemology and ontology are intertwined here. It is this paradoxical-
ity, so intimately held together, that promotes Dionysius' preeminence
as a thinker of radical *apophasis.* Moreover, Dionysius is explicit in the
fact that, when "naming God," he in no way attempts to define God or
to reveal what God's being is, but rather "to sing a hymn of praise for the
being-making procession of the absolute divine Source of being into the
total domain of being."[46]

Hence the assertion in *The Mystical Theology* of a third movement,
beyond both affirmation and negation, which, according to Balthasar
(and Marion following him), "hymn" comes closest to naming. Before
this third movement, one goes through both affirmation and denial, to
a negation of both affirmation and denial:

> Since it is the Cause of all beings, we should posit and ascribe to it all
> the affirmations we make in regard to beings, and, more appropriately,
> we should negate all these affirmations, since it surpasses all being. Now
> we should not conclude that the negations are simply the opposites of the
> affirmations, but rather that the cause of all is considerably prior to this,
> beyond privations, beyond every denial, beyond every assertion.[47]

One's spiritual migration follows two concurrent directions: one descends through perceptible symbols and conceptual symbols (discussed
in *The Celestial Hierarchy* and *The Ecclesiastical Hierarchy*); and, secondly, one ascends beyond all symbols, whether perceptible or conceptual, into silence and the banishment of both language and thought (in
Mystical Theology). Dionysius expands on this double directionality of a
descending and ascending movement, into a plurality of words on one
pole and silence on the other, in *Mystical Theology:*

> The fact is that the more we take flight upward, the more our words are
> confined to the ideas we are capable of forming; so that now as we plunge
> into that darkness which is beyond intellect, we shall find ourselves not
> simply running short of words but actually speechless and unknowing.

> In the earlier books my argument travelled downwards from the most
> exalted to the humblest categories, taking in on this downward path an
> ever-increasing number of ideas which multiplied with every stage of the
> descent. But my argument now rises from what is below up to the tran-
> scendent, and the more it climbs, the more language falters, and when it
> has passed up and beyond the ascent, it will turn silent completely, since
> it will finally be at one with him who is indescribable.[48]

Whether naming God affirmatively or negatively, one must start where
there is the greatest level of certainty or accuracy. In affirmation one
starts at the top of the pinnacle, where there is less to say because what
we say is beyond the perceptible realm; whereas in negation one starts at
the bottom, where our denials of God as "drunken" or "in a rage" are
most sure.[49] In other words, there is a differing range of appropriateness
to both affirmations and negations. It is less appropriate to affirm that God
is a "worm" and to deny that God is "Good" than to affirm that God is
"Good" and deny that God is a "worm."[50] However, at the same time one
must both affirm and negate both God's "goodness" and "wormness."
This is the brilliance of Dionysius' apophaticism.

Dionysius claims that even the word *God* must be relinquished ultimately, for it merely refers to a certain activity of "that Being" which is
apparent to us, namely, to "deify" creation. The word *God*, however, like
all other words, does not pertain essentially or "properly" to that which
is beyond, what Dionysius prefers to refer to as "the absolutely transcendent Cause of all things."[51]

To return to the opening question of this section: Does Dionysius
come to a significantly different conclusion about how language works
and how it can both reveal and hide God than does Gregory? For both,
language is a necessary but inadequate vehicle of divine revelation; language both reveals and conceals the divine. Thus, both affirmative and
negative statements of God are necessary for both writers. We affirm
things of God, negate things of God, and yet recognize that neither affirmation nor negation is adequate to God. Nonetheless, differences
pertain.

For Dionysius, levels of appropriateness of language can be distinguished, whereas for Gregory, all language is equally inappropriate to
name the essence of God. According to Gregory, language strains against
its conventional limits toward a transgression but is found, in the end,
to rely necessarily on the interruptive and gracious transgression of the
divine into the created order. Language is a created human vessel that

nonetheless can overflow with divine grace. However, this is a revelation added "after the fact." For Dionysius, on the other hand, language as part of the divine gift of creation both bears the divine presence and marks its absence (or the divine transcendence). Divinely caused, all things, including language, manifest (and hide) God. Likewise, as divinely caused, all things, including language, are distinguished and separated from God. Analogy and participation are integral to Dionysius' understanding of language, guaranteeing a relation as much as the distance that prevents the relation from collapsing into identification or absorption.

Thus, the theories of language of both Gregory and Dionysius arise out of their particular ontological loyalties and entail distinct strategies to avoid idolatry. In order to strengthen this hypothesis, it will be useful to flesh out the broader implications and presuppositions of their respective philosophies of language.

The World That Language Inhabits: Cosmology, Divinity, and Anthropology

In this section I will employ a binary schematic in order to highlight the different elements of each patristic writer. The philosophies of language articulated by both Gregory and Dionysius presuppose (a) and (b), distinctive cosmological principles that emerge from (c) and (d), distinct doctrines of God, which in turn effect (e) and (f), different understandings of human participation and desire for God. One caveat is necessary. In creating such a comparative binary, the danger is that I have tidied things up far too much. So to be clear: I am *not* saying that Gregory never refers to God as "cause" or to the human desire for God as "natural." Nor am I saying that Dionysius never refers to God as "infinite" or our participation as "endless." Rather, I am trying to draw some distinguishing lines around the concepts where each writer *begins* and what aspects of each theologian's system is the most *emphasized*.

"Diastemic Creation" in Gregory

τὸ διάστημα οὐδὲν ἄλλο ἤ κτίσις ἐστιν.[52] For Gregory, the fact that the world is created carries with it one overwhelming consequence:

there is an unbridgeable gap (*diastema*) between the Creator and creation.[53] This statement is less about God than it is a negative definition of creation: creation is "not-God."[54] As discussed in the previous section, the *diastema* between God and creation results in God's being not only incomprehensible to the created order but also forever utterly unattainable; no created being can ever bridge that gap. The marvel, for Gregory, is that the Creator traverses the distance. As a result, although God's essence remains forever unapproachable, created beings can experience God insofar as God gives of Godself to be known to creation. That is to say, so far as God traverses the *diastema,* creation is able to be in relation with God. But in no way, by seeking out God, can a creature get closer or lessen the *diastema* even infinitesimally.[55]

Furthermore, the fact that the world is created involves it necessarily and eternally in change and movement (*kinesis*). This necessity of mutability is less a characteristic of a particularly "fallen state" of being than a condition for any existence whatsoever. David Bentley Hart articulates this point nicely:

> According to Gregory, creation is in its every aspect a movement. Words such as τροπή and κίνησις retain distinctly opprobrious connotations in the more "Platonizing" climate of, say, Origen's thought, but for Gregory change is simply constitutive of created nature; creation is itself (Gregory employing the traditional argument) a conversion from the darkness of nonbeing toward the light of God, a kind of ontological heliotropism. As utter contingency, it is pure mutability, a motion from moment to moment, place to place, not only in creatures' incessant peregrinations but within their very identities (*De anima et resurrectione; PG* 46:141B–C); the created dies every moment, writes Gregory, to be reborn the next (*In canticum canticorum* 12; GNO 6:351); if it ceased to change, it would cease to exist (*De hominis opificio* 13; *PG* 44:165A–C).[56]

Thus the defining characteristics of creation for Gregory are *diastema* (gap and ontological difference) and *kinesis* (mutability and movement).

"Hierarchical Creation" in Dionysius

Dionysius' most concise depiction of his cosmology is found in *The Divine Names 4:*

> He [God] is yearning on the move, simple, self-moved, self-acting, preexistent in the Good, flowing out from the Good onto all that is and return-

ing once again to the Good. In this divine yearning shows especially its beginning and unending nature travelling in an endless circle through the Good, from the Good, in the Good and to the Good, unerringly turning, ever on the same center, ever in the same direction, always proceeding, always remaining, always being restored to itself.[57]

The "erotic" journey of God processes ecstatically outside of Godself in the creation of the world and, on its return, gathers back to itself all of creation. This is an erotic movement because it emerges out of the divine yearning for creation. Finally, creation is eternally occurring; the movement of creation is circular rather than singular and linear.

God's providential sustenance of the world is accomplished through a "sharing" of divine being. All things participate in the "entire wholeness" of God, not some part. The figure that Dionysius employs is the center point of a circle "shared by the surrounding radii" or the multiple impressions of a seal that nonetheless "all have a share in the original prototype."[58] Dionysius describes the resulting unity thus:

> All the radii of a circle are brought together in the unity of the center which contains all the straight lines brought together within itself. These are linked one to another because of this single point of origin and they are completely unified at this center. As they move a little away from it they are differentiated a little, and as they fall farther they are farther differentiated. That is, the closer they are to the center point, the more they are at one with it and at one with each other, and the more they travel away from it the more they are separated from each other.[59]

This reveals that creation for Dionysius consists of various levels of reality: the celestial, the intelligent, and the material.[60] In other words, creation is hierarchical.

Dionysius coins the term *hierarchia,* which literally translates as "sacred order" or "sacred rule." In *The Celestial Hierarchies* he gives a clear sense of how the hierarchy functions soteriologically as "a certain perfect arrangement, an image of the beauty of God which sacredly works out the mysteries of its own enlightenment in the orders and levels of understanding of the hierarchy, and which is likened toward its own source as much as is permitted."[61]

The soteriological structure and function of hierarchy involves a participatory ontology. Furthermore, this ontology involves a hierarchy of being that is eternally determined. For example, angels "are nearer to

God, since their participation in him takes so many forms."[62] The purpose of hierarchy is to precipitate a "return": "to enable beings to be as like as possible to God and to be at one with him." This occurs, through reflecting the divine light, becoming perfect mirrors, not simply to reflect back to God but also to "pass on this light generously and in accordance with God's will to beings further down the scale," thus becoming a "fellow workman for God" [1 Cor 3:9; 1 Thes 3:2].[63] This movement of light is an act initiated solely by divine grace.[64] Nevertheless, the created being, at whatever level in the hierarchy and whether in the celestial or the ecclesial hierarchy, cooperates.

The hierarchies function anagogically to "lead one upwards" using an "interlocking agency." The first rank of heavenly beings rise up to the source of perfection immediately. "Then by this rank [of angels] the second one, and by the second one the third, and by the third our hierarchy is hierarchically uplifted, in due proportion and divine concord and according to this regulation of the harmonious source of order, toward the source beyond every source and consummation of all harmony."[65] Within this hierarchical system there is a strong emphasis on harmony, which is achieved through proper cooperation. Furthermore, because "order and rank here below are a sign of the harmonious ordering toward the divine realm,"[66] the anagogic "uplifting" through the hierarchies is paralleled in individual human intelligent beings who also have among them hierarchically arranged orders and powers and are uplifted accordingly.[67]

In *The Ecclesiastical Hierarchy*, Dionysius writes that every hierarchy "is the complete expression of the sacred elements comprised within it. The perfect total of all its sacred constituents," and as such, it acts theurgically.[68] As Louth describes, the consequence of the movement of return "is to make of the created order a perfect theophany: each part in its own proportion manifesting the glory of God."[69] Nevertheless, it is also important to take seriously the fact that the hierarchies are qualitatively ordered. For instance, Dionysius uses the metaphors of light and heat, which lessen in power with their diffusion and as they encounter denser or less receptive, less conductive material.[70] Everything "fits" and has its place within Dionysius' cosmology. In the following chapter, I will argue that there is an integral relationship between "hierarchy" and "apophasis," which will complicate Marion's use of Dionysius.

Gregory: God as Infinite

In his recent work, *The Beauty of the Infinite: The Aesthetics of Christian Truth*, David Bentley Hart calls Gregory "the first systematic thinker of divine infinity."[71] Here Hart echoes Ekkehard Mühlenberg's influential work, *Die Unendlichkeit Gottes bei Gregor von Nyssa: Gregors Kritik am Gottesbegriff der Klassischen Metaphysik*, which puts forward as its principal thesis that Gregory of Nyssa was the first to articulate a positive view of infinity and to attribute infinity to God.[72] Both the rationale and the implications for predicating God's infinity are discussed in Gregory's contemplation on the life of Moses.

Gregory's interpretation of *Life of Moses* was written as a contemplation of perfection. Indeed, the work's full title is *The Life of Moses or, Concerning Perfection in Virtue.* Since God is infinite (without limits) by nature and we are finite (limited by our bodies, temporality, and mutability), the question becomes, how are we to "attain" perfection? The work was written in response to the request by letter for "some counsel concerning the perfect life."[73] But Gregory quickly qualifies his capacity to respond: "It is beyond my power to encompass perfection in my treatise [logos]."[74] This is not mere rhetorical humility on Gregory's part, but rather is intrinsically born out of the most centrally held tenet of his theology: God's perfection, which necessitates God's infinity, which in turn implies God's lack of any boundary. Gregory is quite logical here. He begins with an analysis of material perfection, which is marked off by its proper boundaries, and opposes this to the perfection of virtue.

> Quantity, for example, admits of both continuity and limitation, for every quantitative measure is circumscribed by certain limits proper to itself. The person who looks at a cubit or at the number ten knows that its perfection consists in the fact that it has both a beginning and an end. But in the case of virtue we have learned from the Apostle that its one limit of perfection is the fact that it has no limit. For the divine Apostle, great and lofty in understanding, ever running the course of virtue, never ceased *straining towards those things that are still to come* [Phil. 3:13]. Coming to a stop in the race was not safe for him. Why? Because no Good has a limit in its own nature but is limited by the presence of its opposite, as life is limited by death and light by darkness . . . [Thus] stopping in the race of virtue marks the beginning of the race of evil.[75]

Building on this analysis, Gregory argues that God cannot be anything but "infinite, enclosed by no boundary." Something can only be bounded by something different in nature. Furthermore, that by which it is bounded contains the bounded. If God is goodness, then that which bounds it would have to be different: evil. For God to be bounded, bordered, or limited by evil would mean that God is ruled by evil, but this is out of the question. Thus, God must be unbounded and infinite. While this may seem obvious, Gregory was presenting an original argument that flew in the face of the dominant Platonic identification of beauty with form (and hence, with limits).

When Gregory returns to the primary purpose of the treatise, "concerning the perfection of virtue," he postulates that the fundament of virtue, its ground or beginning point, has to do, unsurprisingly, with one's relation to God. Thus in the giving of the divine law, Gregory locates the chief teachings on virtue in "reverence and having the proper notions about the divine nature, inasmuch as it transcends all cognitive thought and representation and cannot be likened to anything which is known."[76] In other words, to say that this work is about the perfection of virtue is always to begin with an understanding of virtue entailing a fundamental stance against idolatry or *hubris* when it comes to God (recalling that idolatry, for Gregory, means "stopping" with one particular definition for God). The believer is enjoined not to search out comprehension of God's nature. "Rather, he should believe that the Divine exists, and he should not examine it with respect to quality, quantity, origin, and mode of being, since it is unattainable."[77] These are the consequences of divine infinity.

Dionysius: God as Erotic (and Beautifully Good) Cause

While Dionysius' *Divine Names* is devoted to the expression of many different titles for God (all of which ought to be employed, although none of which are perfectly adequate), he nevertheless preferences certain terms. God is Good—the erotic, yearning God that gives of itself generously—and God is Beautiful. However, while it is not transparently explicated, another term is used throughout this treatise as well as the entire corpus: "Cause." The constellation of these terms combines to give one coherent image of God, who in God's own yearning (*eros*) causes creation, and in so doing, gives goodness and gives beauty as extensions of Godself. Some key elements can be unpacked from this constellation.

The Good, in going out of itself to become the cause and subsistence of all that is, remains nevertheless removed, whole, and "super-eminent."[78] Indeed, it gives form only by transcending it. Dionysius often utilizes analogies of the dispersion of light, and especially the analogy of the sun, which sheds light on all beings according to their capacity without ever losing the fullness of its light: "It is a single illuminating light, acting upon the essences and the qualities of the many and various things we perceive. It renews them, nourishes them, protects them and perfects them. It establishes the differences between them and it unifies them."[79] As a Good cause, God constitutes, sustains, and fulfills all of being in its particularities and as a whole.

When Dionysius comes to discuss the divine name of beauty, he is driven by a classical notion of harmony equating beauty.[80] Moreover, in a world whose creator is named "Beauty," harmony becomes that to which everything conforms.

> From this beauty comes the existence of everything, each being exhibiting its own way of beauty. For beauty is the cause of harmony, or sympathy, of community. Beauty unites all things and is the source of all things. It is the great creating cause which bestirs the world and holds all things in existence by the longing inside them to have beauty. And there it is ahead of all as Goal, as the Beloved, as the Cause toward which all things move, since it is the longing for beauty which actually brings them into being. It is a model to which they conform ... Hence [i.e., from the One Good and Beautiful], the interrelationship of all things in accordance with capacity. Hence, the harmony and the love which are formed between them but which do not obliterate identity. Hence the innate togetherness of everything. Hence, too, the intermingling of everything, the persistence of things, the unceasing emergence of things.[81]

Finally, given Dionysius' abundant use of the term "cause," that *bête noire* of the critics of onto-theology, some prophylactic defense of Dionysius is warranted. Briefly, "cause" does not have implications of revealing itself through that which it causes ... simply. That is, while beings do reveal their cause, in the same measure do they conceal or hide their cause.

The Human Participant in Gregory: Endless Yearning

As previously mentioned, for Gregory, change is neither good nor bad in itself; it all depends on one's direction, whether one faces or retreats from God.[82] This entails, in Balthasar's terminology, an "anthropology of becoming": "Now, it is certainly required that what is subject to change be in a sense always coming to birth. In mutable nature nothing can be observed which is always the same."[83] To what end might one go, however? How far? Are there limits to what one might become? In order to answer these questions, one must return to Gregory's doctrine of God.

There is a parallel between the infinity of God and the infinity of virtue or perpetual progress in perfection.[84] As a result, perfection is redefined by Gregory: "The perfection of human nature consists perhaps in its very growth in goodness."[85] Moses himself serves as a paradigm of this limitless "growth in goodness" in an eternal search for perfection. Never stopping, despite his achievements, he dies overlooking the promised land to which he led the people without entering it.[86] Hart expresses this as Gregory's insistence that the soul can only be described as "an ἐπέκτασις, an always outstretched, open, and changing motion, an infinite exodus from nothingness into God's inexhaustible transcendence."[87] What is Gregory's understanding of the nature and function of desire in this endless pursuit?

There is no question that Gregory draws a qualitative distinction between the "fleshly" and "spiritual" desires. However, the distinction is not between a desire that originates with one's flesh versus one's spirit. Flesh and spirit make up one being. Rather, the key distinction for Gregory lies in the object, or end of our desire, that to which our desire is directed: the changing and fleeting chance of the material world or the eternally unchanging infinity of God. The danger of the former, according to Gregory, involves a psychology of desire not unlike that of Augustine. As soon as one has one's fill of a material object of desire, once the object itself has been consumed, the desire seeks elsewhere for satiation. The material object has not really filled any appetitive void but has only provided temporary distraction. One remains empty and yearning for more.[88]

Opposed to this, Gregory describes a spiritual desire so vast that it too cannot find satiation. However, the difference here is not that in feeding one's desire (for God) one remains empty. Rather, the difference is that one's capacity to be filled with God is eternally enlarged, so that by its very reception of God's gracious presence it is enabled to receive more, and infinitely so on, without any final consummation or final satiation.[89] Nevertheless, paradoxically, one's desires are always and ever "met" without being finally satisfied. Thus for Gregory, the human being is defined by an endless yearning and an ever-increasing receptive capacity.

The Human Participant in Dionysius: Natural Yearning

Dionysius paints a different picture than Gregory's. For Dionysius, participation of creatures in God, through whom they have their being, protection, and perfection, is characterized by the natural inclination and yearning of individual existents for God:

> The Good returns all things to itself and gathers together whatever may be scattered, for it is the divine Source and unifier of the sum total of things. Each being looks to it as a source, as the agent of cohesion, and as an objective. The Good, as scripture testifies, produced everything and it is the ultimately perfect Cause. In it "all things hold together" and are maintained and preserved as if in some almighty receptacle. All things are returned to it as their own goal. *All things desire it: everything with mind and reason seeks to know it, everything sentient yearns to perceive it, everything lacking perception has a living and instinctive longing for it, and everything lifeless and merely existent turns, in its own fashion, for a share of it.*[90]

Our yearning to return to God not only reflects a natural movement toward our source or point of origin, but it also reflects God's own yearning toward creation:

> And so it is that all things must desire, must yearn for, must love the Beautiful and the Good. Because of it and for its sake, subordinate is returned to superior, equal keeps company with equal, superior turns providentially to subordinate, each bestirs itself and all are stirred to do and to will whatever it is they do and will because of the yearning for the Beautiful and the Good. And we may be so bold as to claim also that the Cause of all things loves all things in the superabundance of his goodness, that because of this goodness he makes all things, brings all things to perfection, holds all things together, returns all things. The divine longing is Good seeking good for the sake of the Good [*o theios eros agathos agathou dia to agathon*]. That yearning which creates all the goodness

of the world preexisted superabundantly within the Good and did not allow it to remain without issue. It stirred him to use the abundance of his powers in the production of the world.[91]

Two aspects of Dionysius' participatory cosmology are significant in comparison with Gregory. First, while God is unknowable and ultimately transcendent, there is simultaneously a strong sense of the presence of God throughout creation. God's presence is necessary since every created being depends upon the immediacy of God in order simply to be, to exist.[92] We have already seen an extension of this necessity: the doctrine of divine names depends, precisely, upon Dionysius' assertion of the immanence of God in creation.

Secondly, how should one understand the process of return, according to Dionysius? Although it is accomplished through and within the hierarchy to which one was "born," Dionysius will also use language that sounds "epectastic" at times. For instance:

> To put the matter briefly, all being derives from, exists in, and is returned toward the Beautiful and the Good. Whatever there is, whatever comes to be, is there and has being on account of the Beautiful and the Good. All things look to it. All things are moved by it. All things are preserved by it . . . Here is the source of all which transcends every source, here is *an ending which transcends completion.* "For from Him and through Him and in Him and to Him are all things" says Holy Scripture [Rom 11:36].[93]

What is meant by this penultimate sentence? Dionysius nowhere expands on the theme. However, a closer analysis of Luibheid's translation reveals an unusual bias. Parker translates this as ". . . it is of all beginning and term, above beginning and term, because from It and through It, and in It, are all things, as says the Sacred Word."[94] This is a more accurate translation: ἔστι πάντων ἀρχή καὶ πέρας [end, termination, completion], ὑπεράρχιον καὶ ὑπερτελές [literally 'beyond the mark']. From the Greek, it is clear that the referent to ὑπερτελές is God and not human desire. In other words, the meaning is that God is beyond the perfection which the individual soul reaches, rather than that the participation is without completion or never-ending as Gregory would say. God is above or beyond the human "term," but there remains a human "term" or end, nevertheless.

How does desire translate with such an anthropology? Unlike Gregory, Dionysius does not draw such a stark disjunctive line between the spiritual and the material as objects of desire. Rather, the material always carries within it the capacity of revelation of God and, by its very existence, a manifestation of God's presence. One comes to the end of one's desire, according to Dionysius, when one "meets" God's own desire in reflection, as a fitting response to the desiring act of God's creation, to the beauty all around one, and above all, in the worshiping praise of God in liturgy.

In the Dionysian world, *eros* possesses a capacity to effect a unity of the Beautiful and the Good. This capacity preexists in the Beautiful and the Good, that is, in God alone: "It is dealt out from the Beautiful and the Good through the Beautiful and the Good. It binds the things of the same order in a mutually regarding union. It moves the superior to provide for the subordinate, and it stirs the subordinate in a return towards the superior."[95] Thus, *eros* has a synthetic quality.

Furthermore, human *eros,* as a reflection of the divine *eros,* is always ecstatic.

> And, in truth, it must be said too that the very cause of the universe in the beautiful, good superabundance of his benign yearning for all is also carried outside of himself in the loving care he has for everything. He is, as it were, beguiled[96] by goodness, by love, and by yearning and is enticed away from his transcendent dwelling place and comes to abide within all things, and he does so by virtue of his supernatural and ecstatic capacity to remain, nevertheless, within himself.[97]

Finally, it is crucial to understand that human yearning is constituted, and even determined, by its divine creation. As such, it cannot resist the call from God to desire God. God is, ultimately, *irresistible:* "The irrepressible cause of all yearning has command and primacy over them and is the cause beyond them all and indeed is the goal toward which everything everywhere strives upward, each as best it can."[98] This phrase, "each as best it can," also speaks of a determinacy, both of the degree of God's presence throughout the cosmos and the corresponding capacity to mirror it in response: "Perfect goodness reaches out to all things and not simply to immediate good neighbors. It extends as far as the lowliest of things. In some beings it is present in full measure, to a lesser extent in others, and in the least measure in yet others. It is there in proportion to the capacity to receive it."[99]

Two main differences between Gregory's and Dionysius' thoughts on desire apply. First, for Gregory desire has no end. This is a central theme not only of *Life of Moses* but throughout his corpus: the creature "never halts at what it has reached, but all that is acquired becomes by participation a beginning of its ascent to something still greater";[100] or again, "the boundary of what has been attained becomes the beginning for the discovery of higher goods."[101] For Dionysius, on the other hand, desire has a point of perfection in the hierarchies. While it does not cease moving "upwards" in an admiring movement or "downwards" in benevolence, desire finds its proper place as a station designated already in God's creation that simultaneously constitutes and determines human yearning.

The second difference involves the value of the material in human desire. For Gregory, one must go "beyond all that is visible" and "believe that the divine is *there* where the understanding does not reach";[102] whereas for Dionysius, one must go *through* the visible and material, using it as God's gracious self-manifestation, partial yet true. Given these two different understandings of human desire for God, how do Gregory and Dionysius understand its perfection or consummation differently?

Notions of Perfection or Desire's Consummation

For both thinkers, the notion of perfection begins and ends with their understanding of God and the divine relation of God to creation: with Gregory, this centers around the notion of infinity, and with Dionysius, the order of a cosmos lovingly brought into being. Thus, while for both the *function* of *eros* is to effect the approach or return of the created order to God, the final understanding of this end will be different for Dionysius than it is for Gregory.

Gregory's Redefinition of Perfection as Its Own Pursuit

As has been shown, for Gregory the notion of perfection is tied to his refusal to predicate any limit of God. In *The Life of Moses* he concludes that, since God is limitlessness, so must the pursuit of virtue (which is nothing other than the pursuit of loving God) be without end or limit. This seems to indicate the impossibility of perfection. He reasons thus:

> The Divine One is himself the Good (in the primary and proper sense of the word), whose very nature is goodness. This he is and he is so named, and is known by this nature. Since, then, it has not been demonstrated that there is any limit to virtue except evil, and since the Divine does not admit of an opposite, we hold the divine nature to be unlimited and infinite. Certainly whoever pursues true virtue participates in nothing other than God, because he is himself absolute virtue. Since, then, those who know what is good by nature desire participation in it, and since this good has no limit, the participant's desire itself necessarily has no stopping place but is stretched out with the limitless. It is therefore undoubtedly *impossible to attain perfection,* since, as I have said, perfection is not marked off by limits: The one limit of virtue is the absence of a limit. How then would one arrive at the sought-for boundary when he can find no boundary?[103]

Yet one is still commanded by Christ to "be perfect, just as your heavenly Father is perfect" (Matt 5: 48). Therefore, perfection needs to be redefined: "For the perfection of human nature consists perhaps in its very growth in goodness."[104]

For Gregory, there is no finally perfect "vision of God." Indeed, true vision comes to be synonymous with invisibility: "This truly is the vision of God: never to be satisfied in the desire to see him. But one must always, by looking at what he can see, rekindle his desire to see more. Thus no limit would interrupt growth in the ascent to God, since no limit to the Good can be found nor is the increasing of desire for the Good brought to an end because it is satisfied."[105] And thus the thesis of the treatise, which consists in a redefinition of perfection as the infinite growth in goodness, is established.[106]

This raises a disputed question in modern scholarship: the status of the term "union" (*henosis*) in Gregory. There is no doubt that he speaks of a union, but what is meant by this is unclear. Does Gregory's understanding of *epectasis* as an infinitely increasing participation in the divine result in an *ontological* union with the divine or not? Jean Daniélou argues that it does, while Ekkehard Mühlenberg argues that, given Gregory's first principle of the *diastema*, such ontological union is impossible.[107] The way one comes to a conclusion about this question will depend greatly on what one means by "union with God." I would suggest two alternative connotations of "union": *identity* or *intimacy*. Mühlenberg overstates his case by denying union in Gregory as Gregory himself uses this language. He is right, however, to argue that any notion of union as ontological identity is impossible, given Nyssen's understanding of divine infinity. Nevertheless, this impossibility may be precisely that which enables a relation of intimacy. This intimate "union" expands infinitely and never reaches final perfection or completion.

Dionysius: Perfection as Harmony within the Hierarchies

Dionysius, unlike Gregory, nowhere gives a clear statement of the *eschaton*. Indeed, his corpus vividly depicts the cyclical, eternal movement of God, rather than a linear history of creation, history, and its end. Nevertheless, he does give some hints regarding a "time to come" as well as his notion of perfection, both now and in the "time to come." A key passage in *Divine Names* gives a tantalizing glimpse of what it will be like in the "time to come"—where "we shall have a conceptual gift of light from him [God] and, somehow, in a way we cannot know, we shall be united with him and, our understanding carried away, blessedly happy, we shall be struck by his blazing light."[108] This passage is followed directly with, and opposed by, a shift to the present moment that, while eternally already partaking of the Divine, lacks the completeness of the glory of that "time to come." He signals the shift thus: "But as for now, what happens is this. We use whatever appropriate symbols we can for the things of God. With these analogies we are raised upward toward the truth of the mind's vision, a truth which is simple and one."[109] It is with this present moment that the rest of the epistle, indeed, one might argue, the rest of the corpus, is occupied. It is vital to keep this in mind. Hereafter, when Dionysius speaks of "perfection," he is speaking of perfection possible now through increasing levels of participation in a loving God who constitutes all beings to a particular perfection of participation. But there is also, just glimpsed at, a further eschatological perfection, which Dionysius describes in the more usual language of the Christian tradition (from which Gregory is distinguished in his refusal of eschatological completion).[110]

Keeping in mind, then, this further eschatological perfection, how does Dionysius understand perfection now? First, it results in a sense of both stability and union: "For just as it is ignorance which scatters those in error, so it is the presence of light of the mind which gathers and unites together those receiving illumination. It perfects them."[111] When Dionysius speaks of a "union in perfection" it is important to understand that he is speaking of a union in which the maintenance of differentiation is guaranteed.[112]

Secondly, perfection is found by taking one's rightful place within the cosmological hierarchies. For Dionysius, perfection has to do with fulfilling one's assigned place in the divine order: "Only the divine source of their perfection could really answer this [the question of how each hierarchy achieves perfection], but at least they know what they have by way of power and enlightenment and they know their place in this sacred, transcendent order."[113] Or again, he says that "the aim of every hierarchy is always to imitate God so as to take on his form, [and] that the task of every hierarchy is to receive and to pass on undiluted purification, the divine light and the understanding which brings about perfection."[114]

One clear difference between Gregory's and Dionysius' understanding of perfection is that for the latter it is accomplished within the hierarchies, and for the former there is no accomplishment of perfection or arrival at perfection, only the pursuit of it. Furthermore, while there is eternal movement in both the "hierarchical perfection" of Dionysius and the "eternal progress" of Gregory, with Dionysius this is an eternal movement *within one's proper place:*

> If all moving things wish never to be at rest but aim always for their own appropriate movement, this too is because of a wish for that divine Peace of the universe which keeps everything firmly in its own place and which insures the individuality and the stirring life of all moving things are kept safe from removal and destruction. This happens as a result of the inward peace which causes the things in movement to engage in the activity proper to themselves.[115]

Expressed oppositely, *stasis,* if it is to be found in Gregory, is found by a single directionality (toward God), whereas *stasis* in Dionysius is found by reaching the perfection of who one is meant and constituted to be, to "become who you are," within a hierarchically ordered universe.

Given the comparison of the broader worlds out of which *apophasis* arises, what can be taken back and applied to a specifically epistemological and linguistic analysis of *apophasis*? The question of revelation offers the final site of comparison of these two figures. How, in the end, does God reveal Godself? To what extent? Through what medium? And how, finally, do our words respond to this revelation?

Revelation: A Return to the Linguistic
Dimensions of *Apophasis*

Both Gregory of Nyssa and Dionysius understand revelation as God's gracious gift. However, precisely how this gift is mediated is understood differently. For Gregory, revelation comes through a divine accommodation to the confines of finitude in both scripture and, most perfectly, in the incarnation. Revelation in this vision is interruptive and saturating, and humans are passive recipients of such a gift. For Dionysius, on the other hand, the gift of revelation comes through God's ecstatic presence and manifestation throughout creation.[116] As a result, creation itself is theophanic. Such a theophany, however, is properly "read" only within the context of the Christian community, specifically within a liturgical setting. The liturgy provides the necessary hermeneutical lens through which one might read God's presence and beauty in all of creation.

Gregory describes an intensification of revelation in sacred history as it is found in the scriptures:

> The Law and the Prophets trumpeted the divine mystery of the Incarnation, but the first sounds were too weak to strike the disobedient ear.... As the trumpets came closer, according to the text, they became louder. The last sounds, which came through the preaching of the Gospels, struck their ears, since the Spirit through his instruments sounds noise more loudly ringing and makes a sound more vibrant in each succeeding spokesman.[117]

Revelation of God is identified, here, simply as the incarnation—first told "quietly" by the Law and the Prophets. When this passage is examined in its context, we find that it directly follows from a passage above that discusses the content of theology as contained fully in the incarnation. Furthermore, it is significant to note that this metaphor of a greater clarity of revelation in history and in scripture goes, paradoxically, hand in hand with Gregory's account of the increasing intensity and volume of God's revelation on Mount Sinai, which deafened the crowd and sent the people running back down the mountain in fear—all except Moses. From this we might extrapolate that the more intense the gift of revelation, the less able one is to receive. In this understanding, Christ, the revelation of God par excellence, becomes the hardest to receive and thus the hardest to speak or name.

Like Gregory, Dionysius claims that God reveals Godself as gift, graciously accommodating Godself to be received by God's creatures, for "the divine goodness is such that, out of concern for our salvation, it deals out the immeasurable and infinite in limited measures."[118] God grants what is necessary for each created being at each and every level of the created order in order to bring about God's soteriological purpose of a return through participation and deification of that order: "By itself it [the Good] generously reveals a firm, transcendent beam, granting enlightenments proportionate to each being, and thereby draws sacred minds upwards to its permitted contemplation, to participation and to the state of becoming like it."[119]

For this reason, Balthasar lifts up Dionysius as an example of a highly developed Christian thinker of theological aesthetics. In *The Ecclesiastical Hierarchy,* Dionysius states such an aesthetic concisely: "It is by way of the perceptible images that we are uplifted as far as can be to the contemplation of what is divine."[120] Liturgy, as the ecclesial reflection of the celestial hierarchies and therefore of the sacred order of the divine procession and return, is also, according to Alexander Golitzin, Paul Rorem, and Balthasar, the key to unlocking his entire theological vision. Liturgy is the link to various worlds or levels of the hierarchies.

> For it is quite impossible that we humans should, in any immaterial way, rise up to imitate and to contemplate the heavenly hierarchies without the aid of those material means capable of guiding us as our nature requires. Hence, any thinking person realises that the appearances of beauty are signs of an invisible loveliness. The beautiful odors which strike the senses are representations of a conceptual diffusion.[121]

Or again, he can say, "Everything, then, can be a help to contemplation."[122] This concept relies on a participatory ontology wherein creation becomes theophanic:

> So, then, forms, even those drawn from the lowliest matter, can be used, not unfittingly, with regard to heavenly beings. Matter, after all, owes its subsistence to absolute beauty and keeps, throughout its earthly ranks, some echo of intelligible beauty. Using matter, one may be lifted up to the immaterial archetypes. Of course, one must be careful to use the similarities as dissimilarities, as discussed, to avoid one-to-one correspondences, to make the appropriate adjustments as one remembers the great divide between the intelligible and the perceptible.[123]

The concept of "anagogy" whereby scripture, liturgy, and the beauty of creation "lifts one up" from representation to divine simplicity is central to Dionysius.[124]

It is important to remember, however, that for both Dionysius and Gregory the vision of God is a vision of darkness. The fact that God is revealed through creation does not mean, for Dionysius, that God is therefore knowable. An oft-repeated refrain in Dionysius is that God is both known in all things and also distinct from all things, as no thing. An extended passage in *Divine Names* expresses the paradox of a God who is simultaneously revealed and concealed through creation:

> If God cannot be grasped by mind or sense-perception, if he is not a particular being, how do we know him? This is something we must inquire into. It might be more accurate to say that we cannot know God in his nature, since this is unknowable and is beyond the reach of mind or of reason. But we know him from the arrangement of everything, because everything is, in a sense, projected out from him, and this order possesses certain images and semblances of divine paradigms. We therefore approach that which is beyond all as far as our capacities allow us and we pass by way of the denial and the transcendence of all things and by way of the cause of all things. God is therefore known in all things and as distinct from all things. He is known through knowledge and through unknowing. Of him there is conception, reason, understanding, touch, perception, opinion, imagination, name, and many other things. On the other hand he cannot be understood, words cannot contain him, and no name can lay hold of him. He is not one of the things that are and he cannot be known in any of them. He is all things in all things and he is no thing among things. He is known to all from all things and he is known to no one from anything. This is the sort of language we must use about God, for he is praised from all things according to their proportion to him as their Cause. But again, the most divine knowledge of God, that which comes through unknowing, is achieved in a union far beyond mind, when mind turns away from all things, even from itself, and when it is made one with the dazzling rays, being then and there enlightened by the inscrutable depths of Wisdom.[125]

Nonetheless, the difference between Gregory and Dionysius on the understanding of God's revelation and its accompanying darkness is particularly apparent in the comparison of their respective exegeses of the same biblical passage, where Moses asks to see God's face and is refused: "You cannot see my face, for no one can see me and live" (Exod

33:20). For Gregory, this passage is interpreted to teach about the fatal danger of satiety. He writes,

> The divine voice granted what was requested in what was denied, showing in a few words an immeasurable depth of thought. The munificence of God assented to the fulfillment of his desire, but did not promise any cessation or satiety of the desire. He would not have shown himself to his servant if the sight were such as to bring the desire of the beholder to an end, since the true sight of God consists in this, that the One who looks up to God never ceases in that desire. For he says: "*You cannot see my face, for man cannot see me and live.*"[126]

Gregory does not argue that a vision of the divine causes death, but rather that in order to "have life" one must recognize the invisibility of God. Since God transcends all characteristics, "he who thinks God is something to be known does not have life, because he has turned from true Being to what he considers by sense perception to have being."[127] (In Heideggerian terms, Gregory argues that to not recognize the "ontological difference," or to not recognize that what we can know is by definition not God, is in some sense to not live.)[128] How does this compare with what Dionysius does with the same biblical passage?

For Dionysius, this passage speaks of impossibility of any unmediated (and, by extension, perfect) knowledge of God. He writes: "Some might claim that God has appeared himself and without intermediaries to some of the saints. But in fact it should be realized that scripture has clearly shown that 'no one has ever seen'[129] or ever will see the being of God in all its hiddenness." Rather, any theophanic visions are initiated and mediated by "the heavenly powers" through created forms.[130]

Encapsulated here, we find the main difference between Gregory and Dionysius. For Gregory, revelation interrupts the created order, filling and overflowing its finite bounds, whereas for Dionysius, revelation is mediated and reflected through the created order, including the beauty of material creation, through the lens of the liturgy.[131]

Summarizing Remarks

In this chapter I have attempted to establish a significant and unavoidable difference between the apophatic visions of these two early Christian thinkers. Their philosophies of language diverge. For Gregory, language is conventional and reflects, primarily, its human speaker; whereas for Dionysius, language is made up of signs that point toward a divine creator as a consequence of his understanding of creation. This divergence was detailed against the backdrop of their distinct cosmological, theological, and anthropological presuppositions. According to Gregory, creation begins with *diastema* (gap) and entails an endless movement toward an infinite God. Human desire mirrors and participates in that infinity in an ecstatic movement without completion. Perfection is here redefined as its own pursuit. For Dionysius, creation is hierarchical; its hierarchies are beautiful and harmonious as they participate in a beautiful and good God. Human desire reflects God's originary and creative desire, and it finds its proper place and perfection within the hierarchies.

For Gregory, language, located as it is within the created order, is implicated by the two elements proper to creation: *diastema* and *kinesis*. The former is, quite simply, the very structure of the created order, and the latter constitutes every created being in irrepressible movement, such that to cease to move is to cease to exist. Scot Douglass neatly communicates the tight imbrication of language, epistemology, and ontology in Gregory's thought:

> In embracing the inescapable espacement [*diastema*] and *kineticism* of the created order, Gregory eventually turned every question and concern about the Trinitarian debate [with which this monograph is primarily concerned] into a question and concern about *diastemic* and *kinetic* language—not language initiated, underwritten and guaranteed by God, but rather language as a recuperative compromise created by man both out of and always within the constantly changing, unstable gaps of creation. *Diastemically* created and *kinetically* constituted, language belonged completely to the economy of human discourse, an economy of constant becoming that [Gregory] consequently argued could never know presence.[132]

Theological language, for Gregory, is simultaneously humble and trusting: humble in the impossibility of its perfection, and trusting in the correct orientation of its approach as a response to God's transgressive revelation.

Dionysius uses a theory of "projection" (or extension), which signifies both the possibility of an ontological and epistemological connection of the created world to its ἀρχη and the "necessity (or inescapability) of signification, that is, of the sign never reaching its ground."[133] In other words, language simultaneously reveals and conceals the divine being upon which it depends and with which it is essentially related. An intricate play between the infinite multiplication of divine names and a movement into silence ushers in a new mode of worship: the hymn. This hymn seeks out and finds, naturally and irresistibly, its proper place within a hierarchically ordered cosmos.

These two different visions of *apophasis* involve quite distinct images of humanity's proper relation to God. Both are "radical" insofar as they simultaneously enable human worship (and even enjoyment) of God and guarantee God's inviolability. However, the way in which this "radicality" is achieved diverges in their distinct understandings of the proper boundaries between God and creation and the different notions of movement within those boundaries. One might say that both Gregory and Dionysius forbid the cessation of activity and movement, but both also forbid a movement beyond permissible boundaries. If both are concerned with idolatry, Gregory fights it with the insistence of never stopping, never arriving, never becoming satisfied with what one has attained, whereas Dionysius guards against idolatry by demanding that one stay within the bounds of possible and permissible exploration. In other words, Dionysius guarantees God's inviolability by firmly setting human beings in their proper place, while Gregory does the same by refusing them a place to rest at all.

The introduction of this study identified Marion's overarching concern with notions of idolatry specific to the philosophical enterprise. Thus the question arises: Which strategy to guard against idolatry is more amenable to Marion's own phenomenology, that of Gregory or that of Dionysius? If this chapter has shown that the two apophatic approaches contain significantly different presuppositions and implications, then Marion's univocal retrieval is not permissible. However, it is not yet clear which ancient thinker is of more service to his own project.

Thus, the next two chapters will turn to a direct comparison between Marion and Dionysius (chapter 3) and Marion and Gregory (chapter 4). Chapter 3 will test the hypothesis that Marion's phenomenological methodology of a "reduction to pure givenness" echoes a Dionysian view of God's self-revelation in the world and of an ontology of

givenness that implies the possibility, if not the necessity, of an originary "Giver." Chapter 4 will explore whether Marion's concept of the
saturated phenomenon, which necessitates an infinite deferral of meaning and presence, does not imply Nyssen's disjunction between God and
creation and the sense of the infinite progression of human desire that
will not, in the end, ever find satiation.

THREE

Giving a Method: Securing Phenomenology's Place as "First Philosophy"

Marion's philosophical enterprise is directed by two primary motivations: first, the desire to free phenomena from all idolatrous restraints and all conditions; and second, the propulsion to show the *possibility* of all phenomena appearing as proper objects of philosophical inquiry. In order to bring these two concerns together, Marion must provide a means by which he can *justify* the entrance of all types of phenomena (including those deemed "excessive") into philosophical discourse without subjecting those phenomena to a set of conditions for their appearance there. Marion's need to provide this justification is in large part a product of the historical and geographical context within which he was writing: the secular university in France (especially after the student revolts of 1968) that demanded an incredibly strict separation between the state and religion and that was explicitly hostile to anything theological within the academy. Thus, in order to risk the inclusion of more "dangerous" phenomena, Marion must provide his philosophical undertaking with a methodology that can claim to be both universal and rigorous (certain, indubitable, unquestionable) qua method without importing any metaphysical implications inherent to the method. In other words, Marion must identify a method that does not determine a specific epistemological outcome a priori. In what follows, I will probe the final coherence of such an undertaking.

I will also demonstrate how this methodological tension illuminates Marion's attraction to, and particular interpretation of, Dionysius the Areopagite. Thus, the same tension that underlies his attempts to establish a universal methodology also explains a certain anomaly in his reading of Dionysius: an acute comprehension of the Dionysian corpus that is often not fully utilized. These dueling motivations, I suggest, explain omissions in Marion's otherwise nuanced and thorough reading of Dionysius. Specifically, they explain his strange and particularly anachronistic translation of *aitia* (discussed in chapter 1) as well as his refusal to acknowledge the hierarchical ontology that Dionysius' apophaticism presupposes (discussed in chapter 2). At the same time, however, the universal "givenness" of creation in Dionysius, and the theological aesthetics established therein, point to a model for the appearance of phenomena that nonetheless remain uncaptured and uncircumscribed. Certain facets of Dionysius' thought remain unspoken, but their presence percolates just under the surface. This tension between Marion's two overarching concerns explains his initial attraction to Dionysius as well as his selective use of the patristic writer.

In order to consider Marion's uneasy retrieval of Dionysius, we must first unravel the various permutations of his methodology. To do this I will proceed through his three major articulations of a phenomenological method: first, in *Reduction and Givenness: Investigations of Husserl, Heidegger, and Phenomenology* (hereafter, *Reduction*);[1] then, in *Being Given: Toward a Phenomenology of Givenness* (hereafter, *Being Given*); and finally, in *In Excess: Studies of Saturated Phenomena* (hereafter, *In Excess*). In the first, we find Marion's original formulation of a method in its historical relation to those of Husserl and Heidegger. In this argument, evidence of a governing allegiance to Husserl's fundamental philosophical aims is apparent in Marion's thinking. In *Being Given,* Marion consolidates the attributes necessary for his phenomenological method: universality (as opposed to the limited region or domain of hermeneutical contextuality and theological dogmatism), and certainty (or indubitability). The rationale for these methodological requirements becomes explicit by the time of *In Excess,* in which Marion defends phenomenology's status as "first philosophy." However, in order to establish this privileged status for phenomenology without allowing it to relapse into a reliance on an a priori method that would determine the content of the method beforehand (and hence become "metaphysical"), Marion must redefine the privileged place of phenomenology as not "first" but "last" philosophy. In this way, the method still yields universal and certain results without being accompanied by metaphysical specificity. Surveying the arc of development in Marion's giving of a method enables one to unpack these tensions along the way. This is the task of the next three sections of this chapter.

The History of the "Reduction":
Breakthrough and Broadening
in Phenomenological Method

In *Reduction*, Marion explores the debate between phenomenology's "father," Edmund Husserl, and his unruly disciple, Martin Heidegger. Both share the common rallying cry of phenomenology—"Back to the things themselves."[2] Moreover, according to Marion, Husserl and Heidegger share a common purpose: an "attempt at a radical founding of philosophy engendered by the twentieth century, which means the century which thinks with and after Nietzsche."[3] In other words, both wish to found phenomenology as "first philosophy," as the condition for (or more correctly, as the method founding the possibility of) all other scientific investigation.[4] However, their agreement ends there. Precisely what the *things* are to which one must return, and furthermore the *way of approach* to those things, remains a matter of great disagreement. In other words, both the method and the content of phenomenology remain contested ground onto which Marion steps, seeking to found his own project. In this chapter, I will discuss the debate regarding the proper *method* and *approach* to the "things themselves." While this will entail reference to the different understandings of the *Sachen selbst*, my argument here is concerned more with their mode of access.[5]

A challenging and deeply provocative work, *Reduction* is meant to be classified within the genre of "history of philosophy." In other words, according to the author's own appraisal at least,[6] it simply narrates the history of a philosophical "breakthrough" with Husserl's phenomenological project and its subsequent "broadenings" by Heidegger and then Marion. There is a straightforward version of the story Marion tells in *Reduction* and also a more complicated one. The easy version runs thus: Husserl orchestrated a "breakthrough" potentially capable of bringing philosophy into the twentieth century (following Nietzsche and the "end of metaphysics"). This breakthrough is constituted primarily in Husserl's method of a phenomenological reduction.[7] The multi-step method of reduction begins with the suspension of the "natural attitude" in which one is concerned with the reality or existence of some transcendent world "out there" to which our internal, or immanent acts of consciousness are required to correlate.[8] This "natural attitude" commits the error of separating the "objects" of cognition from the *intentional* acts of consciousness: perception, imagination, and signification. Husserl's genius lies in his insight that these two elements of cognition cannot be separated but are always found together in an intrinsic relation. This insight results in a revaluation of the epistemological categories of "transcendence" and "immanence." In Husserl's pivotal set of 1907 lectures published under the title *The Idea of Phenomenology*, he defines the phenomenological reduction as an exclusion of "all that is transcendentally posited," that is to say, a method in which "everything transcendent (that which is not given to me immanently) is to be assigned the index zero, i.e., its existence, its validity is not to be assumed as such."[9] For this reason the reduction (*epoche*) indicates a "bracketing," suspending, or putting "out of play" all but that which is evident in consciousness—or better, all but that which "gives-itself" there as a phenomenon of consciousness.[10] Heidegger, while recognizing the potential of this breakthrough, is frustrated with its ongoing enthrallment with the idea of a "pure consciousness" and the possibility of reaching "objectity" therein.

For Heidegger, Husserl remains "metaphysical" insofar as he remains shackled to a Cartesian "ego" that constitutes the objects of consciousness and thus limits them to that of which the ego is capable. Furthermore, Husserl does not take seriously enough the intransigent "embeddedness" of consciousness that is always already in a world that is "at-hand" for it. Consequently, Heidegger broadens the phenomenological method to include an "existential reduction"—broadening the proper domain of phenomenology to include not only objects of consciousness but also their ontological horizon, Being itself (*Sein*).

Marion sees this broadening (in its critical aspects, at least) as "progress" but remains dissatisfied. Because only an ontic (a particular, existing, historical) being (*Dasein*) can perform the existential reduction, Heidegger also remains indebted to a certain type of Cartesian subjectivism that limits the "things themselves" to an arbitrary horizon—that of time and being.[11] Instead, Marion broadens the method again so that the sole horizon is that of *givenness*. In Marion's method, no consciousness intervenes with its constituting intentionality (Husserl), nor does any *Dasein* with its existential particularities and embeddedness within a world (Heidegger). Instead, only the givenness of the "things themselves" as they appear—or more correctly, as they give themselves to appear—remains. All else is bracketed in a radical reduction to what he calls here "the pure form of the call."[12] Marion summarizes this "straightforward" history thus:

More essential than the reduction of objects to the consciousness of an *I*, there intervened their reduction to the rank of beings, and hence the reduction of beings to *Dasein* as the sole ontological being; even more essential again, there was affirmed the reduction of all beings to Being, which claimed the putting into play of *Dasein;* more essential in the end, than this (reduction by the) claim there finally appeared the reduction of every claim to the pure form of the call. After the transcendental reduction and the existential reduction there intervenes the reduction to and of this call. That which gives itself only to the one who gives himself over to the call and only in the pure form of a confirmation of the call, which is repeated because received.[13]

Marion tells a story in which Husserl provides the breakthrough and original methodological insight, which then needs to be broadened by Heidegger and finally again by Marion. It is narrated as a straightforward and linear tale of the progress of an idea. However, closer reading of Marion's argument (for it is indeed an argument and not simply a narration of the history of philosophy) shows a subtler use of Husserl and a more profound engagement with Heidegger than this linear tale implies. Specifically, Husserl is brought in to help Marion turn Heidegger's critique on its head. In this way Husserl offers greater openings, at least potentially, in his phenomenological method than does Heidegger with his first broadening. The technical components of this narrative need to be worked through in order to see just where Marion returns from Heidegger to a rehabilitation of Husserl.

Marion charts the "breakthrough" of phenomenology as a broadening of both the domain of "intuition" and the simultaneous autonomy of "signification." The initial breakthrough comes with Husserl's recognition of the primacy of intuition as a source of knowledge.[14] However, this primacy of intuition—broadened to the point of becoming categorical—is shown to come into conflict with the autonomy of signification, which Husserl also defends.[15] Signification does not rely on a fulfilling intuition in order to signify.[16] How can one be primary (intuition) and the other autonomous (signification)? Marion resolves this aporia by extending toward a third: "givenness."

Both intuition and signification give way to the originary and unconditioned primacy of the givenness of a phenomenon. This is Marion's interpretation of the real breakthrough accomplished in Husserl's phenomenological method. One no longer thinks the *"given* of consciousness," but instead recognizes a *"givenness* to consciousness . . . of the thing itself, given in the mode of appearing and in all of its dimensions (intuition, intention and their variations)."[17] Thus, Husserl's phenomenological "principle of principles" found in §24 of *Ideas* grants privilege to intuition "only to the extent that it interprets intuition first as 'originarily giving.'"[18] Marion cites this key passage in Husserl: "*All originarily giving intuition is by right a source of knowledge, that what offers itself originarily to us 'in intuition' (in its fleshly actuality, so to speak) must be taken wholly as it gives itself, but also only in the limits within which it gives itself (as being) there.*"[19]

Givenness is anterior because it enables, and determines the horizon of, both intuition and signification: "The object, already 'given' in signification, is found 'given' anew by intuition, in 'the same mode' as the latter."[20] Intuition is, therefore, a "mode of givenness." Marion's gloss of Husserl reconciles the competing claims of intuition's primacy with signification's autonomy by way of the more originary notion of givenness. Thus, Marion reads Husserl with this emphasis on givenness always at the forefront. This particular heuristic lens is crucial not only to his retrieval of Husserl but also to the structure of his entire phenomenology.

When Heidegger turns to Being as that which is given par excellence, this turning is framed as a question: the *Seinsfrage*. The "question of Being," simply by turning the primary given into a "question," already involves a critique of Husserl: Husserl names the givenness of Being "without truly thinking it."[21] This is Marion's first formulation of the difference between Husserl and Heidegger: the former opens to the abyss of givenness without staring its excessiveness, its mystery and thus its negativity, in the face. Husserl refuses, in other words, to question what giving means, to question how one is to think "that all that is, is only inasmuch as it is given."[22]

In agreement with Heidegger, Marion argues that Husserl commits an intrinsic betrayal of phenomenology, primarily as a consequence of his fundamental insistence upon certitude in order to secure phenomenology as a rigorous and universal science and as "first philosophy." As we shall see, this aim of securing phenomenology as "first philosophy" is not in itself problematic to Heidegger or Marion. Indeed, both take up the mantle of such an attempt. Instead, the concern is with the identification of securing phenomenology as "first philosophy" with the certitude of a "pure" or "transcendental" consciousness. This is a betrayal because the imposition of consciousness as a limit or horizon prevents one from truly returning to the "things themselves."[23]

Furthermore, Husserl's betrayal is *intrinsic* because it is found already at the very heart of his own formulation of the "principle of principles" of phenomenology (§24, *Ideas*). As cited above, intuition is proclaimed to be a source of knowledge "by right"; we are to take things as they are given in intuition. However, in the last phrase of the principle, Husserl places a limit on what had previously been limitless: ". . . only within the limits within which it gives itself (as being) there." Nothing can be claimed that is not first rendered "evident" to pure consciousness. Therefore, Husserl betrays phenomenology's potential by displacing it from its position as the science of phenomena to that of a science of (and by) consciousness. The aim of founding an indubitable science leads to a determination of phenomenality through consciousness, "by reducing every phenomenon to the certitude of an actual presence."[24] As a result, the revolutionary breakthrough of the principle of givenness is shackled to consciousness rather than the inverse, that is, rather than the determination of consciousness by "the conditions and modes of givenness which are always multiple and discerning."[25] Marion will call the resulting Husserlian phenomenon "reduced" or "flat" because, for all its purity and certitude in appearance, no remainder or excess is permitted "to trouble the equation." Consequently, all sorts of phenomena are disqualified outright as "impossible."[26]

Heidegger seeks to broaden this narrow notion of the phenomenon by first admitting that part of its appearance always also entails a concealment: he recognizes the intrinsic play between the two when he says that "apparition reveals *as such* the unapparent whose contrast haloes the apparent."[27] There is an excess in appearance—an excess that does not appear and yet whose boundary nonetheless marks the shape of that which does appear. Ultimately, the return to the things themselves must entail a return to the question of the phenomenality of Being itself because "that which remains *hidden,* in an egregious sense, or which relapses and gets *covered up again,* or which shows itself only 'in disguise' is not just this entity or that, but rather the *Being* of entities."[28] Heidegger thus locates the first principle of phenomenology, not in §24 of *Ideas,* but in §46 of Husserl's *Cartesian Meditations:* "So much appearance—so much Being."[29] Marion agrees with Heidegger that one must go beyond a reading of phenomena in their "flatness" in order to read "between the lines, so to speak, between the bursts of evident presence, that from which that very presence proceeds."[30] He will disagree, however, that, having gone beyond the objectity of phenomena (as "objects of consciousness"), one arrives and remains with an analysis of Being.

Marion argues that Heidegger's project is still fundamentally *phenomenological* because it is characterized by the two markers for phenomenology: first, it employs the methodology of the reduction; and second, it still returns to the things themselves.[31] Heidegger is distinguished from Husserl insofar as the reduction is broadened, and with it the identity of the things themselves.[32] However, this broadening does not go far enough for Marion, who dedicates much of *Reduction* to charting the various fissures and fault lines in Heidegger's ontological phenomenology. Marion's major concern has to do with what he claims is the substrate of Cartesianism in Heidegger's reliance upon the role of *Dasein*[33] and its capacity to deliver access to ontological difference.[34]

It is at this crucial point in the argument of *Reduction* that Marion switches allegiances: here Heidegger's own criticism against Husserl is turned on its head such that Marion uses Husserl to accuse Heidegger of precisely the same sort of "regionalization" that inevitably betrays the principle of a return to the things themselves. Marion thus imagines reversing Heidegger's critique: Husserl has only failed to return to the things themselves if the *Seinsfrage* is taken as the (most fundamental) *Sache selbst.* However, this in itself may be shown to be a faulty assumption on Heidegger's part. Heidegger is unable to bracket the *Seinsfrage,* and thus, marked "by an evasion or fear before what Husserl had liberated," he too is unable to carry through "the unlimited power of the reduction."[35] Simply put, a preoccupation with Being, or the meaning of Being, prevents Heidegger from reducing to the given and thus thinking givenness. Heidegger stops at Being and does not get beyond to the "givenness" of Being. While neither Husserl nor Heidegger follows the logic of the reduction to its conclusion in givenness, Marion argues that the insight is found in Husserl's writings, although it is a potential never actualized.

> If not, then by not returning, as concerns the thing itself, to the Being of beings, Husserl would in no way have failed but would have attempted an unprecedented and at first glance unthinkable leap: a leap from the region of beings in general (conceived according to objectity) to a phenomenological horizon not determined by Being, properly outside of Being, in traversing without stopping in or trying to satisfy the domain of the question on Being, where Heidegger attempted to lodge—and to block—phenomenology. In other words, Heidegger's slogan against Husserl—

that the possibility of phenomenology surpasses its actuality—could be turned back against the undertaking of *Sein und Zeit:* the *ultimate* possibility of phenomenology would consist in the question of Being no more than it is exhausted in the objectity of the constituted object; beyond the one and the other equally, a final possibility could still open to it—that of positing the *I* as transcendent to reduced objectity, but also to the Being of beings, that of positing itself, *by virtue of the reduction carried out to its final consequences, outside of Being.*[36]

This reduction "carried out to its final consequences" has, of course, been Marion's objective throughout the entire work. It opens up the possibility of a reduction to "pure givenness" or, as he will call it at this stage, a reduction to the "pure form of the call." Marion admits that Husserl does *not* follow this possibility through to its radical end. He insists, however, that its potential remains intrinsic to Husserl's formulation and method. Thus, in order to "outline the thesis of a horizon outside of being," as Marion wants, one must start from "the internal references and requirements of Husserlian phenomenology."[37] Hence, underneath the linear progression of a broadening in method from Husserl, through Heidegger, to Marion, one finds instead a return and rehabilitation of the possibility of Husserl's phenomenological approach that proves a wieldy tool against Marion's more immediate opponent, Heidegger. The rest of the work involves this rehabilitation. It entails a demonstration that, even for Husserl in the end, the *I* cannot escape the reduction. In order to understand this possibility one must attempt "to determine how and in what measure the *I*, which reduces even ontologies, does not itself first have to be."[38]

Employing a phenomenological analysis of boredom, Marion charts the "abandoning of the *I*" in a reduction sufficiently broadened to bracket even its own agent. The "depths of boredom" are described in language reminiscent of profound states of apathy, severe clinical depression,[39] and even the classical notion of ἀκηδία.[40] Such a state enables the reduction (or bracketing) of both Being and the *I* itself: "Boredom relieves the *I* of its character as a being in whose Being Being in general is an issue," that is, the *I* is no longer *Dasein.*[41] Having dissolved the *I*, all beings of the world also disappear. Boredom "deprives them of their whole denomination as beings" by, again, "ceasing from its function of being the being in whose Being the Being of all other beings is an issue."[42] Significantly, Marion's path to givenness is inherently *negative.* It involves the complete effacement of self through a boredom in the depths. This could be compared to the role of apophatic submission of the self in the "death-experience" of baptism in Dionysius. In both one finds a required moment of absolute passivity propaedeutic to reception. I will return to this point below.

Absolute boredom, which renders all beings (including my own being) *as if* they were not, brings one to a certain indeterminacy, a "there" outside of Being (a *Da* unattached to a *sein*). From "there" a call may appear that calls "me"—no longer a constituting *I,* but a witness, a called one, an interrogated and "interlocuted" one, the *interloqué.*[43] This "call" is distinguishable from Heidegger's *Anspruch des Seins* because, by definition, the call is not singular, cannot be identified with any one call, even that of "Being." The call does not issue forth from any predetermined locale:

> For why does the *there,* which I am, stand there? When the *there* is defined as a *Dasein,* a *Being-there,* it stands *there* in order to be . . . [But] if boredom liberates the *there* from the call of Being, it sets it free only in order better to expose it to the wind of every other possible call; thus, the liberated *there* is exposed to the nonontological possibility of another claim, which would qualify it to stand there in favour of another.[44]

One cannot limit this to a specific call, even theological. Marion insists that it is not a matter of invoking revealed authority in order to challenge Heidegger, but rather to show that some other call is also possible, calling into question the sole supremacy of the call of Being.

Here, at the end of this dense work, Marion concludes with a scant two pages of an actual description of his proposed "third reduction." He writes, "Apparition is sufficient for Being only inasmuch as, in appearing, it already perfectly *gives* itself; but it thus gives itself perfectly by the sole fact that it appears only inasmuch as it is *reduced* to its givenness for consciousness."[45] Appearance (in being), in other words, relies on prior givenness: something appears to the degree that it has been given to appear. Moreover, one has access to this appearance (precisely, *as* it gives itself to appear) only to the extent that one has bracketed out ("reduced") anything that might shift or affect that appearance (e.g., the intentionality or constitution of the subject) or particular horizons (of consciousness and, even, of being and time).[46] Marion redefines phenomenology's principle of principles thus: "So much reduction, so much givenness." By this principle he means that the givenness of a phenomenon equals the measure of the reduction: "The givenness that ensues is broadened to a field that is all the more vast insofar as it imposes fewer conditions. The more the reduction reduces (itself), the more it extends givenness. The less the reduction brackets what is in question, the less givenness will be able to render it accessible."[47]

Marion ends with a (somewhat) clarifying comparison of the three reductions according to (a) the one who reduces—the "to whom?" of the reduction; (b) that which it is a matter of giving—"which given?"; (c) the mode and horizon of givenness—"given how?"; and (d) that which givenness excludes—"how far?" In the first reduction (identified primarily with Husserl's transcendental phenomenology but also extended to include the Cartesian and Kantian methodologies of "doubt" and "critique" respectively), the (a) intentional and constituting *I* reduces (b) constituted objects which are taken within (c) regional ontologies in conformity with the horizon of objectity and, thus, excludes (d) everything that cannot be led back to objectity, which cannot become an object. In the second reduction (identified with Heidegger's existential phenomenology) (a) *Dasein* reduces (b) the different ways of Being, or in other words, the "ontological difference in person"—the phenomenon of Being—according to (c) the horizon of time and being itself and, thus, excludes (d) everything that does not have to be. Finally, in his own third reduction, the one who "reduces" is (a) the *interloqué*— the one to whom the call is uttered, and thus the one "to whom" is given (b) the gift itself (here specified as the gift of the possibility of "rendering oneself to *or* of eluding the claim of the call"). This gift is given according to (c) no horizon other than an "absolutely unconditioned call" and excludes (d) nothing.

One must admit that the payoff of Marion's own positive contribution of a "third reduction" remains frustratingly opaque. Leaving aside the question of Marion's reading and application of Husserl and Heidegger, it still remains unclear precisely what such a phenomenality is meant to look like. How does it appear? How does one speak of it? Marion has not yet adequately described how this reduction can result in appearing phenomena. *Reduction and Givenness* leaves one with many unanswered questions. Nonetheless, Marion's complex phenomenological inheritance from both Husserl and Heidegger can be clearly unraveled in this work. In my analysis of the main argument of *Reduction*, the straightforward story of a progressive broadening of the reduction from Husserl, through Heidegger, to Marion, has been problematized. With this analysis, I resist one strand of critical interpretation of

Marion as a fundamental betrayer of the Husserlian philosophical project. Marion returns to Husserl in order to arrive at a radical notion of "givenness" that lacks all horizons. In other words, Marion finds in Husserl a language of givenness that is malleable to his own enterprise: Husserl is used by Marion to critique Heidegger's ontological enclosure of the given. Furthermore, the return to Husserl is rhetorically powerful. His subversion or upending of Husserl is always accomplished within the boundaries of the discourse set by Husserl himself. He places himself securely within phenomenological discourse thus.[48] Marion employs the same rhetorical strategy with Kant. As I will argue in chapter 5, this strategy perhaps confounds Marion's methodology in the end. For now, let me turn to examining the way this depiction of givenness changes by the time of his next major phenomenological work nine years later. We shall see how, in response to many of the critiques of *Reduction,* a greater emphasis is placed on establishing phenomenology as a sort of "first philosophy" with a rigorous methodology.[49]

The Indubitability and Immanence of Givenness

Being Given: Toward a Phenomenology of Givenness is read best as a polemical work, or at least a work written in response to a variety of critics. Hence, in his formulations of both a "new" phenomenological method and its findings (specifically in a type of phenomenon classified as "saturated"), Marion is conscious of warding off criticisms from two directions: that he is too "theological" (Derrida and Janicaud[50]) and that he is not "hermeneutical" enough (Greisch and Grondin[51]). In other words, he is suspected of both "smuggling in" a grand narrative of theological supremacy and, at the same time, of not giving sufficient attention to an explanation of the role of interpretation within such a phenomenological method. Both critiques revolve around the contested issue of universality versus regionality (theological or hermeneutical). Marion's aim in this work is to guarantee the former domain for his method.

Marion summarizes the argument of the book thus: "What *shows itself,* first *gives itself*—this is my one and only theme."[52] *Being Given* is understood explicitly by Marion to be a defense and rearticulation of many of the themes developed in *Reduction,* justifying the privilege Marion affords "givenness" and using an expanded notion of the "saturated phenomenon"[53] as the test case for pure givenness. Marion is energized in this work not simply to defend himself against critics of *Reduction* but also to *justify* the inclusion of all types of phenomena into phenomenological discourse.

The work begins with an expression of frustration arising amidst limitations placed on the practice of phenomenology (and philosophy) in France.[54] He writes that a certain school of phenomenology, in refusing to think comprehensively about the nature of the given and its proper approach, is "powerless to receive a number of phenomena for what they are—givens that show themselves . . . [furthermore] it excludes from the field of manifestation not only many phenomena, but above all those most endowed with meaning and those that are most powerful."[55] Thus, he argues, only a phenomenology employing a radical reduction to givenness actually can achieve what Husserl set out to do: "return to the things themselves"—*all of them*. However, in order to include such excessive phenomena, those most "endowed with meaning" and most "powerful," Marion believes he must justify their appearance by convincing skeptics (especially Janicaud et al.) that his method is universally valid and not simply forwarding a narrow or parochial theological agenda.[56]

In the preface to *Being Given*, Marion claims to have finally articulated a "nonmetaphysical method of philosophy—phenomenology, but a phenomenology thoroughly secured"—something he did not have at hand when he was writing *God Without Being*.[57] In order to understand precisely what Marion means by a "nonmetaphysical method," one must return to his delimitation of the characteristic markers of metaphysics. First, in order to be "metaphysical," the method must impose limitations on the conditions for the possibility of phenomenality: a horizon (temporal and spatial), and the constituting function of the "I" (whether through Kant's "categories" or Husserl's notion of "intentionality"). Secondly, and consequently, the method must uphold the subjective starting place (even the chastened and "authentic" subject of Heidegger's *Dasein*) and privilege the question of Being. In contrast, a "nonmetaphysical" method would not begin from the subject, privilege Being, or submit to any horizon.[58] Precisely what such a method would actually look like must be clarified further.

First, it is important to recall that, as we have already seen, the method of the reduction is *the* essential marker of any phenomenological approach for Marion. In other words, for something to count as phenomenology, it must employ the reduction.[59] But in what does this reduction consist? In a more explicit formulation than that found in *Reduction*, Marion links the reduction intrinsically to givenness:[60] he no longer speaks of a "reduction to the pure form of the call"—a confusing formulation, not least because of its implicit theological implications— but rather, of "the reduction to the given as such" or the "reduction to pure givenness."

Marion contrasts the criterion for grounding knowledge in "science and metaphysics" with that in phenomenology. In the former, it is a question of "proving," which "consists in grounding appearances in order to know with certainty."[61] On the other hand, with phenomenology it is no longer a question of "proving" but of "showing." This implies "letting appearances appear in such a way that they accomplish their own apparition, so as to be received exactly as they give themselves."[62]

How does one reach or access the "apparition in appearance"? Marion argues that to do so one must first bracket every fore-structure and every preconceived idea of what approaches one in the appearance. In Marion's words, one must "transgress every perceived impression by means of the intentionality of the thing itself."[63] One must be ruled or directed by the apparition that gives itself thus, rather than the "subject" to whom it appears. For this reason, Marion will say that the phenomenological method of the reduction should properly be called a "countermethod," that is, a method that undoes method, opening us to pure receptivity.

How is this possible? Marion himself acknowledges the difficulty of knowing how to let something "show itself" as itself when "knowledge always comes from me . . . [and] manifestation is never evident by itself."[64] This difficulty points to the paradox of phenomenological method as Marion would formulate it: "that it takes the initiative in losing it."[65] He gives the analogy of a theater director who is at first necessary to the production but who, by the time of the performance, is no longer noticed or even necessarily present because the spectacle itself dominates and self-directs. The reduction, in other words, does not so much "provoke the apparition of what manifests itself as it clears away the obstacles that encircle it and would hide it," and its sole function is to provide the "conditions for its own disappearance."[66]

One must be very clear about what this method can and cannot secure. On the one hand, it cannot "secure indubitability in the mode of a possession of objects that are certain because produced according to the a priori conditions for knowledge," that is, in the mode of "proving" or "objectifying" phenomena to a subject. On the other hand, this method "should provoke the indubitability of the apparition of things, without producing the certainty of objects."[67] What it *does* secure, in other words, is the indubitable ground or occasion that might alone allow phenomena to give themselves to appear. It is important to observe that one can still talk of a kind of *indubitability*. This fulfills Marion's need for his method to pass a "Husserlian" inspection, to be rigorous and to yield universal rather than quixotic or regionalized results. This (counter-)method does not entail an a priori conditioning that directs (and thus, limits according to its own first principles) the appearance of phenomena. Instead, it "travels in tandem with the phenomenon, as if protecting it and clearing a path for it by eliminating roadblocks," precisely those obstacles that previous phenomenology argued enabled the apparition (Husserl's "intentionality" and Heidegger's "fore-knowledge").[68]

Marion needs to maintain a principle—something that is "indisputable, universal, unconditioned"—that cannot, nonetheless, be shown to direct, produce, or in any way condition the appearance of the given phenomenon.[69] For this reason, he will speak of the "reduction to the given as such" as a last or ultimate principle rather than a first principle because it does not serve a *constituting* function. This is a difficult balance to maintain. Marion attempts it in the claim that the reduction to givenness proceeds as a principle insofar as it dictates that "nothing precedes the phenomenon, except its own apparition on its own basis."[70] The method of the reduction is necessarily found alongside of the appearance without preceding or directing it. Thus, the primacy remains to the phenomenon. The principle of this method ought properly to be called "last" because it "intervenes after the manifestation of appearing, which is displayed freely without any other principle, for the sole purpose of sanctioning a posteriori by reduction what, in appearing, truly deserves the title given phenomenon."[71] In other words, the reduction to givenness functions as a methodological principle *not* by constituting or producing the phenomenon beforehand, but rather by ruling or decreeing, *after the fact*, that the phenomenon necessarily appears by itself.

The other significant aspect of this method is that it does not lead to positing transcendent or theological claims naturally—indeed, it does not allow such claims. Since the reduction "suspends and brackets all that, in appearance, does not succeed in giving itself," it "separates what appears from what does not appear" and "therefore excludes the assumption of any real transcendence and is far from establishing any dogmatism," theological or otherwise.[72] Marion claims that even if he uses the term "revelation," which he does in *Being Given,* he is operating squarely within the field of phenomenology rather than theology.

Marion defends the purely phenomenological nature of his project with two arguments. First, if every phenomenon must be describable necessarily, one ought not to exclude the inversion of this claim—that *every thing describable is a phenomenon of sorts.*[73] Marion objects to the a priori methodological decision to forbid the thinking of events, experiences, and visions that happen to us specifically as phenomenal—"to forbid phenomenality to what claimed it."[74] Secondly, Marion defends the appearance of the term "revelation" within his phenomenological writing by drawing a distinction between outlining a theoretical possibility for revelation (what he claims to do in this work) and making a claim as to its historical actuality or "truth."[75] Marion's method neither inexorably leads to, nor forbids outright, the theoretical possibility of the appearance of "theological" or "transcendent" phenomena. However, were they to appear, by definition they would be transcendent no longer, but immanent in their appearance.

This brings us to another paradox arising from Marion's method: although the given phenomenon emerges from itself and in no way can be constituted or produced by something other than itself (such as the transcendental *I*), nevertheless, appearing on its own, it must give itself *to* one still, to the conscious *I*.[76] In other words, there is no exception to the reduction to immanence. As a result, there is no claim to rely on, or begin from, a place outside of the field of immanence (and here is where, I would argue, Marion most explicitly distinguishes himself from Levinas) and his project remains rigorously *phenomenological,* not theological.

The "advance" of the given comes "in person, without a stuntman, double or any other representative standing in for it"[77]—it gives what it claims to give and nothing else. Thus in *Being Given,* we find further argument for a methodology that yields a potentially unlimited field of phenomena while remaining rigorous, indubitable, and universal due at least in part, if not wholly, to the fact that it wields a principle that is said to be "last."

Phenomenology as "First Philosophy"

As Robyn Horner argues, Marion's aim is to articulate a philosophical method without metaphysical ground, without analogy of being, and without a "self-present" subject."[78] This method, nevertheless, must enable and ensure the status of phenomenology as "first philosophy." I have been arguing that Marion, like Husserl before him, remains committed to this placement of phenomenology. Marion presents this goal most explicitly in the final text discussed in this chapter on his methodology. Published in two slightly different forms,[79] this essay treats various historical attempts to identify the aspect of philosophy that makes it "first."

To begin with, we must understand why the issue of primacy is so significant. Marion argues thus: if it is not judged to be "first," then the purpose of philosophy—to ground all the other sciences—is nullified.[80] Thus the history of a series of attempts to identify what makes philosophy "first" is also a history of various attempts to ground philosophy by developing a methodological principle capable of becoming a universal precondition for all knowledge and thus for all the sciences. Various loci have been given as the proper grounding subjects for any philosophy that would call itself "first." Marion charts these loci chronologically.

Aristotle, Marion's first historical example, locates the proper subject of metaphysics (his "first philosophy") in *ousia*. However, whether *ousia* is understood as "substance" or as "essence," objections can be (and have been) made to its primacy.[81] Thus *ousia* cannot guarantee philosophy's primacy. Marion turns next to Thomas Aquinas and the consideration of the "*causa*" of beings as the subject of "first philosophy."[82] Nevertheless, "cause" also fails to guarantee the primacy of philosophy because the priority of cause and effect can be reversed: cause only *explains,* while effects *prove.* In other words, "existence precedes cause, which only comments on it."[83] Thus it cannot be the guiding subject of a philosophy that seeks to be first.

Marion's third identification of an attempt to define a "first philosophy" comes with the turn to the subject, and hence a shift from metaphysics to epistemology. He locates this in Descartes and Kant primarily and in *the supremacy of the noetic,* of the conditions of knowledge, over both *ousia* and cause. Epistemology, as "first philosophy," is defined as "the science of the *knowledge* of being in general, insofar as it is reduced to what is intelligible, that is to say to the *cogitabile* [conceivable], such that it responds to the *a priori* conditions of its appearance to an *ego cogito*."[84] Here we find ourselves back on the familiar territory upon which Marion concentrates this bulk of his critical energy. Consequently, a rehearsal of the technicalities of the argument against the supremacy of such an epistemology is not necessary here.

Marion argues that phenomenology "takes up again . . . the entire project of 'first philosophy,'" by which he means that phenomenology explicitly aims to guarantee its methodological primacy. As "first philosophy," phenomenology is that with which "it is necessary to begin, in order then to put to work the second philosophies or regional sciences." However, it can succeed in this only if it escapes the metaphysical aporias of *ousia, causa,* and subjectivity.[85] Only thus will phenomenology, with its reduction to givenness, offer the possibility of providing a ground for all knowledge, that is, earn the status of "first philosophy."

In his clearest statement yet, Marion argues for the inexorable capability of the reduction to givenness to yield both *certainty* and *universality.*

> The reduction eliminates all transcendence, that is to say the intentional ecstasy of consciousness toward its objective, which alone allows knowledge of it, but also incertitude, error, illusion, and so on; thus the givenness of the given, on the express condition that it is already reduced, reduced to the pure given, becomes absolutely indubitable.[86]

The reduction eliminates all that is not given, and if it accomplishes this correctly, it becomes "absurd" to say that "givenness does not give the given with certainty."[87] Furthermore, Marion assures the universality of givenness: it is universal because "about what can we say that it does not appear as given?"[88] Phenomenology thus "universalizes the Cartesian result": no longer certifying just an ego, it now certifies and makes a whole world precisely because "it no longer bases it on thought (thinking itself), but on the given as it gives itself (to consciousness)."[89] Thus, Marion argues, he has landed on a method worthy of grounding all other sciences. Yet, is it *properly* called "first"?

Phenomenology cannot be "first" if by that one understands the foundation of a first a priori principle that then governs the constitution and appearance of phenomena. Specifically, phenomenology cannot attain this privileged status through "imposing the transcendental anteriority of the *I*," nor does it restore the primacy of *ousia* or *causa* as first principle. Rather, "the determining originality of its enterprise consists in rendering to the phenomenon an incontestable priority: to let it appear no longer as it must (according to the supposed *a priori* conditions of experience and its objects), but as it gives itself (from itself and as such)."[90] The paradox is that the demands of phenomenology under the dominion of a reduction to givenness both "defines a criterion and opens a crisis."[91] It both enables and simultaneously disables its own possibility. Here is the paradox:

> In all cases, the formula "As much reduction, as much givenness" plays as last principle: not only the last one to be found, but above all the principle stating that the last—the seeming, in its supposed metaphysical fragility—is finally always equal to the single and unique first—to the appearing, the unique screen open to receive all manifestations, all truths, all realities. The last becomes first, the principle is defined as last principle, and thus phenomenology would only retake the title of "first philosophy" in inverting it—"last philosophy."[92]

In other words, phenomenology can gain the traditional domain of "first philosophy" only by supplying the "last" (ultimate) methodological principle. This "last" principle operates successfully only by its disappearance. The method of reduction seeks to clear every obstacle from the pure apparition of the given.

It will become necessary to probe whether the method itself ought to be considered one of the "obstacles" to be swept away. Another way of posing this question is to ask who accomplishes or performs this *method* if subjective limitations on appearance are precisely that which the method seeks to remove. The question of whether it is possible to have a method and a "last" principle without the active involvement of a subject will be pressed in later chapters. It is sufficient for now to note that this is how Marion hopes to achieve his double objective: phenomenology reigns supreme and establishes the possibility of all other sciences without deciding or constituting beforehand its own objects or those of the other sciences. His method establishes the limits by which all phenomena give themselves to be seen and, thus, subjected to further inquiry. They are given first, and givenness, as last word, is also Marion's starting place.

Central Elements of Marion's
Phenomenological Method

Given this survey of Marion's most important phenomenological works—
Reduction and Givenness, Being Given, and *In Excess*—we can draw
together some key elements of Marion's phenomenological method. First,
although he understands his own methodological principles to form a
line of logical continuity with his teachers, Husserl and Heidegger, even
Marion will admit to a dramatic transformation of both of their writings.
Nevertheless, he reveals a continued fascination with, and adherence to,
basic tenets of Husserl's project—not least of which is to provide a method
that can claim for itself the title of "first" (or "last") philosophy. Despite a
radical critique of Husserl's horizon of objectity and its concurrent primacy of the transcendental *I,* Marion remains committed to the search
for a method that can prove itself impenetrable to outside attack—that is,
a method that is both universal and certain or indubitable. This commitment cannot, however, outreach his other commitment to allow phenomena to appear *on their own terms,* rather than having been determined
extrinsically and beforehand. In other words, Marion's method yields
certain and universal phenomena whilst, paradoxically, refusing to allow
for any *metaphysical specificity.* Such specificity would determine the way
in which phenomena appear and the extent of their appearance as well as
the possibility of their appearance. In other words, it might forbid certain
phenomena from appearance, which, of course, is precisely what Marion
seeks to avoid. Understanding this tension provides a lens through which
to view Marion's nuanced and yet uneven interpretation and retrieval of
Dionysius the Areopagite. It is to this that we now turn.

Dionysius: An Ambiguous Source for Retrieval

In order to recognize fully the impact of Marion's methodological commitments upon his retrieval of Dionysius, we must first recall his fundamental
attraction to the anonymous author. Chapter 1 argued that Marion's retrieval of the Fathers often serves as a source of validating "orthodoxy" to
strengthen his position in current epistemological and phenomenological
debates. His relation to Dionysius, however, goes beyond such an apologetic strategy. Dionysius provides a framework within which Marion

might think through several concepts crucial to his phenomenology. Specifically, in his early thinking on the icon and on visibility, Marion sought a way that immanent material might reveal divine glory.[93] Dionysius provides Marion with a "theological aesthetics"[94] that enables the appearance of "transcendent" phenomena without, nonetheless, entailing their circumscription. From Dionysius, Marion can garner the conceptual apparatus to think of language as a gift that reveals, just as it conceals.

The most significant aspect of Dionysius' understanding of revelation and language, according to Marion, is the fact that it is governed by the logic of the gift: "Language, inscribed in the distance of Goodness, must be received as the gift of the unthinkable; it is necessary then all the more that all the claimants, to demand the Requisit, [*requérants, requérir le Réquisit*] receive it as the icon of the invisible."[95] This citation encapsulates many important themes in Marion's interest and use of Dionysius: language as gift received in and from distance, divine incomprehensibility, and the inherent relation between the divine giver (*Réquisit*) and all beings (*requérants*), including those that ask or demand (*requérir*) after them. Concerning the first two themes, Marion's retrieval of Dionysius is unambiguous and straightforward. The latter, however, needs to be interrogated further.

In general, any retrieval of the pseudonymous author comes up against the broad nexus of cosmology, hierarchy, and apophaticism as it is developed in the *corpus Dionysiacum*. I will argue that Marion pays insufficient attention to this integral nexus, ignoring it for the most part. This should not be a surprise since it coincides with Marion's ambivalent relation to universality versus metaphysical specificity in his phenomenological method. As I have been arguing throughout his chapter, Marion desires a method that yields universal and certain results, whilst remaining "non-metaphysical," in other words, without its content having been predetermined by some a priori principle (whether of *ousia*, cause, or subjectivity). This methodological preference, however, at times problematically shapes Marion's retrieval of Dionysius. Thus we find occasion to revisit Marion's quixotic translation of αἰτία as *Réquisit*. Clearly, it is difficult for Marion to simply translate this important word in the Dionysian corpus as "cause" since such language returns Marion to metaphysical connotations that he wants to avoid. It is important to ascertain whether this shift in translation is warranted.

In translating αἰτία as *Réquisit*, Marion not only means to sever the ties between αἰτία and "cause" (especially any metaphysical cause) but also to signify a connection between αἰτία and αἰτέω ('to ask, demand, or request'): "Hence, what we have translated here exactly, but all the less correctly, as 'cause' must perhaps be understood as that which all beings request (αἰτέω, αἰτιάομαι) who for their part fundamentally receive themselves therefrom as requestants (τά αἰτιάτα)."[96] However, when he first makes this etymological connection (in *Idol and Distance*), it is not supported by any of the appropriate lexical apparatus.[97] He has some grounds for alluding to the legalistic and juridical connotations of αἰτία where "cause" refers to the one who caused 'x,' and hence to the one charged with 'x',[98] but this does not necessarily lead to a connotation of "Requisite" or "Requested." His citation of Pachymere's scholia of Dionysius does not further this argument but merely restates the claim: Marion simply translates the Greek into the specific French that he is trying to establish. Citing Pachymere's *Commentary* on *The Celestial Hierarchy*, III, 3, 2, Marion translates thus: "'Called requestants, αἰτιάτα, are the terms that, in order to be in whatever way one might want, need an exterior requisite (αἰτία). Requisites (αἰτίαι), the completed terms, in view of which, in tending toward them, we complete the requestants and those of which they are the terms' (PG, 3, 456c)."[99] This does not in itself provide evidence for a similar translation of the word in Dionysius, for one could just as simply translate αἰτία as "cause" and αἰτιάτα as "caused things," or even "effects"; indeed, to do so would make more sense within the Late Antique context.

Further evidence that αἰτία should be translated straightforwardly as "cause" is found in the profound *lack* of commentary on the meaning of the term in Dionysius amongst Dionysian scholars.[100] No comment is thought necessary, even though this term is used abundantly in *The Divine Names* and throughout the corpus.[101] In other words, one can safely assume that the absence of explanatory commentary and lack of debate around the term points to a general acceptance amongst Dionysian scholarship (which, like any body of commentary, loves to find sources of disagreement) of its straightforward translation as "cause." This is simply not an issue for Dionysian scholars. That it is for Marion is itself enlightening. It reveals, in this case, an importation of concerns and cautions particular to his own context—one in which he seeks to avoid any of the "metaphysical pitfalls" that terms like "cause" seem to veer toward. Quite simply, this is not a concern for Dionysius. Without assuming knowledge of the anonymous author's mind, we can still safely assume that he is not concerned to guard against "onto-theology" or against making ontological and cosmological claims in general. Moreover, little does Dionysius guard against metaphysical specificity. Indeed, the *cosmos* is straightforwardly depicted as having been "given" in a specific manner. To what these specifics are, we must now turn.[102]

The Relation between Apophasis and Hierarchy in Dionysius

As I argued in chapter 2, one cannot separate Dionysius' understanding of language, and specifically his apophaticism, from his cosmology. Language in Dionysius has a specific ontological source, just as its various uses have specific ontological consequences. Language arises out of a cosmology of givenness—God gives Godself in the creation of the world in all its aspects, including language, and this same cosmology of givenness dictates creation's response of praise. (Thus far, Marion accompanies, or is even led by, Dionysius.) More precisely, however, Dionysius' cosmology (and with it, language) is given in a determinedly hierarchical framework. Marion, in his later writings at least, is quite reluctant to take this specific cosmology on board.[103] The question becomes, then, can one properly understand Dionysius' apophaticism apart from the context of the hierarchical world from which it emerges? (This question can be phrased differently in order to expand it to one of the primary questions underlying the logic of this chapter: is it possible to give a universal method that is not in some way determinative, that does not suppose a specific outcome?)

The question of how these two concepts, "apophasis" and "hierarchy," relate to one another in Dionysius' theological system is debated in Dionysian scholarship. Interestingly, only the first term dominates current philosophical discussions and retrievals of Dionysius, while the latter is forgotten. However, the significance of "hierarchy" to Dionysius' corpus is unquestionable. After all, Dionysius invents the term, and its historical impact on Christian ecclesial and imperial developments is massive. I will briefly rehearse three Eastern Orthodox interpretations of the relationship between apophasis and hierarchy before suggesting my own formulation.

Most scholars agree that both apophasis and hierarchy *function* to bring about union with God. However, how this happens remains in question. Representing a common critique, John Meyendorff is suspicious of the possibility of reconciling Dionysius' apophatic (or mystical) union with God with that gained through the hierarchies. "On the contrary," he writes, "it seems that for Dionysius there are two distinct modes of union with God: on the one hand, theology, mystical, individual, and direct; and on the other hand, theurgy, which is the 'activity of the hierarchy' and of its numerous intermediaries."[104] In other words, there is a sense of immediate and individual union through apophasis, while at the same time, Meyendorff thinks one is doomed to seek union through a hierarchy in which one's position and ranking has already been predetermined from all time. Meyendorff argues that these two understandings of union are incompatible with one another. In disagreement, both Andrew Louth and Alexander Golitzin will argue that, far from contradictory elements in the Dionysian system, apophasis and hierarchy necessarily go hand in hand (although which leads the other will remain a matter of subtle distinction between Golitzin and Louth).

Golitzin's rebuttal of Meyendorff begins with the premise of the necessary interrelation between the celestial, earthly, and psychic hierarchies. The saint, he writes, is the "microcosm in whom the heavenly and earthly liturgies are present and mirrored."[105] There is no autonomous intellect or will. Both the liturgy and the ecclesiastical community, themselves as reflections of the celestial hierarchies, are necessary if one is to form or sculpt one's soul into a condition capable of receiving God.[106] Submission to the proper order of the earthly hierarchies helps to bring about proper ordering of the soul. Thus, Dionysius' *Epistle Eight*[107] concerns both harmony between individuals in community and harmony in the soul of one individual. The apophatic disposition is an important step in this act of submission. Demophilus upsets the sacred order of the clergy and the liturgy only because his inner being is also disordered.[108] In this way, Golitzin reads *Epistle Eight,* not as justification for total ecclesiastical power, but as a meditation on the "formation of that receptacle or capacity within us which allows for God's epiphany."[109]

Furthermore, if, as Golitzin argues, the Dionysian corpus can only be understood properly as a coherent unit and not interpreted piecemeal, then there can be no disjunct between the mystical and hierarchical texts. For instance, *Mystical Theology* and *Ecclesiastical Hierarchy* (two seemingly antithetical works) parallel one another in at least one central way: Moses' ascent up the mountain and into darkness (described in *Mystical Theology*) is structurally and philosophically echoed, Golitzin argues, in the worshiper's approach to the altar in *Ecclesiastical*

Hierarchy. In both, the closer one comes to the sacred, the less visible will the sacred appear. Moreover, the identity of the uniting subject toward which one moves in both the "darkness of *Mystical Theology*" and the "altar of *Ecclesiastical Hierarchy*" is, according to Golitzin, Christ.[110] In this way we can see that, in order to accomplish the coherence of the corpus, Golitzin places apophasis firmly in the service of the hierarchies. The emphasis for Golitzin is on the ordered ecclesiastical structures (and even more specifically, finally on Christ[111]).

Louth also argues that hierarchy and apophasis are not antithetical, but in some way co-dependent. Nevertheless, by focusing on the role of "ecstasy" in Dionysius, Louth places a greater emphasis on the function of apophasis in the *corpus*. As a reflection of God's own ecstatic desire or yearning (through which God goes outside of Godself to create the world), so too the individual creature ecstatically yearns to return to God. Ecstasy, here, does not refer to an extra-corporeal experience; rather, Dionysius refers to a radical de-centering of one's life onto another. Louth writes: "In the case of the love of God, it means letting God's love be the principle of one's life. It is 'suffering' in that it means receptivity of such a high degree that the one who loves God is a vehicle for his power and love."[112]

Moreover, it is through the "way of negation" that one surrenders oneself to such a love and such a de-centering of self. Going beyond the signs and symbols, both sensible and intelligible, is "an act of love in which we abandon the *signs* of God's love—the symbols and concepts that reveal him and his love—and come to belong to God himself."[113] For Louth, such apophatic union in love enables one to overcome the static-ness of the hierarchies.[114]

While agreeing with both Golitzin and Louth on the basic coherence of the Dionysian corpus (as opposed to those who find no way to hold apophasis and hierarchy together), I will differ slightly in the way in which this coherence is maintained. It is not achieved, I submit, by subsuming apophasis under a dominant hierarchical structure or, conversely, by dissolving the hierarchies in a final leap into an apophatic abyss. Rather, the corpus coheres, ultimately, only by holding them together in perfect, if paradoxical, balance. Thus the very stability[115] of the hierarchical structure is precisely that which allows a radical apophasis not simply in our language about God but also in our very way of being in relation to God. It is the very *givenness* of the hierarchical cosmos that enables an act of total self-abandonment in the apophatic surrender. We let go of the need for comprehension and adequate language with the "knowledge" of a net somewhere ready to catch us.[116]

There is no requisite disjunct or logical contradiction between a personal and immediate mysticism (seen to be more egalitarian) and union in the hierarchies (which admits of degrees of proximity). On the one hand, both require an apophatic attitude. Whether through linguistic negation or though a de-centering of self in submission, apophasis enables "the last opening up of the soul already formed and prepared, through ascesis and sacramental participation, to become the vessel of God's presence."[117] On the other hand, the hierarchies (represented here by ascetical preparation and sacramental participation) are not simply preparatory devices. They are also, more generally, presupposed as that order to which one might submit. The stability of the contours of a hierarchically ordered cosmos open up an infinite and unknown and unknowable space into which one might travel to "meet her Maker." Dionysius speaks of this in terms of "infinite approximations."[118] While these approximations might appear to be infinitesimal or negligible gestures from the perspective of the cosmos, from one's own perspective they represent an infinitely endless journey.

Paradoxically, then, the radicality of apophasis found in Dionysius is supported by a hierarchical structure of the cosmos wherein one might "rest"[119] and into which one might dissolve, surrendering (through purification and illumination) to one's place in a perfecting union with God. In other words, one does not apophatically surrender to an abyss (even while it might seem so from our limited purview). Although God and therefore the relation or condition one is in vis-à-vis God is radically and eternally unsayable and unthinkable, one nevertheless surrenders to the condition for which one was created. The task of all beings is simply "to become what you are." Negation, denial, unsaying—all rest on this ontological framework, which is not only given but stable and reliable. It is this very stability that frees up language and knowledge to be as creative and loose, as playful even, as it wants.[120]

No one has captured this paradoxical relation between hierarchy and apophasis in Dionysius better than Balthasar (a significant fact, given Marion's reliance upon this theologian's interpretation of Dionysius). Balthasar writes: "If no one has emphasized so strongly as Denys the transcendence of God, [neither] has anyone upheld so decisively the givenness of the essential boundaries and hierarchical ordering of the creation (*because no one has thought through or applied so consistently the consequences of this apophaticism*)."[121] Further, Balthasar does not shy away from the disquieting consequence that in Dionysius' world this leads to a hierarchical understanding of knowledge of God. Balthasar states it plainly: all of reality acts as a symbol or icon of God, yet "images can be interpreted in different ways, the ordinary people remaining standing in front of the symbols while the priests and the contemplatives penetrate more deeply to their spiritual meaning."[122]

Here we arrive at the heart of Marion's uncomfortable retrieval of Dionysius. His commitment to giving a universal method that is rigorous and certain is both attracted and repelled by such a vision—attracted by its universality and repelled not only by its specificity but moreover by the fact that the specificity spells out a hierarchical worldview in which, potentially at least, one might speak of varying orders of knowledge and thus be open to the charge of esotericism. Recalling that this is precisely one of Derrida's complaints about the negative theology he finds in Dionysius,[123] one understands Marion's discomfort in acknowledging its potentiality within the context of a debate with Derrida. This was not always the case.

When writing *Idol and Distance,* Marion is less troubled by an unabashed avowal of the hierarchical presuppositions of Dionysius' understanding of revelation and language.[124] Marion acknowledges the role of hierarchy to "produce relation with God,"[125] places hierarchy under the logic of the gift, whereby that which is given—the "sacred order" that hierarchy is—"does not demean itself when it goes out of itself," and thus, differentiates it from "Plotinian" emanation as a result of its dual-directionality (hierarchy is ascent as well as emanation).[126] Furthermore, this sacred order has a specific ecclesiastical context and consequence or set of possible consequences, positive and negative.[127] Marion is not ignorant of the relation, then, between apophasis and a specifically hierarchical cosmology. (This excuse cannot be made.) However, in his later writings, all reference to or acknowledgment of this connection is dropped. Here again, therefore, we find evidence of Marion's retrieving his patristic sources in a less nuanced way than that of which he is capable.

By the time of his debate with Derrida in "On the Gift" at the Villanova conference, Marion has nothing at all to say regarding hierarchy or even, really, cosmology. Instead, he emphasizes that Dionysius offers a "third way" beyond a false antinomy of apophatic and cataphatic theologies, a way he calls *de-nomination* in order to connote the dual nature of a simultaneous naming and un-naming. He has recourse, here again, to his specific (and, I have argued, somewhat anachronistic) translation of αἰτία as *Réquisit*. Dionysius does not mean to posit God as a "metaphysical cause," he argues, but rather as "what all those who demand [αἰτιάτα, *aitiata*] demand [αἰτέω, *aiteo*] when they aim at the One from whom they come and to whom they return."[128] In other words, αἰτία has no claim either to name God or to deny the name of God. It certainly has no pretences of any cosmological overtones. Indeed, according to Marion, it has no predicative function at all, but only the pragmatic one of enabling a speaker to address that which remains beyond all designation:

> The αἰτία in no way names God; it de-nominates [*le dé-nomme*] by suggesting the strictly pragmatic function of language—namely, to refer names and their speaker to the unattainable yet inescapable interlocutor beyond every name and every denegation of names. With αἰτία, speech does not say any more than it denies—it acts by transporting itself in the direction of the One whom it de-nominates.[129]

It is precisely in this way that Dionysius indicates a "new pragmatic function of language" that will always escape, according to Marion, any onto-theological trappings.[130] Significantly, however, as I have already argued in chapter 1, in fleshing out this notion of a purely "pragmatic function of language," or what he also describes as a "pragmatic theology of absence,"[131] Marion must seek recourse outside of Dionysius' writing. In other words, in his *apologia* concerning Dionysius' potential for the contemporary debates about gift and language, Marion turns, with little explicit acknowledgment, to Gregory of Nyssa. Furthermore, as we can now see more explicitly, in so doing he turns a blind eye to the rich ontological backdrop given with Dionysius' theory of language.

To give one example: Marion might, on the one hand, creatively explore the harmony between the destructive propaedeutic of the "depths of boredom" in his own method of a radical reduction to givenness and, on the other, the role of "death" and "formlessness" in the Dionysian contemplation of baptism. In *The Ecclesiastical Hierarchy* Dionysius speaks of the act of immersion in baptism, which serves to "hide the initiate completely in the water." This is an image of the death into which one enters and shares and the "burial where form is dissolved." This "death" and dissolution of form serves an existential, soteriological, and ontological purpose. One must become formless first in order to be able to become receptive to the divine form with which one then clothes oneself. Through this dying and dissolving, "order descends upon disorder within him. Form takes over from formlessness. Light shines through all his life."[132] Marion misses the opportunity for such rich comparisons, ironically, because of the very methodological commitments that attract him to Dionysius as a source in the first place.

Summarizing Remarks

While Marion is reluctant to translate αἰτία thus, I have argued that "cause" is precisely what Dionysius means, so Marion's own translation is something of a sleight of hand. It is a trick that reveals more than his aversion to anything that veers toward the metaphysical; it also reveals his remaining adherence to a universal method. For Marion does not simply skip over the term; he refashions it to suit his own methodological allegiances. He is both attracted to and wary of the term, just as he is both attracted to and wary of the integral relation between Dionysius' cosmology and his apophaticism.

Were he more willing, Marion could develop an interpretation of Dionysius whereby his understanding of the givenness of creation yields certainty and universality of method without any pretence to *epistemological* certainty. Aside from a certain squeamishness, nothing prevents Marion from exploring in greater depth the ways in which he can augment his rich notion of Dionysian language with an even richer notion of his cosmology. I have argued that hierarchy and apophaticism need not contradict one another but can, indeed, be seen to rely on one another. However, Marion remains wary of such claims. The question remains: can he employ Dionysius' theological aesthetics without also assuming and adopting its underlying cosmological framework?

In emphasizing a particular thrust of Marion's method, I am intentionally pushing him further than many other readers do. I have argued that Marion's primary motivations remain indebted to Husserl before any other. This reading runs directly counter to that of Janicaud, who criticizes Marion for betraying the fundamental aim of Husserl's philosophical project.[133] Differently than Janicaud, my charge is not that he is too theological here but that, ironically, his allegiance to Husserl brings with it an allegiance to grounding phenomenology with a universal method that can assure its privileged status as "first" (or "last"). For the purposes of drawing a connection to his retrieval of Dionysius and illuminating an intrinsic tension running though Marion's thought, I have emphasized the compulsion toward universality and certainty. In the next chapter we shall see how this propensity, paradoxically, is matched strength for strength with Marion's deep antipathy toward anything that would bind or limit phenomena or render them "idolatrous." Following this impulse, Marion draws implicitly more on Gregory. Thus in the following two chapters we shall see how Marion's debt to Dionysius lies in a fundamental tension with his debt to Gregory of Nyssa.

FOUR

Interpreting "Saturated Phenomenality": Marion's Hermeneutical Turn?

In the previous chapter I emphasized one motivational pull in Marion's philosophy: the search for a rigorous philosophical methodology that yields certain and universal results in order to claim a place for phenomenology as "first philosophy." In this chapter I propose to examine a tendency in Marion's thought that is equally strong yet pulls in a different direction. Marion accuses metaphysical philosophy of two crimes, both of which lead to conceptual or intellectual "idolatry": first, metaphysics attempts to determine and clamp down concepts in static formulation; and secondly, it takes its measure from the capacity of the thinking subject. Thus, his determination to exclude the "idolatrous" impulse in philosophy leads Marion to speak less of a universal and certain methodology than of the necessary result of a hermeneutic arising from our experience of phenomena, especially those designated as "saturated."

I will begin this chapter with a discussion of the central notion in Marion's philosophical project: the saturated phenomenon. With this notion Marion posits the possibility of excessive phenomena appearing without limitation, bypassing, as it were, the Kantian categories of experience. This notion raises the question of how one is to receive and interpret such excessive phenomena. How, in other words, do such phenomena actually appear or become visible *to us*? How do we interpret, identify, or speak of them, let alone judge them? On this point Richard Kearney (among others) has challenged Marion to define the role of hermeneutics in the saturated phenomenon. Marion's response to this hermeneutical challenge, I will argue, is unsatisfying for two reasons. First, Marion simply posits a hermeneutic arising from saturated phenomena without telling us how this relates to his insistence on protecting the "pure givenness" of a phenomenon. On the one hand, Marion recognizes the need for hermeneutics; safeguarding against idolatry demands the articulation of a "gap" or "hiatus" that always intervenes between the phenomenon and the subject who experiences it. Indeed, Marion speaks of an "endless hermeneutic" in the face of this gap between the given and our experience of it—the infinite and constant need, therefore, of interpretation and of a plurality of concepts to begin to equal any phenomenon that so saturates our consciousness. Yet on the other hand, this turn to hermeneutics seems to be an about-face from his argument in *Reduction and Givenness* against any horizon in a reduction to pure givenness. In what way can these two aspects of Marion's thought be reconciled?

A second dissatisfaction arises when, in his response, he gestures toward early Christian apophatic writings as a precedent for what he is attempting but without properly explicating how this retrieval shifts the contemporary conversation. Thus, in the second half of this chapter, I attempt to demonstrate how Marion's retrieval might be expanded upon in a way that actually helps Marion satisfy the first lacuna in his response.

I argue that aspects of the contemporary debate can find greater resolution with a more attentive analysis of the ancient source material. Specifically, I will explore the way Gregory of Nyssa's understanding of scriptural interpretation in the face of divine incomprehensibility provides a robust and concrete example of how one might claim to return to the "thing itself" in a way that both guarantees its inviolability and allows for our reception and diverse interpretations of it.

The Saturated Phenomenon

Marion first develops the notion of saturated phenomenality in "The Saturated Phenomenon," an article written, at least in part, as a response to a critique by Dominique Janicaud.[1] He further develops the concept in *Being Given*. To place the development of this crucial notion of Marion's within its original polemical context, we need to understand Janicaud's critique.

Janicaud charges Marion with the betrayal of the original Husserlian phenomenological enterprise: in an act of "strict treason of the reduction that handed over the transcendental I to its nudity, here theology is restored with its parade of capital letters."[2] Janicaud has two fundamental problems with Marion's philosophy. First, he argues, it squanders the basic Husserlian principles of neutrality (in the quest for phenomenology as "rigorous science") and the requisite of immanence (or negatively stated, the prohibition against transcendence). Janicaud insists that the "phenomenologist is neutral, in the sense that he or she is open to the thing itself without any teleological prejudice other than the ideal of rational and scientific truth."[3] Secondly, he argues that "a pure, unconditioned givenness—beyond the horizons of subjectivity (Husserl) and of being (Heidegger)—cannot be rendered phenomenologically evident."[4] Thus he argues that Marion has "reduced" the given to such an extent that he ends up with so arid and empty a concept of the divine as to satisfy neither the "ardor" of the theologians nor the "rigor" of the philosophers: "We have to do, here, with a rather dry mystical night; the superabundance of grace has been put through the Heideggerean ringer."[5]

Marion can respond easily enough to the first critique by turning it round on the accuser: refusing outright the possibility of the appearance of any transcendent (even God) within immanence betrays as much prejudice as does assuming that appearance. Thus Marion can claim to be simply considering the theoretical possibility of such appearance, the conditions of its possibility: what would it be like, were the transcendent to appear immanently? Neutrality is not betrayed here unless there is an expectation for the appearance of some particular transcendent.[6] Regarding the second critique, Marion is somewhat more hard-pressed to show that there still might be the possibility of "description" of such a phenomenon, that such excessive phenomena might be given robustly enough to sustain description. These concerns— the need for neutrality, an appearance in immanence, and the possibility of description—shape Marion's subsequent discussion of a type of phenomena he classifies as "saturated." As we have seen, Marion can dismiss the first concern—the need for neutrality—by simply claiming to remain within a discussion of possibility, not historical actuality: one cannot forbid outright the appearance of any phenomena, but remains open to all phenomena.[7] The other two criticisms require more careful argument.

Marion frames his argument for the existence of "saturated phenomena" with a discussion of the constitutive elements of any phenomenon. He returns to the Kantian-Husserlian definition of the phenomenon as a matching or equating (*adequatio*) between that which appears and the appearance as such, between one's "concept" and the fulfilling "intuition" of it (*adequatio intellectus et res*). Skirting the technical morass of the precise definition of these two terms for now, let me posit the following basic and intentionally broad definition: what is meant by *intuition* is that which gives rise to, or presents, a specific opportunity for cognition, while what is meant by *concept* is that which receives and organizes the "data" given in intuition.[8] Truth (often equated with subjective certainty) is achieved when there is a perfect adequation between concept and intuition. For example, I see a cube, and it perfectly matches my concept of cube as a three-dimensional object with six square sides. However, the intuition of an object is almost always matched insufficiently to our concept or meaning of it. As with the previous example, I only ever see two or three sides of the cube at any given moment. My concept of cube must supply the rest of the information. Thus, intuition is found to be lacking in comparison with one's concepts. The epistemological result of this propensity for insufficient adequation, according to Marion, is the fact that mathematics and logic have traditionally been held to be the most trustworthy of all branches of knowledge, because in them we find the barest and simplest of concepts, which require less intuition to fill them. Only "poor" objects can reach a measure of adequation and can thus pass the test of certainty and truth. Marion asks whether subjective certainty is worth its price. Or does metaphysics not thus "confirm its nihilism by organizing itself around the paradigm of phenomena that do *not* appear, or appear just a bit"?[9]

Marion challenges philosophy to consider another possibility: an inadequation between pairs resulting, not from a lack of intuition, but rather from an *excess* of it, in relation to what our concepts can conscribe. This is not to envision an impossible phenomenon that lacks intuition, but rather the absolutely possible phenomenon that is saturated with intuition.[10] Like a 3000-watt appliance being plugged into a 20-amp outlet, no general concept or pattern is able to receive or contain it. Having demonstrated the *possibility* of such a category of phenomena, Marion goes on to consider its characteristics.

The saturated phenomenon is characterized by four elements following Kantian categories: (1) According to "quantity," it is *invisable*; it cannot be intended, predicted, or "aimed at." It is unforeseeable because immeasurable. (2) According to "quality," it is *unbearable*; it cannot be borne. Here intuition is not blind but is blinding and unsustainable. Marion gives the example of "bedazzlement," which accomplishes adequation—intuition fills that which the concept can contain and then goes further. Like Plato's caveman, one is blinded by the excess of direct, unmediated light. (3) According to "relation," it is *absolute* or *unconditioned* (absolved from any horizon). The saturated phenomenon evades analogy with any other experience; there are no relations between accident and substance, cause and effect. (4) According to "modality," it is *irregardable;* it is irreducible to the "I" and incapable of being looked at.[11] Here the phenomenon will not necessarily "agree" with the power of knowing "I," but will overpower it. It is "seen" but not "looked at."[12] Furthermore, the saturated phenomenon is only seen as "trace" or "counter-experience." Its image is "blurred by the too narrow aperture, the too short lens, the too cramped frame, that receives it."[13] This brings us to Janicaud's other concern: does this not destroy the possibility of description, which is, after all, the cornerstone of phenomenology? Absolutely not, Marion says. Rather, it is this type of phenomenon that qualifies, in the sense of justifies or allows, such description.

This discussion may be somewhat illuminated by expanding our understanding of Marion's use of "visibility" as a quality of the phenomenon. Marion, writing in French, uses both *visable* and *visible:* he uses the former to refer to that which can be literally "aimed at," that which is meant or intended.[14] And so, for instance, the Kantian-Husserlian (empty) concept, which finds no adequate match through intuition or experience, "remains nevertheless *visable* [aimed at or intended] if not *visible* in all the sensory appearances from which it is excluded."[15] To keep straight the difference between Marion's use of *visable* and *visible,* I would suggest that we use *visible* to refer to the former, that which can be aim at or intended, and *apparent* to refer to the latter, that which is encountered, or that which *appears,* through intuition. Given that distinction, we can state that the Kantian-Husserlian phenomenon is perfectly visible, though it never appears fully or completely through intuition. The saturated phenomenon, on the other hand, is invisible (unaimable, *irregardable*) but apparent nonetheless, and therefore describable, albeit, as we shall see, in a fragmented and partial way.

Marion downplays the originality of his notion of saturation. He reminds us that, after all, he remains within the set of terms and relations that Kant used to define a phenomenon. The terms are "intuition" and "concepts," and the possible relations, according to Kant (and Husserl), are *lack* and *equality.* Marion simply states the obvious third possibility of relation: *excess.* He argues, furthermore, that his notion of saturated phenomena is presaged in Descartes' depiction of the "infinite" and Kant's notion of "sublimity."[16] Against Janicaud, Marion insists that such a phenomenon does not subvert the principles of phenomenology, but rather completes it:

> The saturated phenomenon must not be understood as a limit case, an exceptional, vaguely irrational, in short "mystical," case of phenomenality. On the contrary, it indicates the *coherent and conceptual completion of the most operative definition of the phenomenon:* it alone truly appears as itself, of itself, and starting from itself, since it alone appears without the limits of the horizon and without the reduction to an *I.*[17]

This, however, raises the question of Marion's redefinition of the subject who receives the saturated phenomenon. To whom does the phenomenon appear, if it is not to an "I"?

In order to understand Marion's discussion of subjectivity, it is helpful to remember one of the central complaints against metaphysics: its reliance on a *transcendental* (pure, ahistorical, un-embedded) "I," which is then meant to ground and guarantee the subsequent system. Marion's criticism is even more radical. He takes issue with any limitation to a horizon, whether transcendental or hermeneutical.[18] This constraint governs Marion's discussion of subjectivity.

Marion uses different terms to denote subjectivity in different contexts: *l'interloqué* (the interrogated one), *le témoin* (the witness), *l'attributaire* (the receiver), and finally, *l'adonné.* The last is his preferred term, which he translates into English as "the gifted," but which also has the connotations of the "devoted one" or the "one given over," even the "addict."[19] *L'adonné* is constituted by, rather than constituting, phenomena; it no longer has transcendental rank, but comes secondarily.

In every case, the "I" is now in the vocative. There is no longer any nominative subject whose function it is to constitute objects of cognition, but only the called or summoned one, itself constituted in response to the call.[20] Marion is not arguing that the subject is destroyed or suppressed. He opposes his definition of "that which comes after the subject" to the "death of the self." Unlike the latter, *l'adonné* is still

> posited as a center: this will not be contested, but I will contest its mode of occupying and exercising the center to which it lays claim—with the title of a (thinking, constituting, resolute) "I." I will contest the claim that it occupies this center as an origin, an ego or first person, in transcendental "mineness." I will oppose it to the claim that it does not hold this center but is instead held there as a recipient where what gives itself

shows itself. . . . At the center stands no "subject," but a gifted, he whose function consists in receiving what is immeasurably given to him, and whose privilege is confined to the fact that he is himself received from what is received.[21]

L'adonné is utterly subject (and subjugated) to the phenomena and lacks all positive functions of the "I."

The radical passivity with which Marion characterizes receptivity seems to abandon the possibility of hermeneutics. Jean Grondin argues that Marion focuses more on the passivity of the subject than on its "mediation" of, or "presence" to, the phenomenon, which only arrives at the subject. This is very clear, according to Grondin, in Marion's "exuberant doctrine" of the saturated phenomenon, which

wants to describe, better to proclaim, the essential excess of phenomenality in proportion to the concept, indeed to receptivity *tout court*. Far from being constituted by a transcendental subjectivity which would circumscribe its horizon, phenomena in the "full" sense (hear: saturated) of the term, rather, shatters every pre-established horizon.[22]

However, Grondin argues that receptivity is not synonymous with passivity:

At the penultimate page of the work (p. 442), *l'adonné* appears, in effect, as an "allocation placed there where what shows itself [is] that which gives itself," as if it only passively registers the givenness which shows itself. In fact, it [*l'adonné*] is always implicated there, participating in the application of the sense which, without it, has no place. It cannot be otherwise if it is true that it is always con-voked.[23]

Marion would not disagree with Grondin on this point: receptivity requires an active capacity to receive. In fact, *l'adonné* could almost be redefined as that which is (variously) capable of reception. Marion discusses the interplay between the appearance of phenomena and receptivity in *In Excess,* where he describes the process of the given becoming "phenomenal" or "visible" as a projection on *l'adonné,* as if *l'adonné* were a screen reflecting the light of the phenomenon. As such, *l'adonné*

phenomenalizes in receiving the given, precisely because it is an obstacle to it, stops it in blocking it and fixes it in centering it. If *l'adonné* therefore receives the given, it is in receiving it with all the vigor, even the violence of a goal-keeper blocking a shot, of a defender marking, of a receiver sending back a wining return.[24]

We must interrogate this depiction of the reception of saturated phenomena. If phenomena appear only through the force of repulsion or "blocking" with which the given is met by *l'adonné,* surely that repulsion will be peculiar or particular to that specific *l'adonné*? In other words, how do the particularities of the individual resisting the given in reception not inscribe it in yet another subjective horizon? If it does, does this not subvert Marion's initial claim that saturated phenomena are distinguished from other phenomena insofar as they are not limited by any horizon, but show themselves as they give themselves, starting from themselves? With this aporia, we are now in a position to look at the challenge to Marion to clarify the place of hermeneutics within a reduction to pure givenness.

The Hermeneutics of Saturated Phenomena

In October 2001, in a public discussion with Jean-Luc Marion at Boston College, Richard Kearney posed two challenges to Marion: first, most generally, can there be a place for hermeneutics (hence, interpretation and the consequent interpellation of the subject) within Marion's phenomenology and its method of a "reduction to pure givenness"? Secondly, and more sharply, can there be a "hermeneutics of God" in Marion's vision?[25] Kearney opens the debate by delineating the boundary line between Marion and himself:

> It strikes me that your approach is more strictly phenomenological since for you the "saturated phenomenon" is fundamentally *irregardable,* a pure event without horizon or context, without "I" or agent. As such it appears to *defy* interpretation. . . . Whereas I would argue that there is no pure phenomenon as such, that appearing—no matter how iconic or saturated it may be—*always already* involves an interpretation of some kind. Phenomenological description and intuition, in my account, always implies some degree of hermeneutic reading, albeit that of a pre-reflective pre-understanding or pre-conscious affection for the most part. My question, then, would be: how do we interpret—and by extension, how do we judge[26]—the saturated phenomenon without betraying it?[27]

Kearney's articulation of this question gets right to the heart of the challenge to Marion. What is the actual relation between allowing the given to appear as such without any interpretation by the subject, on the one hand, and the subject's actual experience of this appearance, on the other? Or in other words, how can we talk of the appearance itself while totally bracketing out the subject? How does Marion himself respond to Kearney's question during that conversation in Boston?

He responds, first, by dismissing it as an "old question" and referring back to the critiques of both Jean Greisch and Jean Grondin.[28] However, he then goes on to say that we *need* hermeneutics precisely because of the "surplus of intuition."[29] Marion redefines hermeneutics as "always an inquiry for further concepts . . . [thus] hermeneutics is generated when we witness an excess rather than a lack of information."[30] Indeed, an "endless hermeneutics" is required because of the conceptual deficit. Hence, there is no possibility of arriving at "an adequate final concept": "Hermeneutical investigation never completes its mission. It is never finished and should never be finished."[31]

We might extend Marion's response to Kearney to answer him more precisely. The saturated phenomenon does not, in fact, "defy interpretation"; rather, it necessitates interpretation. Regarding Kearney's question of how one might "interpret . . . the saturated phenomenon without betraying it," Marion would agree that this is impossible. The violence that interpretation brings is as unavoidable as is interpretation itself necessary. In fact, we always do betray the phenomenon in our description, the more so, the more excessive the phenomenon. This does not nullify the need to interpret as one's only way of response. It simply qualifies one's response as always fallible, always insufficient, always in need of further interpretative shading. Finally, however, Kearney argues, reasonably from the Heideggerian standpoint, that appearance "always already involves an interpretation." Marion, on the other hand, would say that appearance summons an interpretation; it is "always" there, but not "always already there." But how much can rest on this subtle distinction between "always" and "always already"? Logically, I can make sense of the distinction, yet I am still a little mystified as to what the relationship between the pure givenness of the saturated phenomenon and its endless interpretation would look like "on the ground." Marion simply does not tell us how these two facts work together.

In order to gain further conceptual clarity, I will borrow Shane Mackinlay's critical distinction between an "ontological" and a "derivative" sense of hermeneutics. Mackinlay faults Marion for incorporating only the latter into his philosophy:

> Heidegger established an ontological (or existential) sense of hermeneutics, referring to the network of relations and significations that makes it possible for phenomena to appear to Dasein as part of a meaning-filled world. In Heidegger's understanding, hermeneutics is intrinsic to the actual appearing of phenomena. In contrast to this, Marion confines hermeneutics to a marginal and derivative sense of "subsequent interpretation"—*after* phenomena have already appeared.[32]

Leaving aside the question of Marion's faithfulness to Heidegger, this distinction might actually offer Marion a way out of the seeming contradiction in his thought.[33]

It is clear that Marion is in something of a bind here. His entire philosophical project is at stake in positing this moment of the pure given that we can never access without the "violence of interpretation." It requires a realist ontology (although Marion would never use such "metaphysical" language)—a need for the given to really "be there" and to be there as it gives itself or presents itself. This given has an impact on us, confronts us, changes us. Its reality cannot be denied or controlled. And yet Marion still claims that it is interpreted. To frame this interpretation in terms of an ontological hermeneutics would absolutely subvert all that he has set out to achieve in his reduction to pure givenness—the allowance of the given to reveal itself, starting from itself, as itself. Nevertheless, the very excessiveness of the given demands subsequent interpretation. We can only seek after it, or attempt to follow it, in our interpretative descriptions. Thus a "derivative hermeneutics" is necessary. However, to repeat myself, Marion never elaborates on this relationship between pure givenness and infinite hermeneutics. As I suggest below, this gesture toward an "infinite hermeneutics," defined as an "inquiry for further concepts" in the face of an "excess of intuition," echoes Gregory of Nyssa's depiction of the ardent soul's journey toward the divine in response to the excess of revelation.

Hermeneutics and Religion

In *Being Given,* Marion argues that one encounters the absolute limits of possible phenomenality—the saturation of saturation—in revelation. While reminding the reader that he is merely describing a formal possibility and not a historical actuality, Marion designates Christ as the example of saturated phenomenon par excellence. He articulates Christ's uniqueness in relation to the Kantian categories of understanding: (a) with regard to *quantity,* Christ is unforeseeable because "radically heterogeneous to what it nevertheless completes (the prophecies)";[34] (b) with regard to *quality,* as the Transfiguration shows, Christ's light cannot be borne; (c) regarding *relation,* neither Christ's time nor kingdom are "of this world," but rather are a completely unique instance;[35] and (d) with regard to *modality,* Christ above all constitutes us as "witness," and can never be constituted, himself, according to the whim of the I.

Kearney sharpens his challenge to Marion by situating his question now vis-à-vis religion: "Can we have a hermeneutics of God qua saturated phenomenon?" Kearney is asking two distinct questions: the first reiterates the concern about the possibility of description, while the second has more to do with the question of religious exclusivity and Marion's clearly Christian assumptions. We have already dealt with the question of the possibility of description: saturation, for Marion, necessitates rather than forbids interpretation, even if that interpretation is limited to the role of a subsequent attempt to chase after adequate concepts, images, and narratives in the face of religious phenomena.

Kearney also presses him, however, on the meaning of the "Eucharistic hermeneutics" spoken of in Marion's most well-known work, *God Without Being.* Here the issue rests on the thorn of "exclusivity": who gets to interpret and who has access to the revelation? Kearney initially asks whether Marion would still stand by his very contentious claim that it is "only the bishop that merits in its full sense the title of theologian."[36] Marion insists that he does not mean that only bishops have a warrant to interpret revelation, but that he was harking back to a time when the greatest theologians were also bishops (specifically mentioning Gregory of Nyssa). Patristic theology, he says wistfully, is intrinsically connected to liturgy and homiletics, and this is as it should be.[37] Theology is "originally not supposed to be the outcome of intellectual curiosity, logical dexterity, or academic career . . . [but rather] *grew out of the task of commenting on the scriptures.*" In other words, it is an inherently hermeneutical task, a part of the liturgy, and hence, part of a community.

He insists that this nostalgia for patristic methodology does not equal a yearning for uniform or singular interpretation, however, and offers the example of the Apostles' Creed. While the creed "reveals a set of doctrines shared . . . by the churches," it still remains "open to different interpretations which are not always consistent with each other, even within the same church or the same tradition."[38] Kearney continues to press Marion on whether his hermeneutics of revelation extends to revelation in other religious traditions, and Marion agrees that it must: "If we speak of revelation, then, we have to accept that hermeneutics is still going on, that revelation is open since history is still in the making. There is no contradiction between saying that everything was fully revealed and achieved but that, even today, we don't know, we can't know, how far it reaches."[39]

In sum, then, Marion has stated that interpretation is always present with the saturated phenomenon; however, this interpretation rests on a prior given. This given is a *factum,* which is only afterwards interpreted. The greater the *factum,* the more "real," the higher the intensity of intuition, the more interpretation is needed, including a multitude of interpretative voices. Thus, excessive phenomena require an infinite hermeneutic. With such discussion, Marion moves away from an earlier religious exclusivity to admit, perhaps grudgingly, that his own thought requires a more radical eschatological openness, especially with regard to any phenomenology of God. It is in his later response that we find a nostalgia for patristic methodology and specific citation of Gregory of Nyssa.[40] As I demonstrated in chapter 1, Marion turns to Gregory in order to find a patristic articulation of the "gap" between phenomena and language. However, he ignores Gregory's discussion of the subsequent consequences for the interpretation of scripture and a notion of selfhood whose identity is formed in response to revelation. Thus Marion misses Gregory's eloquent rendering of the "luminous darkness" (λαμπρός γνόφος)[41] of revelation with its paradoxical balance between the necessity of full response to the givenness of revelation and recognition of its eternally deepening obscurity.

Gregory of Nyssa's Theory of Interpretation

In the second part of this chapter I will explore what Marion misses in order to provide a more concrete analysis of what a derivative hermeneutics of revelation might look like. The themes discussed below are found throughout Gregory's writings, yet two texts are particularly instructive in this regard. Book II of *Contra Eunomium* (*CE* II)[42] provides most of the philosophical elements of an argument that Marion might have retrieved in order to get himself out of the hermeneutical bind; and Gregory's more mature work, *The Commentary on the Song of Songs*, displays a complex interplay between divine incomprehensibility, allegorical scriptural interpretation, and his understanding of the self formed in response to revelation. Since divine incomprehensibility remains, even with divine revelation, one's response is both always interpretative and inherently destabilizing. We find in Gregory a notion of selfhood that, like Marion's *l'adonné*, is constituted in response to a prior summoning and that as a result lacks static or substantive identity apart from this summoning.

The most fundamental thesis of *Contra Eunomium* II is the claim that one can neither know nor name God's essence as a result of the basic "gap" (διάστημα) between an infinite God and a temporally and spatially constituted creation.[43] Consequently, *Contra Eunomium* II exposits a theory of religious language with the following main points: (a) language is, by necessity, diverse and multivalent; and (b) it is "conventional" rather than "natural," by which Gregory means that (c) God gives us the "faculty" of speech, or the power of the invention of words, rather than the words themselves. Finally and, Gregory thinks, quite obviously, (d) this gift of the capacity of language is for *our sake*. God has no need of language.

This question about the origin and capacity of language is no abstract or insignificant matter; rather, it gets to the heart of Gregory's understanding of the relation between God and humanity.[44] This impossibility of naming God is not the result of human weakness or sin but a neutral statement of the "irreducible opposition between God and creature."[45] The limitation is primarily positive: it heralds the glory befitting God.[46] Hence Gregory also insists that the naming of God is not merely *impossible,* but it is *impious.*

Furthermore, the debate between Gregory and Eunomius about the origin and status of language is framed within a debate of how to properly interpret scripture, specifically how to interpret the account of creation in Genesis. Gregory's position that language is derived from human concepts (ἐπίνοια) is "blasphemous," according to Eunomius, not only because it denies divine providence but also because it contradicts the literal words of the Genesis narrative. Gregory must counter this critique with his own account of how scripture is to be understood and interpreted.

To begin with, Gregory thinks that one must understand scripture as revelatory only because in scripture God graciously descends to the created order of language.[47] To properly understand what Gregory means here, one must first understand Gregory's depiction of the divine accommodation to the needs of creation in the *kenosis,* the divine self-emptying, of the incarnation. As Sarah Coakley has demonstrated in an article tracking different patristic models of kenosis, Gregory has a somewhat unique understanding of this doctrine, one that is tantalizingly akin to Marion's description of saturated phenomena. Gregory interprets Philippians 2:5–11 (in which the incarnation is described as the kenosis of God) not as a divine self-limiting or constriction into human form, but as a filling, indeed an overflowing, of divinity into the finite vessel of humanity. Here the human is not taken over but is taken up and transformed in its ever-increasing capacity to receive the overflow of the divine being.[48] Gregory extends this understanding of kenosis to the divine accommodation in scripture: revelation in scripture expands to fill and saturate our capacity to receive it in an infinitely extensive way.

A second significant element of Gregory's understanding of divine accommodation in scripture is that revelation does not take the form of dictation. The writers of scripture act not as transcribers but as translators—trustworthy co-workers through whom God entrusts his word.[49] In this way scriptural language also reflects a multitude of particular perspectives and contexts while still laying claim to the inflection of God's truth. For instance, Gregory accepts that Moses writes in a particular way, using specific terms and concepts considered, in his human wisdom, sufficient for the uplifting of his readers:

> Thus Moses' speech *accorded with his upbringing and education,* but he attributes these words to God, as has often been said, because of the infancy of those recently brought to the knowledge of God, to present the divine will clearly, and in order to make the hearers readier to believe, once persuaded of the reliability of the account.[50]

In other words, embedded within Gregory's understanding of scripture as the sacred and uniquely authoritative word of God is nevertheless a historicist, hermeneutical assumption that language arises out of particular contexts to which one must attend in order to better understand the meaning of the text. Thus, Gregory assumes that *scriptural texts are inherently interpretative*—both in their origin and in our reading of them.

It is significant to underline that Gregory's explicit argument about the impossibility and impiety of singly naming God correlates with an implicit argument about the impossibility and impiety of singly interpreting scripture. One must not expect attainment of a single truth in either case. Both phenomena (both God and God's revelation in scripture) far exceed that which can be signified by one word or by one interpretation.

Gregory's mode of reading scripture can be observed in his interpretation of Abraham's journey from his home "into an unknown land." Gregory explicitly says he will interpret the story "allegorically," although the "historical truth of course remains."[51] Allegorically read, Abraham becomes the exemplar of the faithful sojourner in his ascent to ever-greater participation in God. Gregory recasts Abraham's journey as an example of an unceasing movement that does not rest in any attainment of knowledge in its desire to approach God.[52] The culmination of this journey occurs when Abraham reaches the pinnacle of what he can learn about God: the fact that, *essentially,* one knows nothing of God. Gregory writes:

> Rising above all that his own power could grasp, as being less than what he sought, when he had surpassed every verbal description of his nature which might be applied to God, having cleansed his mind of such notions, [Abraham] resorted to faith, pure and unadulterated by any ratiocination, and he took as his indicator, infallible and manifest, of the knowledge of God just this—that he believed God to be greater and higher than any epistemological indicator.[53]

In other words, the height of positive knowledge of God is to recognize God's incomprehensibility. This results in a somewhat cyclical logic. At the "end"[54] of his ecstatic movement, Abraham reaches the highest knowledge, which sets him back where he began, in ignorance. Now, however, he recognizes that state as a positive statement about God rather than a negative one about himself. (Putting this in "Marion-speak," one might say that ignorance is a result of the excess of God, which saturates or overwhelms the natural limitations of finite existence and cognition.) Thus Abraham's journey is a model for the apophatic ascent into ever-deeper darkness. Gregory places no limit on this journey, even in the afterlife.

Finally, Gregory insists that all interpretation is "useful" (ὠφέλιμος)[55] because it teaches the reader something about faith. First, it shows that there is a certain passivity or receptivity that characterizes the journey: "Thus a law of faith is generated for subsequent history, using Abraham's story to teach those who approach God that there is no way to come near to God unless faith interposes and of itself joins the enquiring mind to the incomprehensible nature."[56] Secondly, faith is inherently hopeful and forward-looking. In this way, Gregory opposes faith to knowledge, which, being based on experience, is oriented in the past: "Knowledge adopts a sort of experiential approach, assenting only to what is learnt, whereas Christian faith is different: its assurance is not of things learnt, but of things hoped for."[57] There is, thus, an eschatological openness that includes, by definition, the practice of both humility and hospitality to the unknown.[58] Furthermore, against Eunomius' accusation that, by limiting language of God to derivations of human concepts, the Cappadocians are being disrespectful and impious, Gregory argues that Abraham shows true reverence through a willing acceptance of the limits of knowledge:

> As far above the touch of the fingers as the stars may be, so far, or rather much farther, the nature which transcends mind rises above terrestrial reason. Having learnt, therefore, how great the difference of nature is, we should quietly stay within our proper limits. It is *safer* and at the same time *more reverent* to believe that the divine majesty is more than can be thought of, than to restrict his glory by certain ideas and think there is nothing beyond that.[59]

The claim to reach anything more is not only wrong-headed but also arrogant and idolatrous. One must take one's cue from scripture, which teaches many things about God and "clarif[ies] the way we apprehend God," but says nothing of God's essence.[60]

In concluding this section on Gregory's biblical hermeneutic, we may draw certain practical consequences: first, scripture is to be interpreted diversely, and any interpretation involves a translation. Secondly, scriptural interpretation ultimately serves an apophatic function. On this last point, Joseph O'Leary reminds us of the Cappadocian "conviction that the biblical realities remained irreducible to any metaphysics, and that even the most orthodox dogmatic clarifications had chiefly a negative role, to keep our limited human thinking within its proper bounds."[61] From this notion of scripture as a limiting *horos* (ὅρος),[62] or horizon, out of which arises an unlimited possibility of interpretations, specific practical results are consequent: our intellectual processes must always recall their limits, act with according humility, and remain open to a multitude of diverse possibilities. This understanding of scripture also parallels Marion's example of the Nicene Creed as a limiting horizon that nonetheless yields infinite possibilities for interpretation. Both Gregory and Marion seem to be searching for the same balance between the real boundaries of the given and a radical openness to our receptivity of that given.

Allegorical Constitution of Selfhood in *In Canticum Canticorum*

In one of his final works, *The Commentary on the Song of Songs,* Gregory deepens his understanding of the relation between scriptural interpretation and a subjectivity (or selfhood)[63] formed out of its desire for the ultimately desirable yet finally unattainable God. Reading through the series of homilies, one can immediately see the connection between Gregory's allegorical interpretation of the *Song of Songs* and his apophaticism. I argue that Gregory's insistence upon divine incomprehensibility, the cornerstone of his apophaticism, *arises* out of, *justifies*, and is *performed* in, allegorical interpretation. Furthermore, I argue that the intrinsic relation between the pluriformity of interpretation (especially allegorical interpretation) and apophasis, in Gregory's hands at least, *yields a disruption of identity as much as a formation of it.* Within Gregory's theological vision, the idea and experience of identity is transformed from a static reality to a dynamic and deeply destabilizing "way" of approach that never arrives at a fixed point; furthermore, this way of approach is not only announced in, but also actually formed through, allegorical interpretation.

For Nyssen, as for most other Christian interpreters of the *Song of Songs* before him, the Bride gets read as the soul yearning after the bridegroom, or Christ. The time in which the Bride waits for her Beloved is "night," understood as the "time of darkness . . . the contemplation of what is unseen . . . the darkness of God's presence."[64] Unable to wait, the Bride goes out into the city and asks the watchmen if they have seen "the one whom my soul loves." Yet the watchmen are silent. As the Bride passes on through the city and does not "perceive her love among *immaterial and spiritual beings* . . . she realizes that her sought-after love is known only in the *impossibility to comprehend his essence, and that every sign becomes a hindrance to those who seek him.*"[65] Here language itself is the stumbling block. In other words, the Bride, or soul, learns that her beloved, God, is known only in the recognition of the impossibility of knowing and the concurrent necessity of passing over every sign (whether literal or spiritual). It is clear, then, that an insistence upon divine incomprehensibility arises out of Gregory's allegorical interpretation of the *Song of Songs*. The argument is more circular than this, however, for divine incomprehensibility is simultaneously the presupposition of or justification for interpreting scriptural texts allegorically.

As we have seen in Gregory's debate with Eunomius, the foundation of Gregory's apophaticism is his insistence upon the *diastema* between the infinity of God and the finitude of creation. The infinity of God necessarily thwarts all finite attempts at comprehensive knowledge and thus sends the creature spiraling infinitely toward God in an endless and increasing desire for God. In the Fifth Homily of the *Song of Songs*, Gregory writes:

> So then, when God draws a human soul to participate in himself, he always remains in equal measure superior to the participating soul because of his superabundant goodness. For on the one hand, the soul continually grows through participating in what is beyond it and never stops growing. On the other hand, the good in which the soul shares remains the same [i.e., unlimited] so that the more the soul participates in it, the more she recognises that it transcends her as much as before.[66]

As discussed in chapter 2, God is limited by nothing,[67] and thus one never ceases moving toward God. One can never reach God because reaching would indicate a divine boundary or limitation. The "perfection of knowledge attainable by human nature" only sparks the "beginning of a desire for more lofty things."[68] In other words, the culmination of the perfection of our knowledge is really only the beginning of our desire for God. Gregory thus speaks of an infinite deferral as well as an infinite attainment: "They never cease to desire, but every enjoyment of God they turn into kindling of a still more intense desire."[69] This is another articulation of Gregory's concept of *epectasis* (or eternal progress of the soul toward God). It supplies the justification for allegorical interpretation of scripture: one must continuously look behind the obvious in the search for the hidden. Furthermore, it also bridges over to the third characteristic of allegory: its constitutive capacity to transform the individual soul in the face of divine mystery.

As I have already intimated, Gregory interprets the *Song of Songs* to celebrate the marriage of the "union of the human soul with God."[70] However, this is more than an allegorical interpretation of the *Song of Songs;* Gregory takes it one step further by stating that *the act of interpreting the Song is itself an act of unifying oneself with God.*[71] In the act of spiritual interpretation or allegorization of the *Song,* Gregory commends each person to "go out of himself and out of the material world . . . [to] ascend into paradise through detachment, having become like God through purity."[72] It is important to note that what Gregory is here describing is not abstract and speculative but real and experiential. He is describing the act of interpreting a text together as a community—an activity in which he is presumably engaged while writing and delivering these homilies.[73] He writes that "the interpretation of the Song's prologue according to the two preceding days had the benefit of washing and purifying from the flesh's mire our understanding of its words."[74] Notice, it is not the prologue itself but the (allegorical) interpretation of it that is purifying. In what way is allegorical interpretation formative? In what way does it effect the union of the human soul with the divine? If such interpretation always leads to acknowledgment of divine incomprehensibility, then it is by drawing the self out of any stable, conscribable definition—only by tearing it out of a defined communal identity into the ecstasy and vertigo which, Gregory insists, attends the mystical ascent to God.

To speak of divine *accommodation* gestures to the idea that the divine Word comes according to one's capacity to receive it. This can be seen in Gregory's allegorical reading of the passage in the *Song* in which the Bridegroom knocks at the door and, when it is opened, places his hand through the small opening available to him. Alluding to the incarnation, Gregory writes that "God's creative hand contracted itself to reside in our small, worthless human existence."[75] The Bride "opens the door," signifying the "veil of flesh," in order to bid the Word enter her chamber (heart). But the aperture is too small to contain the infinite Word, thus only the hand appears. "Since Christ, then, is uncreated and before all the ages, eternally incomprehensible and totally ineffable, that which appeared to us through flesh allowed something of him to be known."[76] In this way, the hermeneutical key to the entire journey of the soul remains the kenotic movement of the incarnation, the overflowing of divinity into the limited capacity of human receptivity. This overflowing, in itself, cracks open that limited capacity and enlarges it.

Gregory's strong emphasis on the inherent relation between allegorical interpretation and apophaticism means that there are an infinite number of possible interpretations of scripture through allegory. Since it remains, nevertheless, performed by a finite and limited interpreter, he or she cannot rest with one particular interpretation. Allegory is thus limited and yet vainly pointing to something beyond our comprehension. Through it we engage our whole being—body, mind, and soul— and yet it yields no solid place upon which we might stand and rest. Allegorical interpretation is a speech-act that displaces the self in a confrontation with this divine incomprehensibility. It reveals a selfhood that is called into this particular existence only through a displacement and rupturing of self as much as a formation of it. Finally, that which allows this allegory is the structure of divine accommodation, which gives itself over to be interpreted through an overflowing of finite constrictions.

For Gregory all language, including biblical language, ultimately signifies a lack: "The significance of each word falls short and shows something inferior to the truth."[77] Here is the view that all language is a signifier of the lack of signification. But this signification gives a knowledge that is positive, the knowledge of God's infinity.

Missed Opportunities

I have argued here that there is indeed a hermeneutical "turn" in Marion, a greater emphasis on the need for interpretation *subsequent* to reception of the given. However, he does not adequately treat or argue for this hermeneutical turn. I have suggested one way to supplement this account with reference to Mackinlay's distinction between ontological and derivative hermeneutics. Yet confronting Marion all along was an example of how he might treat an understanding of revelation that both guarantees the inviolability of that which is revealed and summons a subsequent interpretation of the revelation.

Gregory of Nyssa's strong emphasis on the inherent relation between scriptural interpretation and divine incomprehensibility results in the necessity of an interpretative pluralism. Scripture is revelatory. But scripture reveals only by filling and then overflowing our finite capacity to understand and interpret it. In this very act, however, it also transforms and enlarges our capacity to receive more. This, according to Gregory, is an endless movement: revelation, by filling and overflowing our finite capacity, summons a response that calls us into a new being, again and again.

The sole horizon of revelation in scripture is therefore that which reveals itself kenotically: God. And yet to follow this one infinite horizon, an infinite number of finite interpretations are necessary. Through such interpretative practices, one engages her whole being—body, mind, and soul—without finding a solid place on which she might stand and rest. Scriptural interpretation thus displaces the self in a confrontation with divine incomprehensibility. It reveals a subjectivity that is called into this particular existence only through a displacement and rupturing of self as much as a formation of it. Thus, Gregory's treatment of scriptural interpretation as an infinitely open and infinitely transformative response to the excess of revelation provides a rich instance of how Marion might think through the relationship between the pure givenness of the saturated phenomenon and one's subsequent interpretation of it. It is an opportunity that Marion misses.

Richard Kearney continued his discussion with Marion in Dublin in January 2003. Here the conversation turned to the question of desire. Kearney juxtaposed *ontological* and *eschatological* desire. The former, he argues, is based on lack and a return to the One; whereas the latter is based on excess and inaugurates a movement into the unknown—not cyclical, but linear. He cites the *Song of Songs* as a place where such a desire is figured. Marion does not disagree but responds with reference to Gregory. He notes that Gregory's notion of *epectasis* defines an "eternity in paradise" as the "fulfillment of pleasure, where each fulfillment is a new *arche* without end. That is exactly the reverse of our experience of biological desire, which cannot survive its fulfillment." Here, the reverse is the case: fulfillment engenders rebirth of a desire nourished by excess.[78] In the final chapter I shall envision what Marion's philosophy would look like were it to follow more fully this Nyssan instinct.

FIVE

The Apparent in the Darkness: Evaluating Marion's Apophatic Phenomenology

Marion's prose can be obscure. At times such obscurity is unavoidable. Marion plumbs the depths of dark matters: the resistance of given phenomena to objectification, the incomprehensibility of God, the long and deep apophatic traditions of Christianity. Such questions and such retrievals elude the clarity of a bright morning. Yet we must ask: What is hidden in the dark? What lies in the shadows?

One can distinguish three different kinds of "darkness" in Marion's thought: blindness, hiddenness, and invisibility. In this chapter I aim to distinguish between these various strands. First of all, Marion evidences a certain kind of *blindness:* a blindness to the tensions in his thought as well as a blindness to the different ontologies imported in his retrieval of the Fathers. These two blind spots need to be uncovered and, if possible, illuminated.

Second, there is the *hiddenness* of Gregory of Nyssa in Marion's writing. As I will argue, were Gregory to become more of an explicit source, Marion might discover a way forward from two crucial problems in his thought: the troubled relation between "pure givenness" and "infinite hermeneutics," and the lack of clear distinction between "worldly" saturated phenomena and God as the saturated phenomenon par excellence. Gregory might also provide a model for considering bodily and contemplative practices that expand the receptive capacity of *l'adonné,* a topic thus far underdeveloped by Marion.

Third, there is the *invisibility* of saturation. This invisibility characterizes the "luminous darkness" that nonetheless makes an appearance, one that calls us to respond, to love, and to be transformed. Marion's attention to such exceptional and excessive experience, his insistence on its philosophical analysis and discussion, guarantees the importance of reading and studying Marion today, despite my critical comments.

Blind Spots

Unraveling Tensions

Part of what is attractive in Marion's philosophical enterprise is a thought complex and broad enough to elicit criticisms from opposing intellectual camps simultaneously: Marion is both too theological and not theological enough; his phenomenology is too exclusively Christian and also too purely *negative,* with no real content possible. Marion is both not hermeneutical enough (i.e., he does not give an account of subjective interpretation) and not phenomenological enough (i.e., he does not hold to the strict neutrality of the transcendental view). No one of these criticisms, taken alone, does justice to Marion's complex thought. However, taken together they highlight the tensions that emerge when his corpus is read as a whole. Is Marion simply inconsistent, or can these tensions be held together in a tight and generative balance? To answer this question, the different oppositional pressures must be isolated.

That Marion's primary project is phenomenological in that it attempts to return to the "things themselves," in themselves and from themselves, is indisputable. In other words, the return to the things must include their liberation.[1] Marion seeks to free phenomena from all constraints, whether metaphysical or epistemological. This necessitates a radical broadening of the horizon within which phenomena appear, radical to the point of transgressing all horizons (subjective, temporal, spatial) so that all that remains is the "horizon" of the givenness of the phenomenon. Only by removing all horizons does Marion think one might return actually to the things themselves, from and in themselves, as they give themselves. At the same time, the return to the things themselves is a return to *all things.* A key element of Marion's revisioning of phenomenology is its refusal to bar the entrance to any phenomena. Thus, he seeks to secure a place for excessive phenomena at a philosophical table dominated by French secularism.

This twofold motivation, not in itself self-contradictory, determines his articulation of both a phenomenological method and his central concept—a "reduction to pure givenness" and the "saturated phenomenon," respectively—in such a way, however, that tensions arise. On the one hand, in order to secure convincingly that place at the philosophical table, his method must demonstrate a certain level of rigor. It must yield certain and universal results and still claim the valence of "first philosophy" (even if, Marion argues, it is "first" only by virtue of being "last"). But on the other hand, his desire to free phenomena from all constraints directly opposes the former requisite, for here Marion must disavow any claim to predetermine a priori any outcome in the appearance of phenomena. I have discussed this tension in chapter 3.

Secondly, there is a struggle at the heart of Marion's key concept of saturated phenomena, a struggle that is inherited from his earlier articulations of a method. On the one hand, a saturated phenomenon is given to us "purely," overwhelming (saturating) any cognitive or conceptual framework with which we might receive it. On the other hand, it is received, responded to, and even (if only partially and ever-inadequately) interpreted. This tension between pure givenness and subsequent interpretation was discussed in chapter 4. One might distinguish between these two overlapping aporias as a methodological tension and a conceptual tension. I would argue that in the former one side must yield or the tension turns into incoherence. In the conceptual tension, however, there is a way of holding both sides together. Indeed, it is this insight of the paradox between givenness and interpretative response that heralds Marion's main contribution to contemporary philosophy and theology. Let me problematize the methodological tension first.

Marion's methodology cannot be held together as he has articulated it in the past. A reduction to givenness postulates a given so "pure" as to be unattainable, even untouchable, without the consequent pollution of the subjective "I." Such a pure given is, strictly speaking, meaningless. To put it another way, the problem with Marion's method is that it cannot be a *method*, something that one follows (as Marion himself acknowledges by calling it a "counter-method"), because it refuses a productive or volitional role to the subject.

This aporia comes to a head in Marion's recent monograph *The Erotic Phenomenon*.[2] With this work, Marion claims to be finally completing a project that has "obsessed" him since the publication of *The Idol and Distance*: a phenomenological analysis of love.[3] Marion begins *The Erotic Phenomenon* with an inversion of Heidegger: the defining amnesia of philosophy has not been forgetting the question of being, but forgetting the question of love. Philosophy has "renounced its first name, 'love of wisdom,' for that of metaphysics," which "definitively consecrated the primacy of 'being' [*étant*] as the universal object of knowledge."[4] Marion asks whether "the history of the divorce of philosophy and the love within it does not merit at least as much attention and effort as the history of Being [*l'être*] and its withdrawal"?[5]

In order to respond more appropriately to love, to speak love, one must first get beyond an understanding of love as "exchange."[6] This escaping of love from the "order," "measure," "calculation," and "production" of worldly things does not exile love outside the borders of all rationality. Rather, "it suggests that they lie under an other figure of reason, of a 'greater reason'—that which does not restrain itself to the world of things nor to the production of objects, but which rules our heart, our individuality, our life and our death, briefly, that which fundamentally defines us . . . Love reveals an erotic rationality."[7]

Unsurprisingly, Marion insists on starting from the "thing itself": "Finally, a concept of love must attain the experience of the erotic phenomena starting from themselves"[8] without inscribing them in a strange horizon, specifically within the horizon of being, the mistake of metaphysics. For this reason, Marion justifies his method of writing an essay without any citation or reference: "In a word, it is not a matter of recounting, or telling ourselves histories, but of letting appear that which is the question—the erotic phenomenon itself."[9] This lack of citation can be frustrating since Marion certainly is engaged in multiple conversations and debates in the work rather than simply describing love. This again highlights the methodological tension. Can one return to analyze the phenomenon itself, in this case love, outside of various intellectual, historical, and personal contexts in which one always discovers the phenomenon (especially love)? Despite appearances, Marion does not achieve this pristine analysis.

Written in "six meditations," *The Erotic Phenomenon* is intentionally structured to take up the Cartesian enterprise (as Husserl also did), precisely to critique and reappropriate it such that the *ego cogitans* must yield to the primacy of the *ego amans*: "Thus, it will be necessary to take up the *Meditationes* starting from the fact that I love even before being, because I am, only to the extent that I experience love, and [experience it] as a logic. Briefly, it will be necessary to substitute erotic meditations for metaphysical ones."[10] Against Descartes' *cogito*, Marion argues that the phenomenological evidence reveals, at bottom, not a thinking subject but an erotic one.[11]

Claude Romano raises a pertinent question regarding the relationship between the erotic reduction and Marion's reduction to givenness.[12] At first glance, the former would seem to be a particular instance (even if a privileged one) of a reduction to givenness in which the phenomenon to be reduced is "love." Yet Marion claims that "*all* phenomenality finds itself modified by the erotic reduction: the task of the erotic reduction is to give access to a new domain of phenomenality, more originary than that of objects and of beings considered in their being."[13] Thus, in this work Marion identifies his method with love: love is the method of the reduction. The method and the phenomenon it delivers are one and the same. Furthermore, Marion insists that whether we speak of sexual or filial love, whether of ἔρως or ἀγάπη, whether of God's love, maternal love, or fraternal love, in all cases one is speaking of one and the same love: "Univocal, love is only told in a single way."[14] In other words, Marion insists on the *universality* of the phenomenon he is describing. Love *is* just as he describes it, and universally so.

However, a paradox arises, since letting the erotic phenomenon appear itself can only be accomplished *personally*:

> For it is necessary to speak of love as it is necessary to love—in the first person. . . . To love puts in play my identity, my ipseity, my source more intimate to me than myself. . . . Since it is necessary to speak of love as one must love, I will say *I*. And I cannot hide myself behind the *I* of philosophers who suppose it [I] universal, a disengaged spectator or transcendental subject.[15]

Yet between the purpose of the methodological reduction—to let appear that which is the question—and the stated necessity of speaking love "in the first person" does not an implacable contradiction surface? Either love appears as it shows itself (universally and disengaged), or it is always deeply personal and attached to an "I."

If love is the method of the reduction, then, as Marion himself insists, this can only be done in the first person. However, in contradiction to this, Marion's entire project has been to remove any horizons, especially that of the subject. Kevin Hart states the contradiction sharply: "In fact Marion is caught in a paradox. On the one hand, the 'I' is the sole condition of possibility for the reduction . . . while, on the other hand, the reduction dismisses any and all conditions of possibility."[16] In other words, his most recent work lays bare, and indeed fertilizes, the tension that, I have argued, is latent throughout his work: between a universal method that yields pure givenness, and the experience, reception, and interpretation of a phenomenon.

It is precisely the insistence upon holding onto these two things—a rigorous, universal method yielding first philosophy, and the freeing of all phenomena from any constraint (transcendental or existential)— that forces Marion into convolutions that muddy his phenomenological brilliance. His methodological allegiances, as dramatically central to his thought as they are, obscure his project. I argue that, of the two poles of the tension, the least sustainable to Marion's project is the claim of universality in his method. Where does this leave his starting point of a reduction to pure givenness?

Calling the reduction to pure givenness a "counter-method" does not, on its own, solve the aporia. As Marion indeed does, one can speak of a practice of clearing away obstacles to the appearance of phenomena *as much as is humanly possible,* a discipline of cultivating patience, a sense of expectancy, and the capacity for reception. This might even be called a method of sorts, a humble method. But this is to conceive of philosophical method in the broad sense that Pierre Hadot has articulated: the various approaches of philosophy as a "spiritual exercise" or a "way of life."[17] Marion goes one step too far in claiming that this method might *yield* pure, given phenomena or that such a method might *deliver* phenomenology to a place of eminence and secure its status as "first philosophy." His method cannot *yield* such phenomena, for the whole point is that only the phenomena themselves can, and do, contest the subject and resist any objectification or external constitution.

Giving up the claim to universality and the pretensions of establishing phenomenology as first philosophy frees Marion to attend to the things themselves while retaining the conceptual paradox that they are purely given and yet appear only with, and in, one's interpretative reception of the things themselves. Reconceptualizing this as a "counter-method" and taking the "reduction" along Hadot's lines as a discipline or spiritual exercise also fills a void in Marion's thought; it gives one room to consider how habits, bodily practices, contemplative disciplines, might shape our capacity to receive what is given. Marion has thus far given scant attention to the practical application of his theory. This is another place where Gregory's thought on the "training of desire" and "progress in the life of virtue" might be a creative resource for Marion.

Ontological Imports at the "End of Metaphysics"

Marion's philosophical project has been situated at, or indeed after, the "end of metaphysics" both by himself and by his readers. Throughout this work I have reminded the reader that "metaphysics" has a specific, limited usage in post-metaphysical thought: it refers to any system of thought (philosophical or theological) that claims "absoluteness on the foundation of a transcendental I, whose existence and certainty is guaranteed by a term posited beyond the conceptual system."[18] As I discussed in the introduction to this study, Marion amends this general definition to include the following: metaphysics privileges both the subjective starting place and the question of Being.[19] I have addressed the former characteristic at some length, but thus far I have not questioned Marion's desire to escape the horizon of Being.

It is clear with any careful reading of Marion that when he speaks of "God without Being" or "love without Being,"[20] he is not denying the reality of God or love. He is, instead, refuting any attempts to relegate them to the status of *a* being. He is also broadening the power of both love and God to define for themselves the conditions of both their possibility and their manifestation: it need not be within the limits of Being.[21] Thus it is not the language of being in itself that Marion objects to, but rather its reigning supremacy to define and determine what can and cannot become phenomenal. It is precisely a critique of this privileging of Being that separates Marion from Heidegger. Nonetheless, can Marion fully escape from any *ontological* language?[22]

An underlying hypothesis of my argument has been that lurking in the shadows of Marion's project are various ontological assumptions and implications. Marion, unlike Husserl, does not rest content with the analysis of "transcendental consciousness."[23] His phenomenology of givenness is precisely not a study of conscious thought. Husserl redefines the "things themselves" as "objects of consciousness." But Marion radically broadens the horizon so that the thing itself is that which both gives rise to (and resists itself becoming) an object of consciousness. As a result, he cannot avoid, as does Husserl, the dilemma of defining the relationship between "thinking subject" and "thought object." Marion's broadening of the reduction to bracket even the "transcendental I" and the horizon of being takes one back, decidedly, not to a world of objects, but to a *world of givens.*

Marion's "given," beyond or prior to being, is the "really real," which may be but also need not be. Never "*objects* of consciousness," nonetheless, the given are phenomenalized with such a vivid "thereness" as to be impossible to rebut entirely. They are unobjectifiable but also irrefutable. We are confronted by the givens that Marion characterizes as "saturated," and we are irrevocably changed in this confrontation. The consequent "factum," given as a "fait accompli" and with an "unpredictable landing,"[24] cannot be known, spoken, or represented adequately. Nonetheless, one must respond to it, eventually we learn, through love. Indeed, this is the differentiating marker between metaphysics and any donative phenomenology (i.e., any phenomenology that employs the reduction to pure givenness): "To represent or to love—one must choose."[25]

However, in the face of this stark alternative, I would argue that there are different ways of loving in response, different expectations raised in love, and different notions of its consummation. These differences depend, in part, on different ontological assumptions, different "worlds" from which the love is invoked, in which it takes place, and to which it is directed. Thus Marion's importation of various premodern ontologies will point to different notions of love and of its limits and its perfection.

In this study I have argued that patristic sources function in Marion rhetorically as an "authoritative" (orthodox) foundation for his contemporary (often polemical) engagements. For this apologetic reason, Marion retrieves the premodern sources in a strangely univocal manner, despite evidence of a capacity for greater sophistication. This hermeneutic of homogeneity is especially apparent when it comes to his retrieval of Gregory of Nyssa, who is cited in frequent elision with Dionysius the Areopagite. For reasons reiterated below, I have argued that this univocal retrieval unwittingly imports two distinct ontologies into Marion's phenomenology, with two distinct strategies of apophasis and two conceptions of the perfection of a loving response.

In chapter 2 I schematized the different emphases in Dionysius and Gregory as follows. In Dionysius, creation is inherently hierarchical. The interlocking cosmological, ecclesiastical, and anthropological hierarchies facilitate the eternal movement of divine procession and return in a harmonious and ordered way. God is "cause" (αἰτία) of creation. This cause is characterized primarily as resplendent and abundant Eros. Human beings—indeed, all of creation—respond to the erotic causation with a mirroring love. This love, or desire for God, as reflective, is natural. While endless and dynamic, the love still finds its perfection within the hierarchical identity for which a particular being was created (i.e., the love of an angel is more immediately reflective of divine Eros than that of a bishop, which in turn is closer than that of a lay person). At each level, one can reach a perfectly reflective love, but what is perfect is determined by the hierarchy and one's place within it.[26] The point of the hierarchies is not individual "upward mobility" but universal and cosmological harmony and cooperation in which the divine loving energy flows without hindrance.[27] I argued that it is precisely the *stable cosmological structure* of the endless dynamism of "rest, procession, and return" that allows for a radical apophatic surrender of the self.

Revelation of God, here, is a double movement of manifestation and concealment, presence and absence, in which the divine "as Cause of all and as transcending all . . . is rightly nameless and yet has the names of everything that is."[28] When one refers the names of "everything that is" to God, this is only possible because "everything that is" participates in God and likewise both manifests and conceals God. With Dionysius, one guards against idolatrous statements and conceptions by an endless oscillation between affirmation, negation, and, beyond both, the negation of negation,[29] the use of "dissimilar symbols," by the proliferation of different names,[30] and finally by entering into silence.

I have contrasted this Dionysian world with Gregory's. For Nyssen, creation is inherently "diastemic." There is an infinite gap between God and creation that is only unilaterally bridgeable since the created order can never cross that divide but only receive the crossing of the Divine. This gap between God and creation rests uniquely on the difference between God's infinity and creation's finitude. This most basic ontological difference levels all other differences of being within the created order. God is one; creation is many others. As such, all of creation is defined less as substantive being than as kinetic becoming. Revelation occurs through divine accommodation, the most perfect example of which is the incarnation. In all instances of divine accommodation, the divine being "overflows" the finite vessel of the human. This kenotic pouring over of the divine being into the human person and into language (in the revelation of the incarnation or the revelation of divine scripture, respectively), is transformative; it shapes and reshapes created capacities for reception.

Two consequences emerge for interpretation and for desire. First, divine accommodation calls forth an infinitely variable response. Our responses to revelation in the incarnation and in scripture are always interpretative, and each variation is necessary to constitute the πλήρωμα (fullness or completion) of revelation. Secondly, God's revelation meets our desire for God, our desire to see and know God, at our present capacity to receive God. But in filling (and overflowing) our capacity, the revelation also increases it. Our desire is sparked anew, and our capacity to receive more is realized. Thus, human beings (indeed, for Gregory, all of creation) respond to God and God's revelation with an endless yearning, a desire that increases with every moment that it is filled. One guards against idolatrous statements with this twofold recognition: language and concepts can only ever be a chasing-after God's revelation, an interpretation subsequent to the event and ever inadequate. Secondly, God summons more, feeds a desire that is simultaneously met and never satiated. Consequently, there is no rest, whether conceptual, linguistic, or erotic, in Gregory of Nyssa's world.

Given these schemata, I have argued that Marion's double-importation of Dionysius and Gregory (*in voce* Dionysius) is itself interestingly revelatory of a tension that exists within Marion's philosophy in itself. On the one hand, his retrieval of Dionysius is motivated by his desire to find a language to speak about a creation imbued with the presence of the Divine in such a way that it nonetheless never runs the risk of idolatry. Dionysius gives him the language and conceptual framework for thinking revelation as simultaneous manifestation and concealment. On the other hand, Gregory makes his appearance in crucial moments of Marion's writing, especially when he is trying to articulate a theory of discourse as purely pragmatic or of the originary gap (*diastema*) between the "given" and the "phenomenal." To simplify (perhaps overmuch), I have argued that Dionysius satisfies Marion's yearning for a language of givenness that is universal without being idolatrous, while Gregory feeds Marion's more recent discussions of an "endless hermeneutics" arising out of saturated phenomena. I will also argue that Gregory presents Marion with an "orthodox" articulation of a purely pragmatic conception of language that is nonetheless able to facilitate an infinite transformation of the "subject" (*l'adonné*) in response to a revelation necessarily greater than our concepts can manage.

Therefore, I suggest that, while Dionysius was clearly most influential and inspirational to Marion in his early theological works, with his "hermeneutical turn" and focus on saturated phenomena, it is Gregory and not Dionysius who might be of greater help as a patristic source of authority and inspiration. Since Marion does not explicitly differentiate between Dionysius and Gregory, he has not recognized or utilized the two thinkers according to what each distinctly has to offer. Instead, Dionysius continues to function as shorthand for all apophatic philosophy and mystical theology, while Gregory gets summoned to provide the appropriate citation when necessary. This is a blindness on Marion's part, not simply because it elides the two thinkers and misses the significantly different emphases in their corpora, but also because, in so doing, Marion is blind both to a tension in his own thought and to an opportunity offered him in Gregory's thought. It is this opportunity to which I now turn.

The Hiddenness of Gregory of Nyssa

One of the curious elements of Marion's retrieval of the Fathers, as I have argued, is the strange invisibility of Gregory of Nyssa, even when he marginally appears unreferenced in section titles[31] or as an epigraph[32] or unexpectedly in the crucial point of an argument about Dionysius.[33] Nonetheless, Marion offers no sustained interpretation of Gregory and uses him far less than he might. This is partly explained by the fact that, until a quite recent shift in scholarship, Gregory was looked to primarily in the context of the history of doctrine (for his role in the clarification of Trinitarian doctrine) rather than as a vital player within the Christian apophatic tradition.[34] Indeed, as Deny Turner notes, in terms of apophasis, Gregory is most often recognized simply as an important influence on Dionysius, who then in turn plays the role of greater historical importance within the Western[35] Christian tradition.[36] However, one of the aims of this study has been to trouble the easy placement of Gregory and Dionysius together within one tradition of apophaticism as an ascent into darkness. As I have just reiterated, this ascent takes place in substantially different "worlds," with different understandings of language and different understandings of the perfection, or the consummation, of desire. So what, uniquely, does Gregory offer?

Specifically, I will argue that in two overlapping areas Gregory especially illuminates aspects of what Marion is after, without the accompanying verbal obfuscation: (a) the limits of knowledge, and (b) language as pragmatic discourse. These two areas are only artificially separated. Together, they make up a more complex understanding of apophasis wherein the limits of knowledge and language indicate both an ontological reality and an existential response.

The Limits of Knowledge

In *Contra Eunomium* Book II, Gregory gives the analogy of a child playing in a sunbeam who instinctively clasps her hands around the empty air in an attempt to capture the light.[37] However, this attempt to grasp and contain the sunbeam with comprehension merely scatters the light. The child makes the mistake of seeking comprehension when adoration instead would have prolonged and deepened her experience. So, too, human knowledge grasps for what is unattainable and humans "make an idol of their own concept."[38] Balthasar has masterfully analyzed Gregory's critique of knowledge, which has, at the core of its very nature, a "grasping" (κατάληψις) of its objects with the desire to possess and constrain, rather than to love and wonder. Paradoxically, knowledge attains its goal only in relinquishing it, and it accomplishes its purpose only by acknowledging the impossibility of achieving it: "Human knowledge is therefore true only to the degree it renounces by a perpetual effort its own nature, which is to 'seize' its prey."[39] Thus knowledge serves a primarily negative purpose: to isolate and highlight our ignorance.

We might compare *critical* aspects of Gregory's "epistemology" (to use an anachronistic category) with that of modernity. Gregory's "critique of reason" is not motivated by an attempt to secure its own foundations in the way that Descartes, Kant, and Husserl, diversely, all seek to do. Rather, the explicit purpose of Gregory's critique is to return one to a mode of viewing reality in wonder; it is to force one's recognition of the fact that there is an excess beyond which human knowledge can never attain. But it is precisely this "beyond" that should occupy our attention, not that which we can secure. In other words, Gregory's purpose is exactly the opposite of that of modern critiques of reason. Which of these critical projects does Marion follow? His attempt to secure phenomenology's place as "first philosophy" aligns Marion with his philosophical teachers and interlocutors: Descartes, Kant, and Husserl. But his insistence on the remainder, the excess, the refusal of the given to become "objectified," places Marion squarely in the company of Gregory of Nyssa.

More recently, Marion delivered his evaluation of human thought in his inaugural address as the John Nuveen Professor of the Philosophy of Religion and Theology at the University of Chicago. In this address he defends the appropriateness of celebrating the limits of our knowledge. In other words, Marion uses an opportunity traditionally set aside to outline, encapsulate, or focus one's general intellectual research as an encomium to the unknown and unknowable. He argues that none other than this celebration of the human being's incomprehensibility occupies the central question of the philosophy of religion. His essay starts from an Augustinian statement: "*Mihi magna quaestio factus sum*," but at its heart, we again find Nyssen.[40]

Marion asserts that since "every de-*finition* imposes on the human being finite essence, following from which it always becomes possible to delimit what deserves to remain human from what no longer does," philosophy's task ought not to be that of correcting "man's incomprehensibility, as if it were a defect to overcome, but to preserve it as a privilege to reinforce."[41] Thus, Marion argues that we must consider incomprehensibility as no longer failure, but wonderful gift. At the apex of Marion's argument—stating that "man's invisibility separates him from the world and consecrates him as holy for the Holy"—Marion goes on to immediately quote extensively from Gregory, who, he acknowledges, initially formulates this argument:

> The icon is properly an icon so long as it fails in none of those attributes which we perceive in the archetype ... therefore, since one of the attributes we contemplate in the Divine nature is incomprehensibility of essence (τὸ ἀκατάληπτον τῆς οὐσίας), it is clearly necessary that in this point the icon should be able to show its imitation of the archetype. For if, while the archetype transcends comprehension, the nature of the icon were comprehended, the contrary character of the attributes we behold in them would prove the defect of the icon; but since the nature of our mind, which is according to the icon of the Creator (τῷ κατ᾽ εἰκόνα του κτίσαντος), evades our knowledge, it keeps an accurate resemblance to the superior nature, retaining the imprint of the incomprehensible [fixed] by the unknown within it (τῷ καθ᾽ ἑαυτον ἀγνωστῷ)."[42]

There are two consequences of the fact that humans are privileged in bearing the image and likeness of God in their incomprehensibility: first, that the human has the capacity and necessity of transcending, going beyond, and exceeding herself; and secondly, that only that which is originally and infinitely incomprehensible can comprehend the human person: "Only God can reveal man to man, because man only reveals himself by revealing, without knowing it, the one whose image he bears."[43]

It is Balthasar, so influential for Marion's reading of the Fathers, who observes Gregory's originality on this subject within Greek thought: "This is perhaps the first time a Greek thinker considered the incomprehensibility of a thing not only as a sign of its remoteness from us but as a perfection of the thing itself. This discovery is none other than that of the freedom of the spirit to communicate itself and to *allow* itself to be grasped."[44] Gregory raises incomprehensibility as a virtue in the same way as he subverts the regnant Greek valuation of "infinity" and "mutability." Marion adopts all three of these revaluations.

Parenthetically, it is significant to note the way in which Marion rebuts Heidegger's critique of onto-theology (as it is formulated in Heidegger's "Letter on 'Humanism'") at the end of the address. Marion inverts the critique:

> This argument presupposes in its turn that, by invoking creation, the believer confidently knows and thus comprehends what man is, because faith certainly tells him. It is precisely the case, however, that what the Scripture says here establishes nothing certain and procures no clear and distinct knowledge whatsoever; on the contrary, its revelation of man as created in the image and likeness of God institutes an unknowing that is all the more radical in that it is founded in the incomprehensibility of God himself. From a reverse perspective, would it not be he who assumes from the outset that the question of man is inscribed in advance within the horizon of Being and determines man as the being in whom what is at stake is Being?[45]

This rebuttal is illuminating not only because it invokes an *ontological* solution to Heidegger's critique of metaphysics, but also because, in so doing, he brings together a constellation that is uniquely Nyssan: the relation between the incomprehensibility of God with the act of creation and the concurrent inherent mysteriousness of the human person. Invoking creation in this sense, however, is to invoke a created reality that is born of and in the διάστημα (*diastema*) between God and creation. No one thinks this *diastema* more profoundly and thoroughly than Gregory of Nyssa. To this constellation and its relation to Gregory's understanding of language, we now turn.

Language as Pragmatic Discourse

As I discussed in chapter 4, according to Gregory, language is a human invention, established by convention and differing from one time to another and one community to another. Language is not only not divinely given, but it also bears no inherent relation to the essence of created things. It thus has a truly and solely pragmatic function: "Language, then, is a free invention of the human mind, a tool to be used in seeking to represent what cannot be grasped directly."[46]

While Ekkehard Mühlenberg has demonstrated that God's incomprehensibility emerges out of Gregory's commitment to the infinity of God (because infinite, incapable of being limited by any definition or horizon),[47] and Mariette Canévet has taken this principle of divine infinity one step further to examine how it affects Gregory's understanding of scriptural interpretation (the text is open to unlimited interpretations),[48] Alden Mosshammer argues that Gregory's notion of divine incomprehensibility can also be gleaned as a logical outcome from his understanding of language.[49]

Gregory's understanding of language is contingent upon his conception of the original *diastema*,[50] the infinite "gap," between the Creator and creation. This gap arises precisely because of the fact that creation is inherently diastemic (extended in space and time, constantly in motion, moving from ἀρχή to τέλος, divided and divisive), while there is no *diastema* in the divine being.[51] The *diastema* between the created and uncreated world is of the "first-order," and it qualifies all that Gregory writes. It limits human comprehension, human intelligence, and human language to the created level of reality.

> God is beyond all notions of measure, interval, and differentiation, indeed . . . God is beyond all διάστημα and that this is the principal reason that created intelligence can neither know nor speak of the divine.[52] Just as the eye cannot hear, he says, nor the ear taste, even so the created intelligence cannot pass beyond itself—whatever it sees, it sees itself; and it contemplates the διάστημα if it contemplates anything at all.[53]

This "first-order" *diastema* does not signify a *spatial* gap between God and creation, but rather, forbids any notion of ontological continuity between creation and its Creator, and in this Gregory is to be distinguished from Dionysius.[54]

Language belongs to the created order and is, in other words, inherently diastemic. Language mediates between mind and body, between bodies separated in space, and between moments in time. The function of language (to attempt to bridge gaps that it can never traverse) results in its inherently transgressive and futile character: language strains to overcome the *diastema* between one's physical perception and one's thoughts, and between one person and another. This is a futile attempt because, itself belonging to the diastemic order, language "depends for its efficacy on interval and separation."[55] Mosshammer argues that Gregory anticipates Saussure's linguistic theory in his insight that "the meaning of words depends on the whole system of differences"—that *dry*, for instance, refers and depends on its opposite for meaning.[56] We might call this level of difference and separation "second-order" *diastema*. It depends on a more primary ontological gap. Since language is structured on difference, "meaning and interpretation must be multiple, caught up in an unending process of interpretation in which each successive understanding undermines itself so as to point forward to another."[57]

This distinction between what I am calling "first-order" and "second-order" *diastema*—between (1) the radical ontological discontinuity and unilaterally unbridgeable gap between God and creation, and (2) the multiple gaps that language strains to overcome within the created order—provides a model to clarify Marion's discussion of different categories of saturated phenomena. In other words, Gregory provides a more consistent explanation of the difference between the saturation of excessive, but nevertheless created, *banal* phenomena and the saturation of Revelation.

Two inconsistencies pertain here: First, throughout most of Marion's writing, the term "saturated phenomena" refers to exceptional experiences (often religious, or, negatively, traumatic). Yet recently Marion has claimed that *all* phenomena can be saturated.[58] This lack of clarity regarding the range of saturated phenomena is one issue. The second arises with Marion's distinction between the saturation of "banal" phenomena versus the saturation of Revelation. The latter, he argues, transgresses all four of the Kantian categories that determine the four types of banal saturation: (1) the "event" transgresses "quantity" so that it is *invisable;* (2) the "idol" or "painting" transgresses "quality" so that it is *unbearable;* (3) the "flesh" transgresses "relation" so that it is *absolute;* and (4) the "icon" transgresses "analogy" so that it is both *irregardable* and *irreducible.* Revelation, according to this, transgresses all four; it is *invisable,* unbearable, absolute, and irreducible.[59] However, this way of discussing Revelation defines it, strangely, according to Kantian categories rather than, as Marion purports to do, according to the thing itself![60] I argue that Gregory offers a more satisfactory distinction of the two orders of linguistic and conceptual limitation.

For Gregory, these two gaps that language and knowledge strain to overcome take place on two totally different ontological orders. It is not simply a matter of degree or synthesis. Rather, the gaps of the created order are radically dependent on the originary gap that *is creation:* τὸ διάστημα οὐδὲν ἄλλο ἤ κτίσις ἐστιν.[61] To the same degree that God is incomprehensible to humans, God is incomprehensible to celestial beings or angels. This is one of the marked differences between the apophasis of Gregory and that of Dionysius. The originary *diastema* means that the most fundamental ontological difference is not between the sensible and the intelligible, but between the created and uncreated. Gregory again subverts his Greek inheritance on this point.

There are two ways in which language strains to overcome these diastemic obstacles. Within the created order, Gregory recognizes that language is conventional and argues that language serves an intermediary pragmatic purpose. It is thus imperfect, yet it is necessary in order to communicate (even inadequately) our own thoughts to ourselves and to others. However, the futility of our linguistic attempt to transgress the *diastema* between creation and its Creator functions on a different register: its very impossibility serves as positive reminder of the reason for the *diastema:* the infinite, *adiastemic* and incomprehensible nature of God. The very limits of language simply serve to reinforce our own sense of limitation, finitude, and radical dependence. It calls us to wonder and love. These two modes of linguistic transgression come to play in Gregory's understanding of revelation in scripture, our reception of, and response to it.

As I argued in chapter 4, Gregory's understanding of scriptural interpretation puts forth a view of language and of meaning (or the construction of meaning) that defies and repulses objectification. The most basic and, simultaneously, the highest knowledge one can attain is to "grasp" that what one seeks is beyond reach, beyond conception—that what one seeks always avoids, repulses, and eludes capture. Biblical interpretation, then, is not with the aim of attaining a singular truth, but rather to "lead the reader to new horizons of understanding." Scriptural interpretation is *anagogic:* "The goal [σκοπός] towards which Scripture moves is not the revelation of a fixed, metaphysical truth that the language of the Bible translates for us, but a pointing forward to a truth formed and understood only in the act of interpretation itself. Indeed, the purpose of Scripture as a whole is to bring about a change in the situation of the reader."[62] Gregory discusses this transformative quality of scriptural revelation in Homily Five of his *Commentary on the Song of Songs.*

The writings of scripture are anagogic—they lead us onward: "They create in us a desire to see the sun in the open air."[63] This desire stretches out eternally because of the distance from that which it contemplates.[64] The Bride contemplates the "voice" of her Beloved rather than his face in order to demonstrate the cognitive distance from her Beloved. The voice "allows inference rather than certainty about who the speaker is."[65] The text uses a multiplicity of names and images to conjure the Beloved because the Bride "perceives her spouse in different ways at different times and never has the image of what she has comprehended."[66] Thus, scripture's interpretation is open-ended, an endless process with multiple meanings. Both of these qualities point to the inexhaustibility of the divine being.

Were it not to change, human nature runs the risk of becoming "frozen stiff in the cold of idolatry when man's changeable nature has been transformed into the nature of the lifeless objects which he worshipped."[67] Two observations can be made here: first, idolatry is identified with lack of change, remaining fixed on one object or concept (like Marion's phenomenology of the "idol"); and secondly, we are transformed and shaped by that which we worship, for good or ill. For Gregory the determining factor for salvation is one's orientation. Unlike the divine nature, humans have good and evil alternating within their nature; good is limited or opposed by evil. But the divine nature has no limit or opposition. Thus when

> God draws a human soul to participate in himself, he always remains in equal measure superior to the participating soul because of his superabundant goodness. For, on the one hand, the soul continually grows through participation in what is beyond it and never stops growing. On the other hand, the good in which the soul shares remains the same [i.e., unlimited] so that the more the soul participates in it, the more she recognizes that it transcends her as much as before.[68]

There is an unlimited growth in the good.

This progress is initiated through an interpretative response to the revelation in scripture in which God condescends to speak in our own language. Scriptural writers are not "passive secretaries who merely transmit a higher language capable of revealing the truth as it is."[69] They are models for ways in which one strains to describe that which cannot be described, models of the ways to follow, respond, and love, but not to know, God: "The purpose of the Bible is to lead the reader through the writer's words, not back to the original experience of inspiration, but forward to the recreation of a similar experience in himself. Each one must gaze for himself on what cannot be described."[70] Interpretation of scripture can only ever be done in "first person": Gregory's interpretation of Abraham or of Moses is for the benefit of translating narratives into his context; but everyone must eventually do this for him or herself. Gregory has no sense that interpretation ends with him or that his interpretation of the *Song of Songs* somehow cancels or replaces Origen's interpretation of the same text.[71]

To summarize, knowledge and language are limited because finite. They cannot escape or overcome the gap between reality and thought and between thought and word because they are born out of the *diastema* of creation. This limitation exists already within the created order, but it is exponentially multiplied when it comes to the attempt to know or name the divine, uncreated nature. Still, that untraversable gap is bridged by God. This divine accommodation to the needs of creation summons a response as infinite as its source. Finally, the manner of our response determines our very existence.

There is a connection between interpretation and an individual's progress in perfection, between the making and remaking of meaning and a response of "following after" infinitely. This response is also identified as the creature's desire or love for God—to know and see God ever more perfectly in the face of infinite inadequacy. I have already argued in chapter 4 that Gregory provides Marion with a conceptual framework to describe a revelation of pure givenness and its subsequent interpretation.[72] In this chapter I have furthered that thesis by demonstrating that Gregory gives us a way to hold together Marion's notion of love as the response constitutive of subjectivity (one that must always be in the first person) with the endless hermeneutics of saturated phenomena. Gregory is able to do this coherently because he assumes unproblematically that God is the original lover, both radically and eternally unknown and yet eternally beckoning. Having seen what Gregory might offer to Marion, I will briefly compare it to Marion's own discussion of apophasis and erotic discourse.

Marion lays out his ideal vision of the meaning of apophasis in "The Unspoken: Apophasis and the Discourse of Love."[73] Having suggested that mystical theology replaces constative (assertive) and predicative language with a "strictly pragmatic usage," Marion now sets out to prove the success of this replacement. In other words, this essay begins where his response to Derrida at Villanova ended[74] and takes up the challenge with more specificity.

In the abstract of the essay, Marion describes his attempt to delineate a strictly pragmatic discourse as a specifically "Dionysian" enterprise.[75] This descriptive modifier is odd for two reasons: first, Marion nowhere else in the essay cites Dionysius. Thus it would seem that "Dionysius" functions here simply as shorthand for a concept that may or may not actually have anything to do with the pseudonymous writer. Secondly, his claim, that a non-predicative discourse with strict pragmatic usage emerges out of a Dionysian framework, is simply wrong. Language, for Dionysius, offers a richer multivalency than simply predicative and constative discourse, but by no means is language in Dionysius purely pragmatic. On the contrary, Dionysius' theory of language depends on a robust participatory ontology that unequivocally relates signifiers to their signifieds (just as much as that very signification demands a difference, a remainder, and an excess that is not contained in the word). Thus words are not merely pragmatic inventions for human utility (as they are for Gregory), but rather they are ontologically related to the divine, participate in the divine, and reveal the divine just as they simultaneously veil the divine. Despite this curious allusion to Dionysius, then, what precisely is Marion after with his synthesis of apophasis and erotic discourse?

Marion provides an analysis of the statement, "I love you!" It is neither predicative nor constative: it does not say something about something.[76] It does not require the being of the loved one—one can love an unborn or not-yet-conceived child, just as one can love a long-lost friend: "Not only does this absence not stop us from loving and desiring, it reinforces this desire. For the loved one, the person to whom 'I love you!' is spoken, it is no longer about being or not being, nor about being or not being this or that, but only about the fact that one is loved."[77] Marion also insists that the statement is not performative. There is no "conventional procedure," whether public or private, that goes along with the statement: it may be said by those "unqualified," it may not be mutual, and the intention of the one who says it is utterly unverifiable.

Instead, Marion calls it, following J. L. Austin, a "perlocutionary act," an act that one instigates or accomplishes by saying something: "When I say 'I love you!', I try (and in fact always manage) not necessarily to perform the love that I speak, but to move, to influence, and, at the very least, to summon my listener to consider my declaration."[78] There is, in other words, in the speech-act, a reach for power; one seeks a response from the other. However, it is an act that has no inherent power; one cannot control just what that response will be—anger, returned love, jealousy, indifference, fear. Thus the statement, "I love you!" does not say something about something (assertive or predicative language), nor does it bring about a certain reality (performative language); rather, it simply addresses someone and in so doing positions the speaker, orients him, to face that which or whom he addresses. The statement announces the speaker's presence and location and openness to be summoned in response.

> We tell each other nothing in a certain (constative) sense, yet by speaking this nothing, or rather these nothings, *we place ourselves (pragmatically) face to face,* each receptive to the (perlocutionary) effect of the other, in the distance that both separates and unites us . . . neither speaking nor negating anything about anything, but acting on the other, and allowing the other to act on me.[79]

In *The Erotic Phenomenon,* Marion argues that in order to know any other—above all, to know God—is to love the other, to love God. As Robyn Horner has argued, this knowledge that love brings is neither abstract nor static. Rather, it is the knowledge of personal acquaintance (*connaître* rather than *savior*),[80] and it includes elements of interaction, of confrontation and transformation. It is a knowing that also includes an "unknowing." The "face to face" encounter yields no knowledge:

> What do we look at in the face of the other person? Not his or her mouth, nevertheless more expressive of the intentions than other parts of the body, but the eyes—or more exactly the empty pupils of the person's eyes, their black holes open on the somber ocular hollow. In other words, in the face we fix on the sole place where precisely nothing can be seen.[81]

Love requires an infinite hermeneutic because it takes an eternity to envisage the saturated phenomenon that is the face of our beloved.[82]

This discussion of "erotic discourse" seems to raise more questions than it answers. Is love, for Marion, reduced to this bare confrontation? What, positively, is given and received within such a "loving" exchange? The way in which Marion construes the identification of erotic and apophatic discourse seems overly haunted by Derrida's initial criticism that "praise," by addressing one, always remains predicative, or says something about that to which it refers.[83] In an attempt to counter this challenge, Marion goes to extremes in stripping both apophatic and erotic discourse down to the barest of linguistic structures. Yet one might inquire whether what is gained balances what is lost in such a reduction. What is wrong with language being predicative when it is understood as mere human convention? When, in other words, no ontological relationship is claimed between our words and the reality they refer to, what remains dangerous about the substantially humbled claim to talk "about" the divine, to praise, precisely because one must respond in some way, even in the face of an infinite inadequacy so to do?

As I have just shown, Gregory has given a far clearer and richer sense of the way in which a linguistic response, as an expression of our desire or love, is entirely pragmatic (as a human "convention") and yet remains existentially transformative. It may take the form of saying "something about," but such a predication can function only as a reminder of its own inadequacy when the most accurate statement one can make (and the highest knowledge one can arrive at) is, for Gregory, that God is incomprehensible. With this humility, our response says, "Here I am" again and again, in shifting ways and with an openness to be radically changed.

The sense of language's fundamental inadequacy in the face of an excessive force, especially in the face of the plenitude of divine love, is not unique to Gregory. Dionysius shares the same insight. Yet the distinct ontological emphases (the *diastema* of creation versus the *givenness* of creation) of Gregory and Dionysius yield distinct linguistic strategies to respond to this erotic plenitude without claiming to *properly* name it. For Dionysius this strategy ultimately includes a leap beyond language ("beyond saying and unsaying") in an ecstatic union with the Divine, whereas for Gregory the strategy involves an infinitely changing response (in forms of language that remain inherently inadequate) that signals the receptivity to eternally expand one's desire for God, a receptivity that infinitely transforms the person.

These distinct apophatic strategies in the face of the same insight of a plenitude of divine love offer Marion two distinct ways of responding to Derrida. If his primary aim is to demonstrate the purely pragmatic function of language, then he is better served by Gregory than by Dionysius in this context. Gregory has a model of language that is indeed "purely pragmatic" and yet robustly illustrative of the drama of responding with love to love. This is another opportunity Marion misses by his lack of attention to the significant differences between the two Greek Fathers.

The Invisibility of Saturation

Marion characterizes "Truth" (a term with ontological weight if ever there was one) as that which "counteracts."[84] The reception of saturated phenomena transforms one. Marion describes this transformation in language that implicitly echoes Gregory's kenotic language of a divine accommodation that fills and overflows our limited capacity for reception and, in so doing, expands it:

> In seeing what I see, I also see the obligatory *darkness* created by the *all too clear excess of light;* and this obligatory darkness *spills over* the one who sees the truth because it *imposes* on him a dark obligation: that of *revising his own self* to the *(scaleless) scale* of the saturating excess of intuition. That is, since the saturated phenomenon cannot be reduced to the measure of objectivity of objectness, it demands of the one it affects that he see it and admit it in its very excess, without the security of a concept. It therefore demands of the affected that he *give himself over* [*de s'adonner*], let himself be (re-)made, (re-)defined, and, so to speak, (un-)measured by the measure of its own excess. Instead of summing up the given within the limits of my own finitude (of my concept), I undergo the *obscure obligation of letting myself conform* to (and by) the excess of intuition over every intention that my gaze could oppose to it.[85]

This dense paragraph summarizes much of Marion's entire philosophical enterprise: the given's evasion of objectification; the paradoxical quality of lightness that, in its excess, appears as darkness; the imposition upon and subsequent transformation of the recipient—the one given over (*l'adonné*) to the infinite measure of that which it receives.

Here Marion's attention to the stubborn refusal of phenomena to be objectified, to be captured within the constraints of conceptual limits, delineates a truth that unfolds in darkness, a darkness that we nonetheless see: a "luminous darkness."

Marion's work is "apologetic," but not, for the most part, insofar as it seeks to convince "secularists" of the undeniable truths of Christian dogma or of Christianity's inherent rationality. Such an apologetics, he thinks, is doomed to failure. His writing does seek to "convert" its reader, but not, to be fair, necessarily to particular ecclesial allegiances.

Parenthetically, it is necessary to observe that Marion shifts to a more explicitly Christian apologetic aim in *Au lieu de soi*. Nonetheless, this shift represents a dramatic turn away from earlier statements which attempt to remain open to a broader range of religious phenomena. Significantly too, this shift is accompanied by a movement away from the Greek Fathers, Dionysius and Gregory, and toward Augustine. A great deal could be said of the import of this movement, but let me simply isolate three differences between, on the one hand, Dionysius and Gregory, and, on the other, Augustine, that coincide with the shift in Marion's rhetorical strategy and explicit philosophical aims: (1) For both Dionysius and Gregory the mystical ascent of the individual to God is a movement *from lightness to darkness;* for Augustine the inverse is true—it is a movement from ignorance to beatitude, from darkness to light. (2) For Dionysius, and especially for Gregory, the orientation of the self in a loving response to God is an ongoing and infinite process, not a singular decision either "to love or to hate." (3) Finally, for Dionysius and Gregory, the incomprehensibility of the infinite God and the ignorance of the finite human is an unavoidable, neutral, and eschatologically unchanging fact of creation, rather than necessitating the moral culpability of the "deformity of the sinner."[86] I believe this rhetorical shift in Marion—accompanied as it is by a shift from the more closely overlapping apophatic visions of Dionysius and Gregory to that of Augustine—has the unfortunate effect of closing down phenomenological as well as theological possibilities.[87] In this evaluation, I am in agreement with two reviewers of Marion's latest work who argue that it shuts down the possibility of interdisciplinary discourse between phenomenology and theology.[88]

This marks, as I have argued, a significant shift in the rhetorical aim of Marion's corpus. Throughout the majority of Marion's writing, he has sought to arouse his reader's curiosity, to open their eyes to the appearance of unexpected and uncontrolled phenomena.[89] In so doing, he certainly advocates the possibility of returning to the question of God in academic discourse. However, at his best, he does not foreclose how this question will be decided. He leaves this intentionally dark. Marion's "apologetics" offer an enticing invitation to wonder, to allow an openness to experience, rigorous in that it forbids nothing and pre-determines no limitation to what might come except the non-limit of what love might receive.[90] "It is forbidden to forbid": with this gloss on the first principle of phenomenology, Marion provides a valuable cor-rective to all dogmatisms, whether those of theology or those of herme-neutics. Marion brilliantly captures the necessity of attending to what sneaks in, or breaks through, subjective experience without our invita-tion or even our consent. His writing and thought cultivates a fecund expectancy of what might appear both within and out of the darkness.

Conclusion

The aim of this study has been to ask how resilient the tensions in Marion's thought are under the lens of his fascinatingly rich, yet uneasy retrieval of the Greek apophatic tradition. I argued that, despite abundant evidence of the sophistication and comprehensiveness of his knowledge of patristic writings, the Fathers too often function homogeneously as a source of authoritative "orthodoxy" in Marion's thought. I challenged the univocity of his reading of Gregory of Nyssa and Dionysius in particular, arguing that distinct theories of apophasis emerge out of their different ontologies. I then demonstrated the way divergent motivations in Marion's thought were highlighted through an analysis of his use of Dionysius and Gregory. On the one hand, his complicated retrieval of Dionysius drew attention to the finally irreconcilable tension within his methodological enterprise. On the other hand, Gregory proved to be a tapped, though (as yet) underutilized, resource for clarifying the paradoxical relation of pure givenness and its subsequently infinite interpretation.

Throughout these arguments, I have challenged certain aspects of the scholarship on all three of the main figures of this study: Marion, Gregory of Nyssa, and Dionysius. First, I intentionally read outside the parameters of the most dominant debate on Marion: the perennial argument regarding his theological versus his phenomenological identity. I have argued that an overzealous preoccupation with this debate actually glosses over a more integral tension within his thought between a universal methodology that seeks to secure phenomenology's place as first philosophy and the anti-idolatry orientation of Marion's enterprise that attempts to free all phenomena from any constraint.

Secondly, I challenged a long-standing trend in the comparative scholarship on Gregory and Dionysius that elides the apophatic visions of the two and that has, until recently, tended to ignore the original and distinct contributions Gregory makes to notions of Christian apophaticism. In so doing, I am certainly not arguing that Gregory offers a more "radical" or "better" apophaticism than Dionysius (a bizarre claim to make). I am simply insisting on the significant difference between the two. Attention to the difference is not merely a historical issue. It is also significant when one wants to make use of the patristic arguments within contemporary debates.

It remains only to reflect in closing on some of the unresolved issues of this study as well as its broader implications regarding the apologetic value of Marion's thought. Let me first identify issues that invite further exploration than this study has offered. Two related lacunae, in particular, trouble Marion's phenomenological project: a lack of attention to the role of preparatory practices in developing a capacity to receive phenomena as pure givens, and the absence of comment on how, or even whether, we might judge the relative benevolence or malevolence of the phenomena that have such a powerful impact upon us.

One might imagine many practices that cultivate expectancy or receptivity: bodily and contemplative practices as well as social and individual practices. There are a multitude of examples from within the history of Christianity: silent prayer; the contemplation of icons; the practice of solitude, of living in a community, of training one's temporal experience around the liturgical seasons; restrictions on sexual practices and diet; rules about clothing, obedience, poverty, and so on. Marion does refer to one form of practice, Eucharistic contemplation and participation in the liturgy. Yet he never theorizes on the effect of these activities precisely *as a practice,* or what Hadot would call a "spiritual exercise," that might help to clear away obstacles to the reception of given phenomena and thus enlarge our receptive capacity. A debate could occur about which of these practices are more or less conducive to the "clearing away of obstacles" in order that saturated phenomena might appear as they give themselves freely and without constraint. However, Marion never raises the question.

Marion's inattention to preparatory practices might be explained by his wariness to open a place of personal agency for the subject who, as the "gifted" (*l'adonné*), has the sole purpose of receiving an unbidden gift. Nonetheless, this very wariness, along with Marion's inclination to attribute a kind of "agency" or selfhood to the phenomena that give themselves, gives rise to the second lacuna in Marion's thought: How are we to *judge* the intentionality (for good or ill) of the saturated phenomenon and its consequent effect on the one to whom it is given?

Respecting Marion's desire to guarantee the inviolability of the phenomenon to give itself from itself, Marion's rhetorical emphasis here can nonetheless be disturbing. To give one example from many possibilities, he speaks of the reception of saturated phenomena as indubitable in its very *unavoidability:* "The ordeal of excess is actually attested by the resistance, eventually the pain, that it imposes on the one who receives it."[1] This description of the experience of saturated phenomena is not problematic in itself, qua description. Indeed, I think Marion acutely captures some of the violence, the unilateralness, even the trauma, of excessive experience, whether it is "divine" or "demonic." I am, however, critical that this crucial ambiguity within the reception of saturated phenomena does not seem to concern Marion, or at least he never explicitly addresses this as a concern. Marion never discusses how one might begin to establish a mode of judging such phenomena and their intent. Might his analysis of love offer some way forward? If we cannot be protected from the arrival of any particular phenomenon a priori (for this would predetermine the limits of our experience, which is precisely what Marion insists we cannot do), are there other avenues that might at least better equip one to respond to all experiences with discernment and justice as well as love? This aspect of Marion's thought demands further critical exploration.

Finally, a word must be said regarding the implications of my study, specifically in relation to my characterization of Marion's retrieval of the Greek Fathers as "apologetic." Such a retrieval bears the implicit belief that the Fathers have something of value to contribute to the philosophical debates today. Critical questions are raised by such a claim. Some will argue that, in his retrieval, Marion has no license to translate the Fathers creatively.[2] Secondly, there are those who would argue that he should not be retrieving an ecclesial tradition unquestionably as an authoritative source into an intellectual discipline that must remain agnostic in its methodological neutrality. How might Marion be defended on both of these fronts?

First, a creative interpretation of tradition in its "transmission" is nothing new; "tradition" is continually reinterpreted in the face of new intellectual contexts, and it always has been.[3] As I discussed in chapter 4, Gregory argues that even the interpretation of scripture involves a translation of terms and narratives into those that might be understandable to his contemporaries, that Moses' story must be retold for the Cappadocian context. This is not an unusual position for someone to take in Late Antiquity. In fact, the former criticism against creativity in interpretation betrays a particularly "modern" prejudice, one that seeks to guarantee the pristine intactness of some elusive "original meaning" of the Fathers.

Fascinatingly, however, this modern prejudice is one that Marion shares, even as he translates the Fathers. To take the example of Marion's transformation of the term αἰτία (cause) into *Requisit* (the requested or required one), such a translation adds a new shading to the term, a new interpretation of "cause" in Dionysius' theology. In this way, it offers an original way of thinking about Dionysius. Yet Marion argues, unnecessarily and incorrectly, that it represents the "real" or "most accurate" sense of what Dionysius was getting at. While I do not fault Marion for his creative translations in an interpretative engagement with the past, I do fault him for not being up front and explicit about the way the questions that emerge out of his own context shade his reading. To put this another way, even if Marion treats the Fathers as a kind of saturated phenomenon to be received as a pure given, he then ignores his own argument about the necessarily endless interpretation of any such phenomenon.

The second critique, that such a retrieval of an ecclesial tradition is unwarranted,[4] comes from the phenomenological perspective and is more complicated. At least two distinct issues emerge. First, there is the risk that one takes possession of more than was bargained for. Specifically, does Marion's retrieval of the Fathers not involve the importation of a theological (presumed, therefore, to be "metaphysical") solution into a phenomenological question?[5] Secondly, a question arises regarding the authority by which such a retrieval occurs.

How does Marion respond to the cry of "foul play" concerning his retrieval of the Fathers? First of all, Marion himself challenges the instinctive postmodern allergy to any discussion of ontology or even metaphysics. Need metaphysics "always [be] identified as and by presence, or can it also include absence?" asks Marion in the same argument in which he challenges whether all Christian theology is reducible to metaphysics.[6] Furthermore, as I discussed in the introduction, Marion defines the metaphysics at the end of which he locates himself in a technically precise way. His project rails against a mode of metaphysical thinking that, in an attempt to ground its foundation and one's epistemological access to that foundation, limits the possibility of the appearance of phenomena to those that are "possible" within the horizons of that foundation. This attempt to secure a foundation results in the dominance of "Being" and of the subject (whether transcendental or existential) as the determinative horizons of all phenomena.

However, this very narrow definition of metaphysics would sound remarkably strange to the "premodern" ear (i.e., to anyone thinking before Descartes). At the very least, neither Gregory nor Dionysius would recognize such an epistemologically driven enterprise. As I argued in chapter 5, Gregory's critique of knowledge, especially, has the opposite concern: not to secure the foundations of knowledge but, in recalling one's ignorance and the limits of our knowledge, to open one to the wonder and praise of all that exceeds our grasping. A similar understanding of the critique of knowledge underlies most of Marion's own philosophical enterprise (despite his continued commitment to a Kantian framework). Thus one could argue that Marion's retrieval of the Fathers, which imports with it certain ontological assumptions, functions, whether consciously or not, as an implicit challenge to the sweeping application of Heidegger's critique of the history of metaphysics in Western thought.

This still leaves the second question: On what authority are the Fathers an authoritative source for Marion? In his early writings, it is clear that, as part of the Catholic tradition, they function authoritatively *as such*. However, for the vast majority of Marion's writing, this is not the argument Marion makes or wants to make. Are the Fathers retrieved as "authoritative" simply on the strength of their collective and individual wisdom? And if so, to what extent would this appease Marion's critics?

I suggest that, in fact, Marion's retrieval of the Fathers as a resource against present polemics might seem less problematic to some if the retrieval were less univocal. In other words, it is the application of a hermeneutic of homogeneity, which assumes that the Fathers speak the "Truth" singularly, that causes Marion problems. This is yet another reason why Marion would be served by distinguishing between Gregory and Dionysius and by ceasing to allow one to speak for the other, instead acknowledging that he finds the writing of Dionysius particularly instructive in one regard and the thought of Gregory more illuminative in another.

This leaves us with a far broader sense of the "apologetics" being pursued than is often understood by the term. However, I suggest that it is a notion of "apologetics" that, in its breadth, has a greater potential for a constructive engagement between past and present. Apologetics, in this sense, does not aim to convince by rational proof. Rather, its goal is a reciprocal confrontation that may at times appear more like a conversation and at other times more like a wrestling match. But in all cases it represents an openness to receive the unexpected.

I take Marion's work to be apologetic in this broad sense: it challenges two different discourses simultaneously. Marion's astute intelligence and encyclopedic knowledge not only of Continental philosophy but also of the history of Christian thought qualifies him particularly well for the task. Marion challenges theology to think carefully about the claims made concerning the reception of revelation and the conditions of its possibility. He challenges theology to remember always the dynamic, surprising, and uncontrolled quality of revelation, which eternally resists the idolatry of static conceptualization. At the same time, he challenges phenomenology (which must remain strictly agnostic) not to accept religious claims to truth by fiat but to rigorously permit their *possibility*. In demanding that phenomenology attend to saturated phenomena as not merely exceptional cases of experience but as perhaps the most basic and constitutive of a "response-able subjectivity,"[7] Marion dramatically opens up a space for the question of God. Drawing on the traditions of Greek *apophasis,* Marion creates a space for a richer account of all that appears, but most especially of that which appears within a "luminous darkness" and which ignites our desire to follow without end.

NOTES

Introduction

1. He is the subject of several dissertations, three major studies, and two edited volumes in English as well as more than a hundred journal articles in several languages.

2. In 1996 he became the director of the *Centre d'Études Cartésiennes*.

3. An intermediary publication, *Le visible et le révélé* (Paris: Éditions de CERF, 2005), is a collection of previously published articles bringing together themes of visibility and invisibility (manifestation and concealment) and revelation. These articles are treated in chapters 4 and 5 of this study and cited according to their original publications.

4. See Christina M. Gschwandtner, *Reading Jean-Luc Marion: Exceeding Metaphysics* (Bloomington: Indiana University Press, 2007).

5. See, for instance, Jocelyn Benoist, "Le tournant théologique," in *L'Idée de phénoménologie* (Paris: Beauchesne, 2001); idem, "L'écart plutôt que l'excédent," *Philosophie: Jean-Luc Marion* 78 (Paris: Minuit, 2003); Arthur Bradley, "God *Sans* Being: Derrida and Marion and a Paradoxical Writing of the Word *Without*," *Literature and Theology* 14.3 (2000); John D. Caputo, "The Hyperbolization of Phenomenology: Two Possibilities for Religion in Recent Continental Philosophy," in *Counter-Experiences: Reading Jean-Luc Marion*, ed. Kevin Hart (Notre Dame, Ind.: Notre Dame University Press, 2007); Dominique Janicaud, *Le tournant théologique de la phénoménologie française* (Combas: Éditions de l'Éclat, 1991); idem, *La phénoménologie éclatée* (Combas: Éditions de l'Éclat, 1998); Hent de Vries, *Philosophy and the Turn to Religion* (Baltimore, Md.: Johns Hopkins University Press, 1999).

6. See, for instance, David B. Burrell, "Reflections on 'Negative Theology' in the Light of a Recent Venture to Speak of 'God Without Being,'" in *Postmodernism and Christian Philosophy,* ed. R. T. Ciapolo (Washington, D.C.: Catholic University of America Press, 1997); John Milbank, "Can a Gift Be Given? Prolegomena to a Future Trinitarian Metaphysic," in *Rethinking Metaphysics*, ed. L. Gregory Jones and Stephen E. Fowl (Oxford: Blackwell, 1995); idem, "Only Theology Overcomes Metaphysics," *New Blackfriars* 76 (1995).

7. See, for instance, Joseph S. O'Leary, *Religious Pluralism and Christian Truth* (Edinburgh: Edinburgh University Press, 1996); Graham Ward, "Between Modernity and Postmodernity: The Theology of Jean-Luc Marion," in *Postmodernity, Sociology and Religion,* ed. Kieran Flanagan and Peter C. Jupp (London: Macmillan, 1996); idem, "The Theological Project of Jean-Luc Marion," in

Post-Secular Philosophy: Between Philosophy and Theology, ed. Philip Blond (London: Routledge, 1998).

8. See Mark Dooley, "Marion's Ambition of Transcendence," in *Givenness and God: Questions of Jean-Luc Marion,* Eoin Cassidy and Ian Leask (New York: Fordham University Press, 2004).

9. See Ian Leask, "The Dative Subject (and the 'Principle of Principles')," in *Givenness and God.*

10. See, for instance, Jean Greisch, "L'herméneutique dans la 'phénoménologie comme telle,'" *Revue de Métaphysique et de Morale* 96.1 (1991); Jean Grondin, "La phénoménologie sans herméneutique," in *L'horizon herméneutique de la pensée contemporaine* (Paris: J. Vrin, 1993); Richard Kearney, *The God Who May Be: A Hermeneutics of Religion* (Bloomington: Indiana University Press, 2001); idem, "A Dialogue with Jean-Luc Marion," ed. John Manoussakis, *Philosophy Today* (2004); Shane Mackinlay, "Eyes Wide Shut: A Response to Jean-Luc Marion's Account of the Journey to Emmaus," *Modern Theology* 20.3 (2004); idem, "Phenomenality in the Middle: Marion, Romano, and the Hermeneutics of the Event," in *Givenness and God;* idem, *Interpreting Excess: Jean-Luc Marion, Saturated Phenomena, and Hermeneutics* (New York: Fordham University Press, 2009).

11. See Marion, *Being Given: Toward a Phenomenology of Givenness,* trans. Jeffrey L. Kosky (Stanford, Calif.: Stanford University Press, 2002), 4; original publication, *Étant donné: Essai d'une phénoménologie de la donation* (Paris: Presses Universitaires de France, 1997).

12. Robyn Horner has identified Marion's two main insights in a way that indicates the paradox at the heart of his thought: his insights involve the consideration of "givenness as the sole horizon of phenomena, and the possibility of phenomena that saturate intuition to such an extent that all horizons are shattered." See Horner's introduction to Marion, *In Excess: Studies of Saturated Phenomena,* trans. Robyn Horner and Vincent Berraud (New York: Fordham University Press, 2002), ix; original publication, *De surcroît: Études sur les phénomènes saturés* (Paris: Presses Universitaires de France, 2003).

13. Marion defines "first philosophy" as having "at its disposal a domain and operations which, on the one hand, would be absolutely proper to it, such that no other science could either confiscate them from it or be born infiltrating it in order ultimately to dispossess it, and which, on the other hand, impose themselves as the condition of possibility of all other knowledge" (*In Excess,* 3).

14. One of the questions I am not treating here is Marion's silence on the discourses of French feminism and Lacanian psychoanalytic theory. This is a curious silence not only because of the geographic proximity and contemporaneousness of the two but also because of the significant conceptual overlaps between Marion and Kristeva especially. (An interesting study could be done, for instance, comparing Marion's understanding of the subject's repulsion of the saturated phenomenon and Kristeva's notion of "abjection.") Part of the reason behind Marion's silence may have to do with his general avoidance of issues of gender, a

lack of interest that explains his stubborn insistence on non-inclusive language throughout most of his writings. An important critical study is wanting on this question.

15. See Derek J. Morrow, "The Conceptual Idolatry of Descartes' Gray Ontology: An Epistemology 'Without Being,'" in *Givenness and God;* Lilian Alweiss, "I am, I exist," in *Givenness and God.*

16. See Michael B. Ewbank, "Of Idols, Icons, and Aquinas's Esse: Reflections on Jean-Luc Marion," *International Philosophical Quarterly* 42.2 (2002); Wayne Hankey, "Theoria versus Poesis: Neoplatonism and Trinitarian Difference in Aquinas, John Milbank, Jean-Luc Marion, and John Zizoulas," *Modern Theology* 15.4 (1999); Fergus Kerr, "Aquinas after Marion," *New Blackfriars* 76 (1995); Brian J. Shanley, "Saint Thomas, Onto-theology, and Marion," *The Thomist* 60.4 (1996).

17. Marion, "Saint Thomas d'Aquin et l'onto-théo-logie," in *Revue Thomiste* 95 (1995); "Thomas Aquinas and Onto-theo-logy," trans. B. Gendreau, R. Rethy, and M. Sweeney in *Mystics: Presence and Aporia,* ed. Michael Kessler and Christian Sheppard (Chicago: Chicago University Press, 2003).

18. See Timothy Mooney, "Hubris and Humility: Husserl's Reduction and Givenness," in *Givenness and God;* Paul Gilbert, "Substance et presence: Derrida et Marion, critiques de Husserl," *Gregorianum* 75.1 (1994); R. Kühn, "'Sättinung' als absolutes Phänomen. Zur Kritik der klassische Phänomenalität (Kant, Husserl) bei Jean-Luc Marion," *Mesotes. Zeitschrift für philosophischen Ost-West-Dialog* 3 (1995); John Manoussakis, "The Phenomenon of God: From Husserl to Marion," *American Catholic Philosophical Quarterly* 78.1 (2004); James K. A. Smith, "Respect and Donation: A Critique of Marion's Critique of Husserl," *American Catholic Philosophical Quarterly* 71.4 (1997); Ruud Welten, "Saturation and Disappointment: Marion according to Husserl," *Bijdragen* 65.1 (2004).

19. See Jeffrey Bloechl, "Dialectical Approaches to Retrieving God after Heidegger: Premises and Consequences (Lacoste and Marion)," *Pacifica: Journal of the Melbourne College of Divinity* 13 (2000); Brian Elliott, "Reduced Phenomena and Unreserved Debts in Marion's Reading of Heidegger," in *Givenness and God;* Jean Greisch, *Le cogito herméneutique: L'herméneutique philosophique et l'heritage cartésian* (Paris: Vrin, 2000); Laurence Hemming, "Reading Heidegger: Is God without Being? Jean-Luc Marion's Reading of Martin Heidegger in *God Without Being,*" *New Blackfriars* 76: 895 (1995).

20. See Victor Kal, "Being Unable to Speak, Seen as a Period: Difference and Distance in Jean-Luc Marion," in *Flight of the Gods: Philosophical Perspectives on Negative Theology,* ed. Ilse N. Bulhof and Laurens ten Kate (New York: Fordham University Press, 2000); J. E. Drabinksi, "Sense and Icon: The Problem of *Sinngebung* in Levinas and Marion," *Philosophy Today* 42 (1998).

21. See Arthur Bradley, "God *Sans* Being"; John D. Caputo, "Apostles of the Impossible," in *God, the Gift and Postmodernism,* ed. John Caputo and Michael Scanlon (Bloomington: Indiana University Press, 1999); Robyn Horner, *Rethinking God as Gift: Marion, Derrida, and the Limits of Phenomenology* (New York: Fordham University Press, 2001); idem, "Aporia or Excess: Two Strategies for

Thinking r/Revelation," in *Other Testaments: Derrida and Religion,* ed. Kevin Hart and Yvonne Sherwood (London: Routledge, 2004).

22. See Robyn Horner, *Jean-Luc Marion: A Theo-logical Introduction* (Burlington, Vt.: Ashgate, 2005), 3.

23. See, for instance, "Distance et beatitude: Sur le mot capacitas chez Saint Augustin," in *Résurrection* 29 (1968): 58–80; "Ce mystère qui juge celui qui le juge," in *Résurrection* 32 (1969): 54–78; "Penser juste ou trahir le mystère: Notes sur l'elaboration patristique du dogme de l'incarnation," in *Résurrection* 30 (1969): 68–93; "Amour de Dieu, amour des hommes," in *Résurrection* 34 (1970): 89–96; "Distance et louange," in *Résurrection* 38 (1971): 89–118; "Les deux volontés du Christ selon saint Maxime le Confesseur," in *Résurrection* 41 (1972): 48–66.

24. Two strong articles have begun to explore this relationship, but far more remains to be said. See Martin Laird, "Whereof We Speak: Gregory of Nyssa, Jean-Luc Marion and the Current Apophatic Rage," *Heythrop Journal* 42.1 (2001), and Mary-Jane Rubenstein, "Unknow Thyself, Apophaticism, Deconstruction and Theology after Ontology," *Modern Theology* 19.3 (2003). Also, John Panteleimon Manoussakis's recent work, *God After Metaphysics: A Theological Aesthetic* (Bloomington: Indiana University Press, 2007), has some overlap with my study insofar as it is deeply influenced by the thought of Marion and brings the writings of the Fathers into the contemporary conversation. However, Manoussakis does not analyze Marion's interpretation and use of the Fathers, nor is he interested in parsing differences between them.

25. Marion, *Au lieu de soi: L'approche de Saint Augustin* (Paris: Presses Universitaires de France, 2008).

26. See Marion, "Réponses à quelques questions," *Revue de métaphysique et de morale* (1991): 68.

27. See Marion, *Being Given*, 328.

28. See, for instance, Bert Blans, "Cloud of Unknowing: An Orientation in Negative Theology from Dionysius the Areopagite, Eckhart, and John of the Cross to Modernity," in *Flight of the Gods,* 75; Daniel Bulzan, "Apophaticism, Postmodernism and Language: Two Similar Cases of Theological Imbalance," *Scottish Journal of Theology* 50.3 (1997): 284; Luke Ferreter, "How to Avoid Speaking of the Other: Derrida, Dionysius and the Problem of Negative Theology," *Paragraph* 24.1 (2001): 50; Jeffrey Fischer, "The Theology of Dis/similarity: Negation in Pseudo-Dionysius," *Journal of Religion* 81.4 (2001): 530; Kevin Hart, *The Trespass of the Sign: Deconstruction, Theology and Philosophy* (New York: Fordham University Press, 2000), 183; Eric Perl, "Signifying Nothing: Being as Sign in Neoplatonism and Derrida," in *Neoplatonism and Contemporary Thought,* part 2, ed. R. Baine Harris (New York: SUNY Press, 2002).

29. See, for instance, John D. Caputo, *The Prayers and Tears of Jacques Derrida: Religion without Religion* (Bloomington: Indiana University Press, 1997), 1–19; David E. Klemm, "Open Secrets: Derrida and Negative Theology," in *Derrida and Negative Theology,* ed. Robert Scharlemann (Charlottesville:

University Press of Virginia, 1992), 8–22; Mark C. Taylor, *nOTs* (Chicago: Chicago University Press, 1993), 47–49; *idem*, "nO nOt nO," in *Derrida and Negative Theology,* especially, 188–89; Hent de Vries, "The Theology of the Sign and the Sign of Theology: The Apophatics of Deconstruction," in *Flight of the Gods,* especially, 184–94.

To this debate one must, of course, add Derrida's own self-positioning vis-à-vis negative theology. He has two slightly different moments in this debate. Originally, Derrida distanced himself from any "negative theology" that, he argued, ended in "hyperessentiality" or a "being beyond Being." See Derrida, "How to Avoid Speaking: Denials," in *Derrida and Negative Theology,* ed. Harold Coward and Toby Foshay (Albany: SUNY Press, 1992), 77. A later essay modifies his stance slightly to speak of saving negative theology (from itself) by universalizing it rather than overcoming it. See *"Sauf le nom,"* in *On the Name,* ed. Thomas Dutoit (Stanford, Calif.: Stanford University Press, 1995), 47.

30. See Marion, "The Unspoken: Apophasis and the Discourse of Love," trans. Arianne Conty, *Proceedings of the American Catholic Philosophical Association 76* (2002): 39–56.

31. G. W. H. Lampe, *A Patristic-Greek Lexicon* (Oxford: Clarendon Press, 1961). Ivana Noble expresses this even more paradoxically: *apophasis* "has two basic meanings, namely 'revelation' and 'negation'" (323). See Noble, "The Apophatic Way in Gregory of Nyssa," in *Philosophical Hermeneutics and Biblical Exegesis,* ed. Petr Pokorny and Jan Roskovec (Tübingen: Mohr Siebeck, 2002), 323–39. In this article Noble argues that Gregory's "apophatic way" is not merely a question of epistemic negation but a recognition that both positive and negative language are inadequate: "[T]he apophatic approach is a safeguard against any temptation to think that God can be defined by any system, be it positive or negative" but advocates instead a plurality of discourses to signal the incomprehensibility of God (326).

32. More on the possibly controversial application of this term to Marion's corpus in chapter 5 below.

33. See Thomas A. Carlson's introduction to *The Idol and Distance: Five Studies,* trans. Thomas A. Carlson (New York: Fordham University Press, 2001): "Such a critique on the subject, in both the theological and the phenomenological registers, is carried out primarily in terms of some overwhelming or inconceivable 'gift' or 'givenness' whose presence can be excessive to the point of appearing as absence" (xii). Original publication: *L'Idole et la distance* (Paris: Éditions Bernard Grasset, 1977).

34. See Martin Heidegger, "Introduction to 'What Is Metaphysics?'" in *Pathmarks,* ed. William McNeill (Cambridge: Cambridge University Press, 1998), 279.

35. Ibid., 281.

36. Martin Heidegger, "The Onto-Theo-Logical Constitution of Metaphysics," in *Identity and Difference,* trans. Joan Stambauch (Chicago: University of Chicago Press, 2002), 58.

37. Ibid., 62. See also George Kovacs, *The Question of God in Heidegger's Phenomenology* (Evanston, Ill.: Northwestern University Press, 1990), 126.

38. See Marion, "Thomas Aquinas and Onto-theology," trans. B. Gendreau, R. Rethy, and M. Sweeney, in *Mystics: Presence and Aporia*, ed. Michael Kessler and Christian Sheppard (Chicago: University of Chicago Press, 2003), 43.

39. Marion, *God Without Being*, trans. Thomas A. Carlson (Chicago: Chicago University Press, 1991), 34; original publication, *Dieu sans l'être: Hors-texte* (Paris: Fayard, 1982).

40. Ibid., 37.

41. With this second characteristic, Marion argues that Heidegger, too, falls prey to the very metaphysics he sought to overcome: *Dasein* is just as much a subjective starting point as is Husserl's "transcendental ego," and of course it is Heidegger who preeminently privileges the question of Being.

42. See Horner's introduction to Marion, *In Excess*, xiii.

43. See *The Idol and Distance*, 15, 35; *God Without Being*, 34–42; *Being Given*, 4; *In Excess*, 128; *On Descartes' Metaphysical Prism*, 2–4; "Thomas Aquinas and Onto-theology," 39–43; and especially, "Metaphysics and Phenomenology: A Summary for Theologians," in *The Postmodern God*, ed. Graham Ward (Oxford: Blackwell, 1997), 280–83.

44. Denys Turner, "Atheism, Apophaticism, and 'Différance'," in *Theology and Conversation: Towards a Relational Theology*, ed. J. Haers and P. De Mey (Leuven: Leuven University Press, 2003), 692.

45. See Martin Laird, "'Whereof We Speak'," 1.

1. Sightings

1. Marion refuses to apply the modifier "pseudo" to Dionysius, interpreting Dionysius' pseudonymity differently: "This is obviously a religious name: Denys does not pretend *to be* the convert of Saint Paul (Acts 17:34) but assumes the name as that of a role model and patron saint. Otherwise, why would he confess his spiritual father to be not Saint Paul but 'the divine Hierotheus' . . . ? It takes some naivety to imagine Denys and his ancient readers more naive and ignorant of monastic practices than we have become" (*In Excess*, 134 n. 12).

2. Marion clearly includes Dionysius within his canon of "orthodox" Christian writers, although Dionysius' position within this canon has been disputed, especially within the traditions of Eastern Christianity.

3. Amongst the works that I will not be discussing in this chapter are the following: *Sur la théologie blanche de Descartes* (Paris: Presses Universitaires de France, 1981) cites Gregory of Nyssa once, Dionysius 14 times, and Augustine, 22. *On Descartes' Metaphysical Prism: The Constitution and the Limits of Onto-theo-logy in Cartesian Thought*, trans. Jeffrey L. Kosky (Chicago: University of Chicago Press, 1999) cites Augustine 4 times, Dionysius 4 times, and John

Damascene once. *Cartesian Questions: Method and Metaphysics* (Chicago: University of Chicago Press, 1999) cites Augustine 8 times, Dionysius 2 times, Nazianzen 3 times, and Gregory of Nyssa 2 times. *Reduction and Givenness: Investigations of Husserl, Heidegger and Phenomenology,* trans. Thomas A. Carlson (Evanston, Ill.: Northwestern University Press, 1998) cites Augustine once. *The Crossing of the Visible,* trans. James K. A. Smith (Stanford, Calif.: Stanford University Press, 2004) references the Second Council of Nicaea, John of Damascus, and Theodore the Studite within the context of a defense of icons.

4. As we shall see, concurrent to this positive appraisal, "heretics" in Marion's writing (most especially, Eunomius) function as representatives of various dangers in thinking, both past and present.

5. "God and the Gift: A Continental Perspective," in *God's Advocates: Christian Thinkers in Conversation,* ed. Rupert Shortt (Grand Rapids, Mich.: Eerdmans, 2005), 150.

6. Ward, "Between Postmodernism and Postmodernity." Here Ward is drawing on a theoretical category of the French sociologist Pierre Bourdieu. See Bourdieu, *Homo Academicus,* trans. Peter Collier (Cambridge: Polity Press, 1988).

7. Ward states this negatively in "Between Postmodernism and Postmodernity," 190: "Marion is a Roman Catholic influenced by the anti-liberal and Neopatristic theology of Daniélou, du Lubac and von Balthasar."

8. Ibid., 191.

9. Marion, *The Idol and Distance: Five Studies,* trans. Thomas A. Carlson (New York: Fordham University Press, 2001), 22. Hereafter cited as *ID.*

10. This is not to say Marion was not influenced by his theological teachers; however, for the most part this must be argued rather than simply indicated since he rarely cites any secondary sources on the Fathers—with the one important exception of Balthasar, whose writings are referenced throughout his articles.

11. Marion, "Presence et distance: Remarque sur l'implication reciproque de la contemplation eucharistique et de la presence reelle," *Revue Résurrection* 43–44 (1974): 31–58.

12. Marion, "Le splendeur de la contemplation eucharistique," *Revue Résurrection* 31 (1969): 84–88.

13. Louis Bouyer, a convert to Catholicism and fierce critic of the liturgical reforms begun by Pius XII, was asked by Maxime Charles (the rector of Sacre-Coeur, Montmartre) to form a study group with some of the more promising graduate students of Ecole Normale Supérieure among whom were Remi Barque and Marion. This group called itself "Résurrection," and their discussions and writing formed the nucleus of the journal that would become the French edition of *Communio,* i.e., *Revue Résurrection.* See Bouyer's obituary notice at http://nouvelletheologie.blogspot.com/2005/09/obituary-for-louis-bouyer/913-2004.by .html.

14. Marion, "Ce mystère qui Juge celui qui le juge," *Résurrection* 32 (1969): 54.

15. See Marion, *Being Given: Toward a Phenomenology of Givenness,* trans. Jeffrey L. Kosky (Stanford, Calif.: Stanford University Press, 2002), 367 n. 90.

16. Marion, "Ce mystère qui Juge celui qui le juge," 68–69 n. 20.

17. See Marion, "Penser juste ou trahir le mystère," *Résurrection* 30 (1969): 12. We shall see another example of this in his use of Eunomius as a foil against a "Dionysian-Nyssen" view of language in *In Excess*.

18. Marion, "Distance et louange," *Résurrection* 38 (1971): 117.

19. Ibid., 104–105 and n. 57.

20. Marion, *Being Given*, x.

21. Indeed, *Sur la théologie blanche de Descartes* is the only book published between these two works.

22. By his own admission, Marion was dissatisfied with the scope of this response; according to him, a "nonmetaphysical method of philosophy," i.e., a "phenomenology thoroughly secured" was needed to complete the response (*Being Given*, x). According to Marion, theology was insufficient, not because it could not respond, but because the initial critique was directed foremost at philosophy, or more properly, metaphysics. Theology, only insofar as it bound itself to metaphysics, became suspect. Outside of that, theology has no part—in either the critique or the need of defense. In this evaluation, theology is understood by Marion as essentially rooted in its apophatic mode.

23. *ID*, 21.This work is also significant insofar as it marks one of the first engagements with Derrida over the question of the nature of 'negative theology' as it is envisioned by Dionysius, although this is not the central conversation Marion is having in the book. See *ID*, 229.

24. See Horner, *Jean-Luc Marion: A Theo-logical Introduction*, 51–60, for an excellent discussion of the various permutations of this term in Marion's thought.

25. *ID*, 91.

26. Marion goes on to say here: "There is nothing more suitable, then, to honor Hölderlin and that god of whom Nietzsche suggests that he wants to be praised, than to meditate on the *Divine Names* and *Mystical Theology*" (*ID*, 138).

27. *ID*, 139.

28. *ID*, 140, citing Dionysius, *DN* 7. 2, PG 3, 868a. This has a further consequence of significance: "As a censure and as a condition, distance requires one to think the doubly unthinkable according to excess (supremacy over beings in general) and according to lack (withdrawal as insistence, without being)" (ibid).

29. *ID*, 145. Marion argues convincingly that the "and also" [τε καί] (found in *DN* 7.3. 872a; *DN* 2.4. 641a; and *MT* 1.2. 1000b: "beyond all negation and affirmation") is the linguistic marker for Dionysius' attempt to "contradict the categoric antinomy of the true and the false in order to reach, without saying it or being able to say it, the (un)speakable that exceeds the very opposition between speakable and unspeakable" (*ID*, 149 n. 18).

30. *ID*, 147.

31. Thus, one cannot simply oppose affirmation with negation to avoid idols: "The closure of discourse and the reference to a supreme being come together on this point, which distance rejects: to treat God as an object (attainable or not)" (*ID*, 140).

32. *ID*, 141.

33. See *ID*, 142: "The Name appears as gift, where, in that same gesture, the unthinkable gives us a name as that in which it gives itself, but also as a gift that gives the unthinkable, which only withdraws in the distance of the gift. The name therefore delivers the unthinkable, as the unthinkable that *gives* itself." However, as I shall argue in chapter 3, in the Dionysian corpus this is not simply a gift of revelation but is also a gift of being—not simply of epistemological import but also ontological. I will uncover Marion's uneasy relationship with these implications later.

34. I am following Thomas Carlson's translation of Marion's *Requisit* (for αἰτία) as "Requisite" and *requérant* (for αἰτιάτα) as "requestant."

35. *ID*, 151 n. 21.

36. This is the straightforward definition in both classical and patristic Greek. See both Henry George Liddell and Robert Scott, *A Greek-English Lexicon* (Oxford: Clarendon Press, 1968), and G. W. H. Lampe, *A Patristic-Greek Lexicon* (Oxford: Clarendon Press, 1961).

37. *ID*, 161.

38. *ID*, 161 n. 43.

39. *ID*, 151. See *DN* 1.1. 588b: "ὑπερλάμποντα. . . ."

40. *ID*, 151: "*MT* 4. 1040d; *Ep.* 5. 1076a; *MT* 5. 1048b; and *DN* 1.5. 593c.

41. *ID*, 152, citing Maximus the Confessor, *Scholia on the Divine Names*, 5.8 PG 4. 328a.

42. *ID*, 162.

43. Regardless of where one is situated in the perennial debate concerning Dionysius' Christian, Neoplatonic, or Christian-Neoplatonic identity, his strong engagement with the thought of Iamblichus is apparent and widely acknowledged.

44. *ID*, 162.

45. Αἰτία (in its various declensions) occurs 109 times in the corpus, 82 of which are in *DN*.

46. Some of the clearest citations to illustrate the anti-idolatrous thrust of Marion's argument do not come from Dionysius (although they are dropped into an exposition of him). For example, the following statement cites the Fourth Lateran Council and not Dionysius: "[B]etween the creature and the creator can be seen no resemblance so great that there would not also have to be seen between them a greater difference" (cited in *ID*, 152). This gives us a glimpse of the way Dionysius is beginning to function as shorthand for Marion's entire anti-idolatry enterprise, especially in the identification of a non-predicative discourse of praise.

47. *ID*, 162.

48. Interestingly, Marion concedes, nevertheless, that this crude interpretation is only too often "transpose(d) . . . uncritically and without precaution to the ecclesiastic and therefore spiritual aspects of divinization" (*ID*, 164).

49. τελείωσις is defined by Liddell and Scott as "a becoming perfect, completion, accomplishment, consummation." Marion's translation is actually

more literal here than that of Luibheid or Parker, who translate this as "perfection," a translation that would more appropriately render τελειότης.

50. Dionysius, *CH* 3.2. 165a and b, cited in *ID*, 164.

51. *ID*, 164–65. Marion credits Louis Bouyer's *L'Eglise de Dieu* (Paris: Cerf, 1970), 317, for this interpretation of "hierarchy." Bouyer, as stated above, was one of Marion's teachers—a conservative Catholic convert who wrote on the rite of Eucharist and liturgy. In this work he is highly critical of the liturgical reforms of Vatican II. This backdrop of an ecclesial and liturgical debate offers an interesting subtext on Marion's argument here, particularly in light of his controversial comments in *God Without Being* concerning the bishop as "the only true theologian."

52. *ID*, 165.

53. One could problematize Marion's caricature of Plotinian metaphysics. Here again we can see how Marion is less interested in parsing different emphases than in establishing an "orthodox" position of the Christian *kerygma* over against any "heretical" variants.

54. *ID*, 165. The seeds of Marion's later work on the gift are already here apparent.

55. *ID*,166.

56. *ID*,167.

57. Ibid.

58. For a clear discussion of the complicated relationship between Neoplatonism and Dionysius regarding emanation and the hierarchies, see Andrew Louth, *Denys the Areopagite* (New York: Continuum, 1989), 81–87. Louth argues that there are "levels of being," yet distinguishes Dionysius from Neoplatonic ontology insofar as all creation receives being *directly* from God; that is, "being" is not mediated through the "levels of being."

59. According to Marion, it is the Logos who first delivers the *logia* (Scripture), and this becomes the standard of all our praise (*ID*, 181). Thus praise is imitative of an original gift rather than generating within the human mind.

60. *ID*, 184. Marion cites several Dionysian passages in support of this argument: *DN*, 593c–d; 596a–c; 637b; 641d; 701c; 709b; 713c; 816c; 820c; 842b; 868a; 872a; 909b; 969a, c; and *MT* 1025a. He notes the following passage, especially: "We must recall that this discourse does not aim to bring to light (ἐκφαίνειν) the superessential essence inasmuch as superessential (for it remains unspeakable, unknowable, and hence, totally impossible to bring to light, withdrawing from all union), but much rather to praise the procession that makes essences and that comes to all beings from the [trinitarian] Thearchy, the principle of essences (*DN*, V, 1, 816b)."

61. *ID*, 186.

62. *ID*, 189.

63. *ID*, 193. Marion will go on to develop this idea outside of "theology" in *Reduction and Givenness*.

64. See *ID*, xiv, xv, xxxvi–xxxviii, 22, 89, 142, 155, 157, 158, 184, 245, and 249.

65. See *ID* xxxviii: "To H. Urs von Balthasar my approach owes much, save the weaknesses in its implementation; the proportions of what is involved here nevertheless forbid me from transforming a dependency into an affiliation."

66. *ID*, 155 n. 32. See Tamsin Jones, "Dionysius in Hans Urs von Balthasar and Jean-Luc Marion," in *Re-Thinking Dionysius the Areopagite*, ed. Sarah Coakley and Charles M. Stang (Oxford: Wiley-Blackwell, 2009).

67. See Horner, *A Theo-logical Introduction*, 51–53.

68. See Hans Urs von Balthasar, *Presence and Thought: An Essay on the Religious Philosophy of Gregory of Nyssa*, trans. Marc Sebanc (San Francisco: Ignatius Press, 1995), 27.

69. Gregory of Nyssa, *v. Mos.* 2.165 (PG 44. 337b).

70. See *ID*, 198: Marion does not cite the source in Gregory.

71. *God Without Being*, trans. Thomas A. Carlson (Chicago: University of Chicago Press, 1991), xxiv. Hereafter *GWB*.

72. See, for instance, *GWB*, 106: "We are in the process of discovering, as much through Denys the Mystic as through Nietzsche, that it is not self-evident that an *ousia* or that a concept should be able to determine in what way this might be Gød. It remains to be glimpsed, if not with Heidegger, at least in reading him, and, if really necessary, against him, that Gød does not depend on [*relève de*] Being/being, and even that Being/being depends on distance."

73. *GWB*, 34.

74. *GWB*, 35.

75. Ibid., citing Heidegger.

76. *GWB*, 36. Given this Heideggerian critique of positing God as cause/ highest cause/*causa sui*, it is apparent just how high the stakes are for Marion to reconfigure "*aitia*" in Dionysius.

77. As I mentioned in the introduction, Marion has since revised this somewhat flat appraisal of Thomas Aquinas in the face of a host of criticisms. See "Saint Thomas d'Aquin et onto-théo-logie," *Revue Thomiste* 95 (1995). Interestingly, this article also appears as a sort of postscript in the second French edition of *Dieu sans l'être* (Paris: Presses Universitaires de France, 2002).

78. *GWB*, xxiii.

79. *GWB*, 78.

80. *GWB*, 74–75.

81. *GWB*, 76.

82. *GWB*, 155.

83. *GWB*, 225 n. 13.

84. See *GWB*, 29: ". . . the concept on its part can take up again the essential characteristics of the 'aesthetic' idol: because it apprehends the divine on the basis of *Dasein*, it measures the divine as a function of it."

85. *GWB*, 203 n. 4.

86. *GWB*, 221–22 n. 19.

87. *GWB*, 173–74, and in *Dieu sans l'être*, 245–47.

88. *GWB*, 174–75.

89. *GWB*, 173–74.

90. *GWB*, 174.

91. John Caputo, ed., *God, the Gift, and Postmodernism* (Bloomington: Indiana University Press, 1999).

92. This was then translated into English as "In the Name: How to Avoid Speaking of It," in *In Excess: Studies of Saturated Phenomenon*.

93. "In the Name," 134.

94. This critique is found primarily in Derrida's essay "How to Avoid Speaking: Denials" ("*Comment ne pas parler: Dénégations*") in *Derrida and Negative Theology*, ed. Harold Coward and Toby Foshay (SUNY Press, 1992). This article represents Derrida's most direct disavowal of any methodological (or teleological) relation between deconstruction and "negative theology," which he hypothetically defines as that which "consists of considering that every predicative language is inadequate to the essence, in truth to the hyperessentiality (the being beyond Being) of God" (74).

95. See Derrida, "How to Avoid Speaking: Denials," 76: "Every time I say: x is neither this nor that, neither the contrary of this nor of that, neither the simple neutralization of this nor of that with which it *has nothing in common*, being absolutely heterogeneous to or incommensurable with them, I would start to speak of God, under this name of another."

96. "In the Name," 132.

97. See "How to Avoid Speaking: Denials," 77: " 'Negative theology' seems to reserve, beyond all positive predication, beyond all negation, even beyond Being, some hyperessentiality, a being beyond Being."

98. Ibid.

99. Ibid., 88.

100. Ibid., 93. Furthermore, Dionysius himself is a member of the secret society: "Like all the initiated, he must purify himself, step aside from the impure, separate himself from the many, join 'the elite of the priests' " (91).

101. "In the Name," 128.

102. This is an important admission. Marion acknowledges ways of thinking "metaphysically" that fall prey to the critiques of neither Heidegger nor Derrida.

103. Derrida, Marion argues, likes maintaining the duality between positive and negative because, by keeping the two in a false binary, it allows him to object that negative theology actually re-establishes, hyperbolically, affirmation ("In the Name," 137).

104. "In the Name," 139–40. Marion provides three important quotations from Dionysius (*DN* 7.3. 869d–872a; *MT* 1.2. 1000b; *MT* 5.1004b), showing that there are not two terms but three. He also argues that even those who follow Dionysius less well in other respects (such as Thomas Aquinas) follow him in this tripartite division—though the latter will, according to Marion, invert Dionysius' order by starting with negative, moving to positive, and finally going to eminence; whereas Dionysius, he says, goes from affirmation, to negation, to negation of the negation in praise.

105. Marion refers to this previous work as an excuse for not justifying his somewhat quixotic translation further: "I will not go back over this translation or the interpretation of this concept, which have not been contested" ("In the Name," 139 n. 23). I have begun to contest this translation and will do so more forcibly in chapter 3.

106. Ibid., 140.

107. Ibid.

108. Ibid., 142.

109. Ibid.

110. Ibid., 143.

111. Ibid.

112. Ibid.

113. Ibid.

114. Ibid., 150–52.

115. Ibid., 152.

116. Ibid., 153–54.

117. Ibid., 155.

118. See ibid., 139–40.

119. Gregory of Nyssa, *v. Mos.* 2.163 (PG 44, 377).

120. See *De Surcroît,* 182: "*Car c'est en cela que se trouve la vraie connaisance de ce qu'on cherche (sc. voir le Dieu invisible et incomprehensible—* ἀκατάληπτὸν), *en ceci que le voir se trouve dans le non-voir* (τὸ ἰδεῖν ἐν τῷ μή ἰδεῖν), *parce que ce que l'on recherche surpasse toute connaissance, comme enveloppé de toute part par une nuée d'incompréhensibilité.*"

121. See *La Vie de MoVse,* Sources chrétiennes, n. 1 *bis,* ed. J. Daniélou (Paris: Les Éditions du Cerf, 1968), 211–13: "*. . . parce que celui qu'il cherche transcende toute connaissance, séparé de toute part par son incompréhensibilité comme par une ténèbre.*"

122. *The Life of Moses* (New York: Paulist Press, 1978).

123. "In the Name," 156.

124. Ibid.

125. Ibid., 157.

126. Ibid.

127. Marion, *Au lieu de soi: L'approche de Saint Augustin* (Paris: Presses Universitaires de France, 2008), 383–84. Here and throughout my discussion of this book, I am relying on my own translation.

128. Joeri Schrijvers, "In (the) Place of the Self: A Critical Study of Jean-Luc Marion's 'Au lieu de soi: L'approche de Saint Augustin,'" in *Modern Theology* 25.4 (2009): 666.

129. *Au lieu de soi,* 37.

130. Ibid., 159.

131. Ibid., 158.

132. Ibid., 179.

133. Ibid., 217.

134. Ibid., 163.

135. Ibid., 255.

136. Schrijvers sharply captures the decision made by Marion in this work. No longer to be accused of producing a "covert theology," Marion here plays his cards plainly: "[Y]es, givenness can be linked to creation, and yes, the gift is not all too different from grace, and surely 'love could risk' (*Being Given*, p. 101) to identify the giver in/of givenness" ("In (the) Place of Self," 679–80).

137. *ID*, 22.

2. How to Avoid Idolatry

For the first epigraph, from Gregory of Nyssa, *V. Mos.* 2.239, I am using the *Classics of Western Spirituality* translation by Abraham J. Malherbe and Everett Ferguson in *The Life of Moses* (New York: Paulist Press, 1978), 116. Hereafter, if I use this translation the page number will be found in parentheses after the classical designation: e.g., *V. Mos.* 2.239 (116).

For the second epigraph, from Dionysius the Areopagite, *DN* 3.3, I am using the *Classics of Western Spirituality* translation by Colm Luibheid in *Pseudo Dionysius: The Complete Works* (New York: Paulist Press, 1987). Hereafter, if I use this translation the page number will be found in parentheses after the classical designation.

The third epigraph is from Hans Urs von Balthasar, "Denys," in *Glory of the Lord: Theological Aesthetics*, vol. 2, *Studies in Theological Styles: Clerical Styles*, trans. Andrew Louth, Francis McDonagh, and Brian McNeil C.R.V., ed. John Riches (San Francisco: Ignatius Press, 1984), 171. Hereafter "Denys."

1. See Alexander Golitzin, *Et Introibo ad Altare Dei: The Mystagogy of Dionysius Areopagita, with special reference to its predecessors in the Eastern Christian Tradition*, Analecta Vlatadon 59 (Thessaloniki: Alexander Golitzin, 1994), 287. Hereafter, *Et Introibo*.

2. This undertaking does not constitute a comprehensive comparative analysis of Gregory and Dionysius, although such a comparison is long overdue.

3. Thus, the chapter will follow more of a thematic comparison than a genealogical one. The latter is a worthy task that, hopefully, someone will soon accomplish. However, the argument of this study does not require such genealogical work, nor does space allow for it. Therefore, in this chapter, I do not assume that Dionysius "read" Gregory. Some of the commentators I discuss will assume this (whether or not they make it part of their explicit argument), especially those who are attempting to "rescue" Dionysius from the smear of "pseudonymity" and reclaim him in line with an "orthodox" Christian tradition. Such an assumption is complicated by the fact that Gregory in all probability read Plotinus and certainly read Iamblichus—both of whom are likely influences on Dionysius. Ascertaining whether Dionysius was directly influenced by Gregory or

whether similarities cannot be just as adequately explained by the fact that both read and were influenced by the same Neoplatonic texts seems an impossibly uncertain decision (which is not to ignore the confessional impetus for figuring out such genealogies).

4. For this reason also, contemporary readers of Dionysius often neglect the ontological implications of his apophaticism.

5. Andrew Louth, *The Origins of the Christian Mystical Tradition: From Plato to Denys* (Oxford: Clarendon Press, 1981); Bernard McGinn, *The Foundations of Mysticism* (New York: Crossroads, 1991); J. P. Williams, *Denying Divinity: Apophasis in the Patristic Christian and Soto Zen Buddhist Traditions* (Oxford: Oxford University Press, 2000); Dierdre Carabine, *The Unknown God. Negative Theology in the Platonic Tradition: Plato to Eriugena* (Louvain: Peeters Press, 1995).

6. Golitzin, *Et Introibo.*

7. Balthasar, "Denys."

8. Jeffrey Fisher, "The Theology of Dis/similarity: Negation in Pseudo-Dionysius," *Journal of Religion* 81.4 (2001).

9. Henri-Charles Puech, "La Ténèbre mystique chez le Pseudo-Denys l'Aréopagite et dans la tradition patristique" in *En Quête de la Gnose: La Gnose et le temps et autres essais* (Paris: Gallimard, 1978).

10. Kevin Corrigan, "'Solitary' Mysticism in Plotinus, Proclus, Gregory of Nyssa, and Pseudo-Dionysius," *Journal of Religion* 76.1 (1996). While one might have sympathy with his project of complicating a too-neat division between Christian and "pagan" mysticism, Corrigan does employ some spurious interpretations of the "Christian" side of this equation. For example, he takes Dionysius' discussion of the monastic state as a statement of the definitive ideal of the religious life. Although this fits with Corrigan's thesis about "solitude," it requires taking the monastic vision entirely out of the liturgical context within which it is found in the *Ecclesiastical Hierarchies.*

11. Golitzin attempts to show that Dionysius is indebted to Gregory not only for his depiction of the ascent of the soul as eternal, his emphasis on divine incomprehensibility, a particular conception of theological language, and the paradoxical relation between God's transcendence and immanence but also for his basic trinitarian and christological doctrines. Some of these arguments for Dionysian precedence stand up better than others. At times, however, he takes the similarity one step too far. See, for instance, *Et Introibo*, 312, 315, 290–92.

12. According to Louth, Dionysius went "beyond Gregory of Nyssa, to whom otherwise he had been so close" insofar as he will speak of the soul's proper ecstasy. Dionysius speaks of the soul's ecstasy, however, only because he first spoke of God's ecstasy in *DN* IV. 13. In this way the "soul in ecstasy meets God's ecstatic love for herself" (175, 176). Louth claims that, for Gregory, there is no ecstatic moment where the soul unites with God: "The gulf between uncreated and created is such for Gregory that there is no possibility of the soul passing across it: there is no ecstasy, in which the soul leaves its nature as created and passes into the uncreated" (81).

13. For instance, Fisher's explicit statement of his aim, to show that "Dionysius engages in an apophaticism of the most radical kind, that it is radical in a quite particular semiotic fashion, and . . . that Dionysian negative theology is significantly compatible with certain aspects of Derridean deconstruction" ("Theology of Dis/similarity," 530), already tells us much about his project: first, the switch to the terminology of "negative theology" rather than *apophasis* or mystical theology places him already in a circle of contemporary writers interested in Dionysius especially insofar as he is helpful in articulating a postmodern, deconstructive mode of theology. Secondly, in line with the first, he want to show that Dionysius and Derrida have much in common. Thirdly, there will be a strong emphasis on a "semiotic" reading of Dionysius.

Interestingly, both Fisher and Williams apply some statements to Dionysius that seem to apply at least equally, if not preeminently, to Gregory's writing. See, for instance, Fisher, "Theology of Dis/similarity," 548, and Williams, *Denying Divinity,* 91. In the latter, Williams makes a curious and illuminating choice of language. She argues that Dionysian apophasis is "an infinitely recursive process, an intrinsically *epectasic* commitment to recognize the theological deficiency of all the forms under which God is worshipped, to go beyond them in search for union with the transcendent God." This use of a term, which is only constructed in the twentieth century and then only applied directly to Gregory of Nyssa, is a sleight of hand that Williams only partially acknowledges in a footnote. Here she admits that Dionysius does not actually use the term *epectasis* but she still argues that this does not mean that he does not share Gregory's view. Williams points to some passages (*CH* 180A, 193B; *EH* 401C) that seem to speak of a ceaseless ascent. Yet it is not convincing when one is trying to show the radicality of one writer (Dionysius) over another (Gregory) to use a term and idea found primarily in the latter! Furthermore, it does not equally treat the vision of perfection within Dionysius' hierarchical understanding of the cosmos—a fact that Williams eventually admits (92).

14. See, for instance, Puech, "La Ténèbre mystique," 141.

15. See Balthasar, "Denys," 165: "The more deeply our wonder experiences the unmanifest God, and does not simply know him (*ou monon mathon alla pathon ta theia,* DN II.9), the more the aesthetic relationship is transcended, the more it is possible to discern in the manifestation *what* is really manifest, the more the truth of the aesthetic emerges. *This relationship between negation and affirmation was laid down by Plato and determined the mysticism of Plotinus and Proclus as also of Gregory of Nyssa and Augustine;* but only with Denys did it receive its balancing counterpoise: in that the tremendous ascending movement of negation, often rising to a pitch of sheer frenzy, which sets the apophatic (rejection of names) over the cataphatic (affirmation of names), is kindled only—and ever more brightly—by God's movement of descent as he imparts himself in manifestations" (emphasis added).

16. Ibid., 171.

17. Ibid.

18. Ibid., 194.

19. Ibid.

20. Indeed, the extent to which Dionysius echoes (in *Mystical Theology* 1.3) Gregory's description of the ascent is one of the pieces of evidence that scholars point to if they are interested in showing a reliance of Dionysius on the fourth-century Cappadocian bishop.

21. Dionysius, *MT* 1.3. 1001A.

22. Gregory of Nyssa, *v. Mos.* 2.163, line 9, 6.

23. For instance, in *DN* 7. 2 (107), Dionysius writes, "We posit intangible and invisible darkness of that Light which is unapproachable because it so far exceeds the visible light."

24. Gregory uses this word rarely, but it has become the standard term for describing this movement. I will follow Daniélou's usage while noting that it involves an overly systematic classification of Gregory's thought into the modern categories of "philosophical" versus "mystical" texts.

25. *V. Mos.*, 2.225, line 5.

26. As we shall see later, this statement must be qualified; there is a movement "toward," but it is not one that lessens the gap between the desiring person and the Beloved.

27. Moses signifies this moment by removing his sandals before ascending Mt. Sinai. See *v. Mos.*, 2.22 (59).

28. *V. Mos.*, 2.162–69 (94–97).

29. *V. Mos.*, 2.233 (115).

30. *V. Mos.*, 2.243–44. Golitzin paraphrases Gregory's *epectasis* thus: "our repose is the journey itself" (*Et Introibo*, 306).

31. *MT* 1.1 (135). The phrase that Luibheid renders as "brilliant light" (ὑπέρφωτων γνόφον) is literally closer to "the darkness beyond light."

32. *MT* 1.1 (135).

33. *MT* 1.3 (136, 137).

34. *V. Mos.*, 2.162 (95).

35. See Balthasar, *Presence and Thought*, 94: "This is perhaps the first time a Greek thinker considered the incomprehensibility of a thing not only as a sign of its remoteness from us but as a perfection of the thing itself."

36. *V. Mos.*, 2.163 (95).

37. *V. Mos.*, 2.165 (95–96).

38. Lampe's *Patristic-Greek Lexicon* defines κατ' ἐπίνοιαν as, most basically, a "thought, or conception." He notes that both Gregory and Basil of Caesarea use it to denote a "reflection on a concept already formed, opposed to direct conception or perception." For Eunomius the term clearly refers to an idea or concept based solely on human invention and is for that reason "fanciful." See Eunomius' *Apology for the Apology*, in *Eunomius: The Extant Works*, ed. R. P. Vaggione (Oxford: Clarendon Press, 1987). See also G. C. Stead, "Logic and the Application of Names to God" in *El 'Contra Eunomium I' en la Produccion Literaria de Gregorio de Nisa*, VI Coloquio Internacional sobre Gregorio de Nisa (Pamplona:

Ediciones Universidad de Navarra, 1988), 303–20; Theo Kobusch, "Die Epinoia— Das menschliche Bewusstsein in der antiken Philosophie," in *Gregory of Nyssa: Contra Eunomium II. An English Version with Supporting Studies. Proceedings of the 10th International Colloquium on Gregory of Nyssa (Olumouc, September 15-18, 2004),* ed. Lenka Karfíková, Scot Douglass, and Johannes Zachhuber (Leiden: Brill, 2007), 3–20. Hereafter *Contra Eunomium II.*

39. As Brooks Otis comments: "The logic of Aetius and Eunomius seems to us now almost puerile in its verbalism, yet it had the effect of awakening the Greek Christian world to the whole problem of the knowledge of God and the nature of God." See Otis, "Nicene Orthodoxy and Fourth-Century Mysticism," in *Actes du XIIe Congrès International des Etudes Byzantines. Ochride 10–16 Septembre 1961.* Vol. 2 (Beograd: n.p., 1964), 480.

40. Scot Douglass, "A Critical Analysis of Gregory's Philosophy of Language: The Linguistic Reconstitution of Metadiastemic Intrusions," in *Gregory of Nyssa: Homilies on the Beatitudes: An English Version with Commentary and Supporting Studies, Proceedings of the Eighth International Colloquium on Gregory of Nyssa,* ed. Hubertus R. Drobner and Alberto Viciano (Leiden: Brill, 2000), 449.

41. Gregory's dynamic view of the interpretation of scripture will be treated at greater length in chapter 4.

42. Douglass, "Critical Analysis of Gregory's Philosophy of Language," 451. See also his monograph, *Theology of the Gap: Cappadocian Language Theory and the Trinitarian Controversy* (New York: Peter Lang, 2005), which expands on many of the themes in this article.

43. Douglass, "Critical Analysis of Gregory's Philosophy of Language," 449. Again, we observe the impossibility of separating an analysis of Gregory's philosophy of language from his cosmology.

44. Gregory of Nyssa, *C. Eun.* 3.1. (104–105), in *Gregorii Nysseni Opera* (hereafter GNO), vol. 2, ed. W. Jaeger.

45. *DN* 1.5–1.6 (54). In the preface of *Pseudo-Dionysius: The Complete Works,* Paul Rorem sums up the brilliance of his system thus: "Whatever the origin of these names—biblical or philosophical—all are related to the same method, to a double and apparently contradictory axiom that the whole creation reveals God (Rom 1:20), while on the contrary, no one has ever seen God (Ex 33:20; Jn 1:18; 1 Jn 4:12). Hence, God will receive many names, an infinity of names ('polyonomous,' 'apeironomos'); or, on the contrary, he will remain without a name, above every name ('anonomos,' 'hyperonomos')," (6).

46. *DN* 5.1 (96).

47. *MT* 1.2 (136). See also *MT* 5 (41): "There is no speaking of it, nor name or knowledge of it. Darkness and light, error and truth—it is no one of these. *It is beyond assertion and denial.* We make assertions and denials of what is next to it, but never of it, for it is both beyond every assertion, *being the perfect and unique cause of all things,* and, by virtue of its preeminently simple and absolute nature, free of every limitation, beyond every limitation; it is also beyond every

denial" (emphasis added). Note, the closest thing to a predication of God is "Cause."

48. *MT* 3 (139).

49. *MT* 3 (140).

50. Gregory manifests a very different understanding of language from Dionysius' careful weighing and ordering of different levels of adequacy and proximities of words to the God they signify when he levels all language as equally inadequate: "But if we name such a God [i.e., the 'Only Begotten God'] 'tabernacle,' the person who loves Christ should not be disturbed at all on the grounds that the suggestion involved in the phrase diminishes the magnificence of God. For neither is any other name worthy of the nature thus signified, *but all names have equally fallen short of accurate description, both those recognised as insignificant as well as those by which some great insight is indicated*" (*v. Mos.,* 2.176 [99]).

51. *DN* 2.7 (64). It is interesting to note here that Dionysius refers to God most often as "Cause" (αἰτία) rather than God, Good, One, or any other terms one might expect. See also *CH* 4.1 (156); 13.3 (178). We have already discussed Marion's translation of this term in chapter 1, but it will be further problematized in chapter 3.

52. Gregory, *In Eccles.* 7.1.729 C: "'Diastema' is nothing other than creation," or, "Creation is nothing other than 'diastema.'"

53. See D. L. Balás, "Eternity and Time in Gregory of Nyssa's Contra Eunomium," in *Gregor von Nyssa und die Philosophie*, ed. H. Dörrie, M. Altenburger, U. Schramm (Leiden: Brill, 1976), 128–55; A. A. Mosshammer, "Disclosing but Not Disclosed: Gregory of Nyssa as Deconstructionist," in *Studien zu Gregor von Nyssa und der christlichen Spätantike*, ed. H. R. Drobner and C. Klock (Leiden: Brill, 1990), 99–123; and also Balthasar, *Presence and Thought.*

54. See Balthasar, *Presence and Thought,* 27.

55. On this subject see Louth, *Origins,* 80–97. Louth argues that Gregory's understanding of *epectasis* arises directly out of his understanding of creation: "It is clear that this doctrine of *epectasis* springs out of Gregory's profound apprehension of the unbridgeable gulf between the soul and God implied by a radical doctrine of creation out of nothing" (81).

56. David Bentley Hart, *The Beauty of the Infinite: The Aesthetics of Christian Truth* (Grand Rapids, Mich.: Eerdmans, 2003), 189. See also Balthasar, *Presence and Thought,* 57–69.

57. *DN* 4.14 (83); see also 4.17 (84).

58. *DN* 2.5 (62).

59. *DN* 5.6 (99–100). This trope is very different from one Gregory would use because it describes a reality that is one at root or source and only different insofar as the radii travel outward.

60. See *DN* 4.1 (71). Each level has characteristics of being and participation in its source that are particular to it, for instance, the celestial realm possesses

"immunity to motion, to flux and to all that goes with change" (*DN* 4.1 [72]). Again, in the celestial realm we can see in this characteristic of "immunity to motion" a difference from Nyssen, for whom the entire created order is necessarily and eternally in flux.

61. *CH* 3.2 (154).

62. *CH* 4.2 (156).

63. *CH* 3.2 (154).

64. *CH* 3.3 (155).

65. *CH* 10.1 (173).

66. *CH* 1.3 (146).

67. *CH* 10.3 (174).

68. *EH* 1.3 (197).

69. Louth, *Origins*, 170. In his work on Dionysius, *Denys, the Areopagite* (London: G. Chapman, 1989), Louth admits that creation seems not to be of primary significance to the Areopagite; indeed, he never once refers to a *creatio ex nihilo*. Louth argues that neither is emanation central, however: "We have to find another word for what is central to Denys' understanding of God's relationship to the world: and a good candidate for that word would be *theophany*. The world is a theophany, a manifestation of God, in which beings closer to God manifest God to those further away" (85).

70. *CH* 13.3 (177).

71. Hart, *Beauty of the Infinite*, 29. Gregory acts as the "heart of this essay"—in the second part of which Gregory's "account of desire and *epektasis* is offered as an answer to Nietzsche's account of the will to power and finite becoming, and his understanding of the infinite as an answer to a certain postmodern understanding of the sublime" (ibid.).

72. Ekkehard Mühlenberg, *Die Unendlichkeit Gottes bei Gregor von Nyssa: Gregors Kritik am Gottesbegriff der Klassischen Metaphysik* (Göttingen: Vandenhoeck and Ruprecht, 1966), 103.

73. *V. Mos.*, 1.2 (29).

74. *V. Mos.*, 1.3 (30).

75. *V. Mos.*, 1.5–1.6 (30).

76. *V. Mos.*, 1.47 (43).

77. *V. Mos.*, 1.47 (43). Knowing *that* God is, but not *what* God is, is a common theme in Gregory. See also *De an. et res.* (MG 46.40C); *C. Eun.* 2.13 (GNO 1, 230); 2.71 (GNO 1, 248); and 2.98 (GNO 1, 255); *In Cant.* 11 (GNO 6, 335).

78. See *DN* 1.2 (146): "Of course this ray never abandons its own proper nature, or its own proper unity. Even though it works itself outward to multiplicity and proceeds outside of itself as befits its generosity, doing so to lift upward and unify those beings for which it has a providential responsibility, nevertheless it remains inherently stable and it is forever one with its own unchanging identity. And it grants to creatures the power to rise up, as far as they may, toward itself and it unifies them by way of its own simplified unity. However, this divine ray can enlighten us only by being upliftingly concealed in a variety of sacred

veils which the Providence of the Father adapts to our nature as human beings." The "sacred veils" represent scripture and liturgy.

79. *DN* 5.8 (101); see also *DN* 4.2 (72); 4.4 (74).

80. It is just this classical aesthetic against which Gregory rebels by "predicating" the formlessness of infinity to God. There can be no order, rank, or harmony when there is no form and no stability. This was the concern of the Greeks that biased them against infinity as a category.

81. *DN* 4.7 (77–78).

82. *V. Mos.*, 2.2 (55).

83. *V. Mos.*, 2.3 (55).

84. Compare *V. Mos.*, 1.5–10 and 2.236.

85. *V. Mos.*, 1.10 (31).

86. As Everett Ferguson notes in the "Introduction" to *Life of Moses:* "Moses' attainments throughout the work serve to emphasize the truth that from each summit attained new horizons continuously open out." *V. Mos.*, 12.

87. Hart, *Beauty of the Infinite*, 115. Again: "One is, to use the imagery of Gregory of Nyssa, a vessel that expands in receiving the infinite (*vide infra*), which offers itself in an infinitely various series of icons" (144).

88. See, for example, *V. Mos.*, 2.60–61 (68): "Those who yearn after the pleasures of clay and keep on filling themselves with them never keep the space which receives them full; for although it is always being filled, it becomes empty again before the next pouring. In the same way the brick maker keeps on throwing yet more clay into the mould while it is constantly being emptied. I think that anyone can easily perceive the meaning of this figure by looking at the appetitive part of the soul. For if he who fills his desire in one of the things which he pursues should then incline his desire to something else, he finds himself empty again in that regard. And if he should fill himself on this, he becomes empty and a vacant container once more for something else. And we never stop doing this until we depart from this material life."

89. It is important to understand the polemical context out of which Gregory's understanding of the lack of satiation arises. It is, at least in part, a response to the Origenist controversies and a desire to distinguish his thought from the aspects of Origen's thought being called into question. Gregory is in many respects deeply indebted to Origen, especially with regard to his understanding of the allegorical interpretation of scripture and his belief in the universal salvation of creation (*apokatastasis*). Nonetheless, Origen's teaching that the soul can become "sated" in its contemplation of God was one that Gregory clearly wanted to distinguish himself from.

90. *DN* 4.4 (75) (emphasis added).

91. *DN* 4.10 (79–80).

92. *DN* 13.2 (128).

93. *DN* 4.10 (79).

94. John Parker, *The Works of Dionysius the Areopagite* (London: James Parker and Co., 1897), 44.

95. *DN* 4.12 (81).

96. Parker translates this as "cozened." The Greek is θέλγεται, from θέλγω: "to stroke with magic power, charm, enchant, seduce." In any case, it is a remarkable verb to apply to God in the passive.

97. *DN* 4.13 (82).

98. *DN* 4.16 (83).

99. *DN* 4.20 (86).

100. *c. Eun.* 3.6 (74) (GNO 2, 212).

101. *In Cant.* 8 (GNO 6, 247). I am following, with some caution, Casimir McCambley's translation, *Commentary on the Song of Songs* (Brookline, Mass.: Holy Cross Press, 1987). Hereafter, if I use this translation the page number will be in found in parentheses after the classical designation. I may also cite the GNO reference. See also *In Cant.* 12.6 (366) (GNO 6, 245–46).

102. *V. Mos.,* 1.46 (43).

103. *V. Mos.* 1.7–1.8 (31) (emphasis added).

104. *V. Mos.* 1.10 (31). Scripture will act as a "beacon light" or "guide" in this endless pursuit (1.11 [32]).

105. *V. Mos.* 2.239 (116).

106. Gregory can still speak of "standing still" because the more one remains firmly in the Good, the more one progresses in virtue (2.243 [117]); stillness consists in a singularity of orientation or directionality. Moreover, the "Rock" upon which one can "rest" is not simply the Good, but Christ (2.244 [117]).

107. See Jean Daniélou, *Platonisme et théologie mystique: essai sur la doctrine spirituelle de saint Grégoire de Nysse* (Paris: Aubier, 1953), and Mühlenberg, *Die Unendlichkeit Gottes,* especially, 147. C. W. Macleod agrees with Mühlenberg. See Macleod, "Allegory and Mysticism in Origen and Gregory of Nyssa," *Journal of Theological Studies* 22 (1971): 363: "In so far as Gregory conceives of a consummation, it is a God-likeness, not union or vision." On the other side of this debate, Martin Laird defends Daniélou's position. He argues that when *pistis,* or faith, is properly understood to function as the "faculty of apophatic union," then we find how Nyssa ensures a "union beyond knowledge" that nevertheless does not risk the "loss of ontological status as a creature" ("By Faith Alone: A Technical Term in Gregory of Nyssa," *Vigiliae Christianae* 54 [2000]: 77–78).

108. *DN* 1.4 (52–53).

109. *DN* 1.4 (53).

110. The full text, brief as it is, which points to Dionysius' vision of a "time to come" follows in its proper context: "This is the kind of divine enlightenment into which we have been initiated by the hidden tradition of our inspired teachers, a tradition at one with scripture. *We now grasp these things in the best way we can, and as they come to us, wrapped in the sacred veils of that love toward humanity with which scripture and hierarchical traditions cover the truths of the mind with things derived from the realms of the senses.* And so it is that the Transcendent is clothed in the terms of being, with shape and form on things

which have neither, and numerous symbols are employed to convey the varied attributes of what is an imageless and supra-natural simplicity. *But in time to come, when we are incorruptible and immortal, when we have come at last to the blessed inheritance of being like Christ, then, as scripture says, 'we shall always be with the Lord'* [1 Thes 4:17]. In most holy contemplation *we shall be ever filled with the sight of God shining gloriously around us as once it shone for the disciples at the divine transfiguration. And there we shall be, our minds away from passion and from earth, and we shall have a conceptual gift of light from him and, somehow, in a way we cannot know, we shall be united with him and, our understanding carried away, blessedly happy, we shall be struck by his blazing light"* (1.4 [52], emphasis added). Eschatologically, we will be in the center of the divine light that swathes us, rather than now, where even the celestial hierarchies can only hope to circle around, ever closer to the divine light to which they return.

111. *DN* 4.6 (76). See also *DN* 7.4 (109–10): "If knowledge unites knower and known, while ignorance is always the cause of change and of the inconsistency of the ignorant, then, as scripture tells us, nothing shall separate the one who believes in truth from the ground of true faith and it is there that he will come into the possession of enduring, unchanging identity. The man in union with truth knows clearly that all is well with him, even if everyone else thinks that he has gone out of his mind."

112. God "brings everything together into a unity without confusion, into an undivided communion where each thing continues to exhibit its own specific form and is in no way adulterated through association with its opposite, nor is anything of the unifying precision and purity dulled" (*DN* 11.2 [162]). This results in "peace": "And perfect Peace is there as a gift, guarding without confusion the individuality of each, providentially ensuring that all things are quiet and free of confusion within themselves and from without, that all things are unshakeably what they are and that they have peace and rest" (*DN* 11.3 [123]).

113. *CH* 6.1 (160).

114. *CH* 7.2 (162). See also "The process of handing on from angel to angel can be a symbol for us of that perfection which comes complete from afar and grows dimmer as it proceeds from the first to the second group" (8.2 [168]). In other words, perfection is hierarchically doled out and found in degrees. I will discuss this implication of "hierarchy" in Dionysius in the following chapter.

115. *DN* 11.4 (123).

116. *DN* 4.4 (75).

117. *V. Mos.*, 2.159 (93–94).

118. *DN* 1.1 (49).

119. *DN* 1.2 (50).

120. *EH*, 1.2 (197).

121. *CH* 1.3 (146).

122. *CH* 2.4 (151).

123. *CH* 2.4 (151–52).

124. *CH* 4.1 (156).

125. *DN* 7.3 (108–109).

126. *V. Mos.*, 2.232–33 (115).

127. *V. Mos.*, 2.234 (115).

128. *V. Mos.*, 2.235 (115).

129. Luibheid's translation of Dionysius here cites not only the passage where Moses asks to see God's face and is refused (Ex 33:20–23), but also Jn 1:18; I Tim 6:16; I Jn 4:12.

130. *CH* 4.3 (157).

131. Louth writes: "The whole of creation has been brought into being by God to manifest His glory, and each creature, as it fulfils the role that God has assigned to it, manifests His glory and praises him" (Louth, *Denys,* 166).

132. Douglass, *Theology of the Gap,* 6.

133. Fisher, "Theology of Dis/similarity," 532.

3. Giving a Method

1. Marion, *Reduction and Givenness: Investigations of Husserl, Heidegger, and Phenomenology,* trans. Thomas A. Carlson (Evanston, Ill.: Northwestern University Press, 1998); original publication: *Réduction et donation: Recherches sur Husserl, Heidegger et la phénoménologie* (Paris: Presses Universitaires de France, 1989).

2. This formulation of the "things themselves" (*Sachen selbst*) rather than the "thing-in-itself" (*Ding-an-sich*) critically evokes Kant by insisting on attention to that which Kant had banished to the realm of the noumenal. See E. Husserl, *Ideas Pertaining to a Pure Phenomenology and to a Phenomenological Philosophy. First Book. General Introduction to a Pure Phenomenology,* trans. F. Kersten (The Hague: Martinus Nijhoff, 1983), §19, 35; see also §52, 118, 122, and §62, 142.

3. *Reduction,* 40.

4. See Edmund Husserl, "Phenomenology" in *Encyclopaedia Britannica* (1927): "The term 'phenomenology' designates two things: a new kind of descriptive method which made a breakthrough in philosophy at the turn of the century, and an a priori science derived from it; a science which is intended to supply the basic instrument (*Organon*) for a *rigorously scientific philosophy* and, in its consequent application, to make possible a methodical reform of all the sciences" (emphasis added). See also Husserl, *Cartesian Meditations: An Introduction to Phenomenology,* trans. Dorion Cairns (The Hague: Martinus Nijhoff Publishers, 1960), especially §§1–2, 1–6. Similarly, in *The Basic Problems of Philosophy* (Bloomington: Indiana University Press, 1982), Heidegger defines phenomenology as the "name for the method of ontology, that is, of scientific philosophy" (20). Thus for Heidegger this is a question of philosophy seeking out its proper "scientificity," just as earlier Husserl had sought out "rigor."

5. Briefly, for Husserl, the things themselves are identified as the "objects of consciousness"; whereas for the early Heidegger, there is only one ultimate thing itself: Being, or more precisely, the meaning of Being.

6. See *Being Given*, "Preface," ix.

7. Interestingly, "reduction" has the opposite meaning in phenomenology than its more common usage in the humanities, where calling a description "reductive" signals a critique of the "thinness" or insufficient complexity of a discussion of some phenomenon. In phenomenology, the term is used in a way that more closely reflects its meaning in French culinary practice: to *reduce* a sauce, for instance, is to cook it down to arrive at its condensed essence.

8. Famously, this involves a bracketing of any consideration of the "reality" of the world. Against those who would see this as evidence of a radical transcendental idealism, or even solipsism, it is important to understand the difference between the method of "bracketing" and that of "doubting." Unlike Descartes, Husserl does not start by calling the reality of the world into question; rather, he simply puts its being or non-being aside (or "out of play") as not pertaining to the appearance of the world in consciousness. See *Ideas* §31, especially 61. For more on the debate about idealism versus realism in Husserl's philosophy, see Karl Ameriks, "Husserl's Realism," *Philosophical Review* 86 (1977): 498–519, and Hermann Philipse, "Transcendental Idealism," in *The Cambridge Companion to Husserl*, ed. Barry Smith and David W. Smith (Cambridge: Cambridge University Press, 1995).

9. Husserl, *The Idea of Phenomenology*, trans. William P. Alston and George Nakhnikian (Dordrecht: Kluwer Academic Publishers, 1990), 4.

10. Husserl, *The Idea of Phenomenology*, 5 and 34–42.

11. Marion goes so far as to state that Heidegger's choice to identify *Dasein* as the only being capable of such a reduction is "proof of a regression toward anthropology." See *Reduction*, 69.

12. Marion will later clarify this ambiguous phrase in an attempt to cleanse it from "theological" overtones that critics such as Dominique Janicaud would hear in the phrase. The move to a "pure form of the call" is less a specifically Christian influence, however, than a demonstration of the strong influence of Emmanuel Levinas on Marion's thought. (Janicaud will also accuse Levinas of the same theological betrayal of phenomenology.)

13. *Reduction*, 197–98.

14. Despite the essential role "intuition" plays in Husserl's thought, he seldom speaks *about* it or defines what is precisely meant by the term. It is clear that it is related to self-evidence, which is "rooted in each case in an act of intuition." Furthermore, intuition involves an "absolutely immediate seeing" in consciousness such that doubt can be ruled out when intuitive evidence is present. See Joseph Kockelmans, *Edmund Husserl's Phenomenology* (West Lafayette, Ind.: Purdue University Press, 1994), 83. Moreover, we can say of intuition that it is not merely sensible, as with Kant, but is broadened to include the "ideal" or "intelligible." Ideas can be intuited just as "real" objects. For

example, the "principle of a parallelogram" is just as much of an object of thought as is the "city of Paris." With Husserl, what had previously been taken as the subjective acts of thinking are now taken to be objects of thought (something Husserl refers to as "objectity") that may be intuited. This means that one might have intuition, not simply of a particular house, but of "house" in general—that, in other words, universal essences may also be intuited. See *Reduction*, 13, 15.

15. This is the crux of the critique that Derrida yields against Husserl, that he opens up the possibility for fully autonomous signification and then closes the door on it by demanding that each signification (or "meaning-intention") needs to be met with adequate fulfilling intuition. Husserl, according to Derrida, betrays signification by again having it require the guarantor of intuition. This means, in Derrida's thought, that signification is haunted always by presence. See Jacques Derrida, *Speech and Phenomena and Other Essays on Husserl's Theory of Signs,* trans. David B. Allison (Evanston, Ill.: Northwestern University Press, 1967).

Marion counters this critique by arguing that one can have presence without intuition—that, indeed, if intuition most often proves inadequate to fulfill the intentionality of signification, as Husserl shows it to be, then signification has existence outside and without intuition. Signification presents a new *sui generis* mode of presence in which signification is also said to be "given" in conscious-ness. In other words, Derrida is not radical enough, or at least not as radical as is Husserl who was, at least, able to see that signification also had its own mode of presence with its autonomous ability to appear as a given in consciousness. See *Reduction,* 22–35.

16. See Husserl, *Logical Investigations, Volume One,* trans. J. N. Findlay (London: Routledge & Kegan Paul), §19, 303–304. For example, the signification of a "straight line" or "triangle" never finds adequate fulfillment through intuition. Neither a sensible experience nor an ideality can provide perfectly adequate intuition of what "straight line" signifies; thus signification is autono-mous. As Marion notes, there is a certain irony to this: "Everything happens as if intuition were liberated from sensuousness only . . . in order to allow signification then to be liberated from intuition" (*Reduction,* 30).

17. *Reduction,* 32.

18. Ibid., 33.

19. Ibid., 49 (original emphasis). Marion's translation into French differs significantly from Kersten's translation into English, which drops all overtones of "giving" intuition. Kersten translates this principle thus: "that every originary *presentative* intuition is a legitimating source of cognition, that everything originarily (so to speak, in its 'personal' actuality) offered to us 'in intuition' is to be accepted simply as what it is *presented as being* but also only within the limits in which it is *presented* there" (*Ideas,* trans. Kersten, 44, my emphasis). In terms of the debates surrounding Marion's work, the difference between the transla-tions is significant—between language of "giving" and "presenting." Returning to the German original, however, we see that Marion's translation is technically

warranted: "*daß jede originär gebende Anschauung eine Rechtsquelle der Erkenntnis sei, daß alles, was sich uns der 'Intuition' originär, (sozusagen in seiner leibhaften Wirklichkeit) darbietet, einfach hinzunehmen sei, als was es sich gibt, aber auch nur in den Schranken, in denen es sich da gibt.*" See Husserl, *Ideen zu Einer Reinen Phänomenologie und Phänomenologischen Philosophie, Erstes Buch*, in *Husserliana III* (The Hague: Martinus Nijhoff, 1950), §24, 52 (my emphasis). While the various cognates of *geben* are translated by Kersten as "presenting," Marion renders them as "giving." Both are warranted, although Marion's does bring in the most basic and common sense to *geben*. Still, one can recognize in Marion's rendition of Husserl's "principle of principles" a significant shift in emphasis from the primacy of intuition to that of the "givenness" that determines it.

20. *Reduction*, 49.

21. Ibid., 36. As Marion puts it, "For here, the one who is most sober before the fascination of the over abundant and unconditional presence is doubtless not the one expected. Husserl, indeed, completely *dazzled* by unlimited givenness, seems not to realize the strangeness of such an excessiveness and simply manages its excess without questioning it" (*Reduction*, 38).

22. Ibid., 36.

23. See *Reduction*, 47: "The primary concern that guides [Husserl] is the *idea of an absolute science*. This idea, that *consciousness is to be the region of an absolute science,* is not simply invented; it is the idea which has occupied modern philosophy since Descartes. The elaboration of pure consciousness as the thematic field of phenomenology is *not derived phenomenologically by going back to the matters themselves* but by going back to a traditional idea of philosophy."

24. Ibid., 51.

25. Ibid. See also 54: "Consciousness thus radically determines phenomenality by imposing upon it the actuality of presence, the absoluteness of intuition, and the test of lived experience. The return to the things themselves is limited to a 'return to the sources of intuition.' The phenomenon that so emerges receives, with its purity, its limit—the 'reduced phenomenon.'"

26. Ibid., 56. Marion's second fundamental motivation, to justify the potential inclusion of all types of phenomena—even the "excessive" or "impossible"—is clearly in conflict with such a consequence. This term "impossible" will signify something different in Marion's later writings: the impossible marks the portal to the theological, where God is defined as "the impossible to Man." However, in this context the term does not yet have this sense.

27. Ibid., 59.

28. Martin Heidegger, *Being and Time*, trans. John Macquarrie and Edward Robinson (San Francisco: Harper and Row, 1962, §7, 59. Note the play between visibility and invisibility here that will, eventually, lend to Heidegger's project a mode of the "mystical" attractive to Marion. See also *Reduction*, 61: "To render phenomenal not that which, being invisible, could become visible, and therefore become a being, but, paradoxically, to render phenomenal that which, invisible as

such, could not in any way become visible on the mode of a present being." This resonance points to a clear line of influence from Heidegger to Marion's analysis of the modes of visibility in the idol and icon.

29. See also ibid., §7, 60.

30. *Reduction*, 62, 3.

31. Despite Marion's interpretation here, it is important to note that Heidegger himself does not use the term "reduction."

32. One must look at beings according to their horizon—not that of consciousness, but instead, of the Being of each and every being. This results in a shift from the ontic to the ontological.

33. Heidegger's broadening of the transcendental reduction to the existential "passes from being to the 'meaning of Being' only by working *that* being which is determined above all by the Being of being," i.e., *Dasein* (*Reduction*, 70). Furthermore, the Cartesian ego and *Dasein* share important characteristics, especially "finitude" and "mineness" (98–99). For these reasons, Marion will argue that the "*Ego cogito, sum* states less a countercase of *Dasein* than a territory to occupy, a statement to reinterpret, a work to redo" (106). The extent to which Heidegger is exercised by his engagement with Husserl (and through Husserl, Descartes) is large precisely because he remains haunted and indebted to them both.

34. As we have seen, because *Being and Time* still preferences the "question of Being" and therefore *Dasein* (which provides the only access to the *Seinsfrage*), this very intervention of *Dasein* prevents Heidegger from properly thinking ontological difference. See *Reduction*, 135: "Thus, in *Sein und Zeit*, the ontological question had to fade behind the question of Being—had to let itself be covered over by the 'ontological difference' between the way of Being of *Dasein* alone and that of other beings—precisely because the question of Being *is Dasein* itself." In other words, the "ontological difference" operative in *Being and Time* is between the being of *Dasein* and other beings, rather than the difference between Being and being. Thus it is "necessary to see *Dasein* not only as the driving force behind the appearance of the question of Being in *Sein und Zeit*, but even as that which blocks its access to the ontological difference" (ibid., 136). Marion argues that Heidegger himself was aware of this weakness in *Being and Time*, as §83 attests (140). Marion identifies this as Heidegger's admission that the breakthrough remains incomplete because of the unquestioned primacy of *Dasein* in its formulation.

35. See *Reduction*, 162.

36. Ibid., 162. Emphasis in final sentence added.

37. Ibid. The purpose of this study is not to evaluate the justification for, or accuracy of, Marion's reading of Husserl. However, this is clearly an innovative and controversial interpretation, one that seems, at times, antithetical to Husserl's primary philosophical aims: i.e., an analysis and description of "objects of consciousness." For further critical discussion of Marion's inheritance of Husserl, see Timothy Mooney, "Hubris and Humility: Husserl's Reduction and Givenness," 47–68, and Robyn Horner, *Rethinking God as Gift*, 82–114.

38. *Reduction,* 166.

39. See, for example, Marion's description in *Reduction,* 191: "Boredom leaves beings in place, without denying them, deprecating them, or suffering their absent assault. It leaves beings in place without affecting them, above all without being affected by them . . . boredom defuses the explosion of any call, whatever it might be; it covers itself, refuses to expose itself, defuses the conflict by deserting the field."

40. Marion draws this connection explicitly with reference to Thomas Aquinas's treatment of *acedia* (see *Reduction,* 247 n. 71).

41. Ibid., 192.

42. Ibid.

43. Ibid., 198–99. Marion later changes the term for subjectivity from *interloqué* to *adonné.* With this reference to the "there," Marion's notion of the "call," and the consequent understanding of subjectivity, one can readily see the strong influence of Levinas on Marion.

44. *Reduction,* 196.

45. Ibid., 203.

46. In later chapters I question the success of this endeavor at the level of methodology.

47. Ibid.

48. In a public debate with Derrida moderated by Richard Kearney (published as "On the Gift: A Discussion between Jacque Derrida and Jean-Luc Marion" in *God, the Gift, and Postmodernism*), Marion plays his hand: "But, with *Reduction and Givenness,* the question of the gift turned out to be profoundly modified for me by the discovery of the issue of givenness, *Gegebenheit,* in phenomenology, and by phenomenology I mean Husserl, and by Husserl I mean the early Husserl, the Husserl of the *Logical Investigations*" (56).

49. This concern is present in *Reduction,* but it remains a somewhat subterranean presence until *Being Given.*

50. See Jacques Derrida, *Donner le temps: I. La fausse monnaie* (Paris: Éditions Galilée, 1991); English trans. by Peggy Kamuf, *Given Time: I. Counterfeit Money* (Chicago: University of Chicago Press, 1992); Dominique Janicaud, *Le tournant théologique de la phénoménologie française,* English trans. by Bernard G. Prusak, "The Theological Turn of French Phenomenology," in *Phenomenology and the "Theological Turn": The French Debate* (New York: Fordham University Press, 2000).

51. See Jean Greisch, "L'herméneutique dans la 'Phénoménologie comme telle'"; Jean Grondin, "La phénoménologie sans herméneutique." The following chapter treats the hermeneutical critique more fully.

52. *Being Given,* 5.

53. This concept, so central to Marion's thought, will be discussed in chapter 4.

54. For a concise description of this background context, see Graham Ward, "Between Postmodernism and Postmodernity: The Theology of Jean-Luc Marion," 190–205.

55. *Being Given,* 4. See also Marion, "Metaphysics and Phenomenology: A Summary for Theologians," in *The Postmodern God: A Theological Reader,* ed. Graham Ward (Cambridge: Blackwell, 1997), 279–96.

56. This quasi-apologetic move brings a basic ambiguity or tension to his entire corpus. In chapter 5 I will question both the necessity and the possibility of this move.

57. *Being Given,* x.

58. Ibid., 4.

59. Ibid., 13.

60. He justifies this connection both conceptually and through a series of textual references to Husserl's texts (*Being Given,* 14–18). Significantly, when Marion seeks textual justification for the validity of his method, he returns to Husserl, strengthening my thesis that he is closer to Husserl (although a radicalized reading of Husserl) than he is to Heidegger, or any other teacher.

61. Ibid., 7.

62. Ibid.

63. Ibid., 7–8.

64. Ibid., 9.

65. Ibid.

66. Ibid., 10. This analogy is flawed since it is the director who, although invisible during the performance, previously "directs" what will later appear as a finished play. In other words, this analogy posits precisely the sort of invisible yet determinative subjective constitution of the phenomenon that Marion seeks to avoid with his reduction to givenness. I will return to this unavoidable paradox in chapter 5.

67. Ibid., 9.

68. Ibid.

69. Ibid., 11.

70. Ibid., 18.

71. Ibid.

72. Ibid., 16.

73. It remains to be discussed (as Marion does later in *Being Given*) *what sort* of phenomenon is described without in any way capturing or equaling it.

74. Ibid., 5.

75. See *Being Given,* 5: "The hypothesis that there was historically no such revelation [speaking here specifically of Christ] would change nothing in the phenomenological task of offering an account of the fact, itself incontestable, that it has been thinkable, discussable, even describable."

76. This furthers Marion's argument about the relationship between the reduction and givenness. See *Being Given,* 16: "If one admits that . . . the phenomenon appears all the more as it gives itself perfectly to be seen and received, but also that it can give *itself* thus only by giving itself to the conscious I, that is by letting itself be led back to it, which is equivalent to being reduced to it, then apparition gives itself perfectly based solely on the

fact that it appears, only insofar as it is *reduced* to its givenness for consciousness."

77. Ibid., 69.

78. Robyn Horner, *A Theo-Logical Introduction*, 149.

79. Marion, "The Other First Philosophy and the Question of Givenness," in *Critical Inquiry* 25 (1999); subsequently published in slightly revised form as the first chapter in *De Surcroît: Études sur les phénomènes saturés* (Paris: Presses Universitaires de France, 2001); English translation, *In Excess: Studies of Saturated Phenomena*, trans. Robyn Horner and Vincent Berraud (New York: Fordham University Press, 2002).

80. *In Excess*, 2. (Unless otherwise noted, I will cite from *In Excess*.)

81. First, as Descartes has shown, substance cannot be conceived without attributes, for only the latter are shown to, or known by, us. From this, both Hume and Kant will argue that substance is merely a function of our understanding. Secondly, understood as essence, *ousia* is no less problematic once it has been reduced to "abstraction from general ideas" (by Hume and Locke) and to "significations" (by Wittgenstein) (ibid., 5–6).

82. Here Aquinas identifies God, not simply with ontic causality (God is cause of created beings), but also with ontological causality (God is cause of the beingness of beings, their *esse*). Thus, the consideration of *causae* leads back to a consideration of God. However, Marion insists that Aquinas limits this approach necessarily by excluding *ousia* from cause and "is exercised as (coming from) pure *esse*," from being as act rather than substance.

83. Ibid., 8. Marion then goes on to defend Aquinas as himself fully understanding this conundrum when, "after having reached God following the guiding thread of causality, he vigorously refused to conceive God according and subject to cause, in rejecting the pertinence of any *causa sui* and in leaving the divine *esse incausatum*" (ibid.). See also Marion, "Saint Thomas d'Aquin et l'onto-théo-logie."

84. Ibid., 11.

85. Ibid., 14.

86. Ibid., 18.

87. Ibid., 19. See also "On the Gift," in *God, the Gift, and Postmodernism:* "The ultimate determination of the phenomenon implies not to be, but to appear as—*given* . . . [As a result], one of the most decisive characters of any phenomenon establishes it as an event, which definitely happens" (57).

88. Ibid., 21.

89. Ibid., 20.

90. Ibid., 25.

91. Ibid., 26.

92. Ibid., 26–27.

93. Horner, *A Theo-Logical Introduction*, 62.

94. The influence of Hans Urs von Balthasar on Marion's reading of Dionysius is evident here. Balthasar's entire interpretation of Dionysius is framed

by his recognition of an essential paradox in the manifestation of a God who, through that very manifestation, is also concealed. See, for example, Balthasar, "Denys": "If, on the one hand, any manifestation makes itself known as the manifestation of the One-and-Only not merely contingently (as is often the case with members of a class) but rather of necessity, then indeed this One is truly visible, everywhere announced, in the all which is his manifestation, but only as the eternally One and therefore eternally mysterious, hidden One who can never be fully comprehended in any of his manifestations; and therefore the wondering admiration of his beauty—as manifestation, as relation between manifestation and non-manifestation—is grounded in the worship of what is not manifest" (165). Marion is also distinctly influenced by Balthasar's depiction of the relationship between the cataphatic and the apophatic in Dionysius.

95. *ID*, 117.

96. Ibid., 160.

97. Nor is this support brought in elsewhere when the translation comes up. The reason for this is simple: such supporting evidence is not to be found.

98. Though he does not do so, he could reference both classical Greek and patristic Greek lexicons for this connection.

99. *ID.*, 161. This citation is also inaccurate: Pachymere is commenting here on *The Ecclesiastical Hierarchy* 3.3, 2 (not *The Celestial Hierarchy*).

100. None of the following major works of Dionysian scholarship supply a treatment of the meaning of αἰτία: Alexander Golitzin, *Et Introibo ad altare Dei*; Andrew Louth, *Denys the Areopagite*; Paul Rorem, *Pseudo-Dionysius: A Commentary on the Texts and an Introduction to their Influence* (New York: Oxford University Press, 1998); idem, *Biblical and Liturgical Symbols within the Pseudo-Dionysian Synthesis* (Toronto: Pontifical Institute of Mediaeval Studies, 1984); not even in the dense and highly technical work of Stephen Gersh, *From Iamblichus to Eriugena: An Investigation of the Prehistory and Evolution of the Pseudo-Dionysian Tradition* (Leiden: Brill, 1978) is it found. Finally, René Roques's work on Dionysian cosmology, *L'univers Dionysien: Structure hiérarchique du monde selon le pseudo-Denys* (Paris: Aubier, 1954), simply translates αἰτία into the French "*cause*"—as in "ὑπερούσιος αἰτία" (translated as *cause suressentielle*) (320); see also p. 80. Furthermore, Roques has no hesitation in making such *risqué* statements as giving God the "*titre de cause première*," citing *CH* 304a (ἐπὶ θεὸν μὲν ὡς αἴτιον) (151 n. 10) or even translating *The Ecclesiastical Hierarchy* 428c thus: "*Remontons des effets* (αἰτιατῶν) *aux causes* (αἰτία) . . ." (262 n. 4).

101. According to the *Greichisches Register* in the critical edition of Dionysius, *Corpus Dionysiacum II*, ed. Günter Heil and Adolf Martin Ritter (Berlin: Walter de Gruyter, 1991), αἰτία and its cognates appear a total of 164 times in the corpus, 127 of which occur in *DN* (270). Given the frequency with which Dionysius uses the word, one would expect a definition or discussion of it, especially in the context of the *DN*. This is not given. However, a major influence of Dionysius, Proclus, does define the term in his *The Elements of Theology*, trans. E. R. Dodds (Oxford: Clarendon Press, 1963): cause is "that which fills all things naturally

capable of participating in it, which is the source of all secondary existences and by the fecund outpouring of its irradiations is present to them all. But by its mode of being, which has no admixture of the spatial, and by its transcendent purity it is nowhere" (87). While Marion may be troubled with this definition, it is one with which, we might assume, Dionysius would be comfortable.

102. It is important to observe, however, that while I have argued that Marion's translation of αἰτία is not *warranted*, this does not mean it is not a *justifiable* translation. Marion's translation is interesting and thought-provoking. It brings something new to a reading of Dionysius that is worthwhile considering. Thus, I do not challenge the translation per se, but only the implication that it somehow gives us Dionysius' "real" intention or meaning. Such a claim involves a sleight of hand that is unnecessary.

103. As we shall see, this discomfort shifts in the historical development of Marion's writing. While he is comfortable with the hierarchical world as it translates into ecclesiastical structures in *Idol and Distance,* by the time of his later debates with Derrida over proper interpretation of Dionysius, Marion has dropped all such reference and emphasizes instead the mystic as a source for a purely "pragmatic theory of discourse." Here "praise" may be liturgical, but there is no longer any explicit mention of it as issuing from and occupying a hierarchical order.

104. John Meyendorff, *Christ in Eastern Christian Thought* (New York: St. Vladimir's Seminary Press, 1987), 108.

105. Golitzin, "Hierarchy versus Anarchy? Dionysius Areopagita, Symeon the New Theologian, and Nicetas Stethatos," in *New Perspectives on Historical Theology: Essays in Memory of John Meyendorff,* ed. Bradley Nassif (Grand Rapids, Mich.: Eerdmans, 1996), 263. See also ibid., 235: the hierarchy is "the icon of the inner man."

106. See here *CH* 1.3, 121d.

107. Dionysius' stern letter to Demophilus, *Epistle Eight,* in which he chastises the monk for daring to disrupt the sacred clerical order by challenging the actions and authority of a priest, is often cited by those wary of Dionysius' hierarchical vision and its conservative impulses. See Rorem, *Pseudo-Dionysius: A Commentary on the Texts and an Introduction to their Influence,* 19; Meyendorff, *Christ in Eastern Christian Thought,* 91–111.

108. Golitzin, "'Suddenly,' Christ: The Place of Negative Theology in the Mystagogy of Dionysius Areopagites," in *Mystics: Presence and Aporia,* 34.

109. Ibid., 35.

110. Golitzin, "'Suddenly,' Christ," 35. Eric Perl also claims that creation is to be identified as incarnation, without distinguishing any historical particularity to Christ but simply on a continuous line of emanation. See Eric Perl, "Saint Dionysius the Areopagite," *The Greek Orthodox Theological Review* 39.3–4 (1994), 336: "Dionysius does indeed . . . present the Incarnation in terms of pattern of procession and return, but for this very reason the entire motion of God to the world comes to be seen as incarnational."

111. Space does not allow us to delve into Golitzin's strongly christocentric interpretation of Dionysius, though it is an intriguing argument. See Golitzin, "'Suddenly,' Christ." Even more interesting is the fact that this article was first presented at a conference in Chicago at which Marion also presented his reappraisal of Thomas Aquinas as a mystic, or at least, *not* as an onto-theologian. It is interesting to imagine his response to Golitzin's argument.

112. Louth, *Denys*, 103.

113. Ibid., 107.

114. Louth argues that if, as in Neoplatonism, the hierarchies mediate being as well as illumination/salvation, then one would indeed find oneself in a predicament where in order "to ascend to the One is to recapitulate the procession through the hierarchies" (106). However, because God creates every level of reality immediately, union is also immediate from one's designated place in the hierarchy. Thus the mutual ecstasy of God's love (in creation) with ours (in deification) bypasses the hierarchies without destroying them. The hierarchies remain determinative but without ranking one's union with God as greater or lesser according to one's position within a hierarchical cosmos.

115. Again, by making a claim about the "stability" of the hierarchical structure, I am not saying that the cosmos is immovable or non-dynamic in Dionysius. The opposite is the case: creation is an eternal movement of procession and return. Yet the structure of this movement is given and stable.

116. One might say that the where, when, how, and why are all unknown—but not the whether.

117. Golitzin, "'Suddenly,' Christ," 47.

118. See Balthasar, "Denys," 172.

119. Any language of "rest" in Dionysius must always be understood as the eternal movement of the simultaneous rest (*mone*), procession (*proodos*), and return (*epistrophe*). In other words, "rest" is always moving.

120. As I will demonstrate in the next two chapters, Gregory presupposes a significantly different ontology, one that opens up more *abysmally*.

121. Balthasar, "Denys," 166 (my emphasis).

122. Ibid., 169.

123. See Jacques Derrida, "How to Avoid Speaking: Denials," 88–89, for Derrida's expression of a more appropriate complaint of Dionysius than Marion perhaps allows.

124. See *ID*, 164–73. In this section Marion begins by reminding us that Dionysius coined the term *hierarchy*. He also refers to Louis Bouyer's *L'Eglise de Dieu* (Paris: Cerf, 1970) as one of his sources for the following material. This is significant since Bouyer, with whom Marion studied, was one of the foremost critics of the liturgical changes of Vatican II. There is, in other words, a polemical and ecclesiastical debate in the background to Marion's own commentary on Dionysius here.

125. *ID*, 164.

126. See *ID*, 165. This is again governed by the logic of the gift: "The essential perhaps is this: each member receives the gift only in order to give it, such that this gift, in the same gesture, regives the gift in redundancy ('emanation') and, giving, sends the original gift back to its foundation ('ascent')" (165). This passing forward or "transmission" of the gift is necessary since "the gift cannot be received unless it is given. . . . Only the abandonment of that which fills it permits that the stream to come should fill it without cease" (166). One cannot grasp at the "content" of the gift but only transmit the "giving act." Here Marion acknowledges a "diminishing transmission of the gift" in the hierarchies, not as a result of any limitation of the original gift or the generosity of its Giver, but rather due to "the relative and variable impotence of each among the givers/recipients to carry out the redundancy themselves also 'without envy'" (167). As such, each person becomes not only recipient and giver of the gift but "interpreter" of it according to his or her own capacity (167). Here, intriguingly, is one of the sole places Marion hints at a possible theory of hermeneutics to emerge out of his Dionysian retrieval.

127. See *ID*, 168–69: "The hierarchies (legal: Old Testament; ecclesiastical: Church of Christ; celestial: angelic world) constitute the models of spiritual intelligibility of the community of saints, that is, of the rigorous, absolute, and hidden interdependence of spirits in the transmission of charity. Far from passing into some kind of gnosis [against Derrida's critique], Denys deploys in intelligibility the most concrete logic of a double solidarity, in charity as in its refusal. Here each person relies rigorously on the other, since the gift of grace arrives only through redundancy. The other becomes my neighbour since grace comes to him only inasmuch as it can, through me and, so to speak, as me, reach him or miss him." According to Marion, hierarchy, and most especially ecclesiastical hierarchy, necessarily carries with it the potential for both grace and sinfulness.

128. Marion, "In the Name," 139.

129. Ibid., 140.

130. Ibid.

131. Ibid., 155.

132. See Dionysius, *EH* 2, 3, 7–8, p. 208.

133. See Janicaud, "Theological Turn," 31, 91.

4. Interpreting "Saturated Phenomenality"

1. Jean-Luc Marion, "The Saturated Phenomenon," in Dominique Janicaud, Jean-François Courtine, Jean-Louis Chrétien, Michel Henry, Jean-Luc Marion, and Paul Ricœur, *Phenomenology and the "Theological Turn": The French Debate* (New York: Fordham University Press, 2000); originally published in *Phénoménologie et théologie*, ed. Jean-François Courtine (Paris: Critérion, 1992) and first translated into English by Thomas Carlson in *Philosophy Today* 40.1–4 (1996).

2. Dominique Janicaud, "The Theological Turn," in *Phenomenology and the "Theological Turn,"* 27.

3. Ibid., 48.

4. Ibid., 8. As we will see, Kearney shares this concern with Janicaud.

5. Ibid., 63.

6. See *Being Given:* The reduction "suspends and brackets all that, in appearance, does not succeed in giving itself . . . [it] separates what appears from what does not appear . . . [and thus] excludes the assumption of real transcendence and is far from establishing any dogmatism" (16).

7. Marion describes his frustration with phenomenology, which, in refusing to think justly about the given, is "powerless to receive a number of phenomena for what they are—givens that show themselves . . . it excludes from the field of manifestation not only many phenomena, but above all those most endowed with meaning and those that are the most powerful." Against this refusal, he argues that only a phenomenology of givenness can achieve that which Husserl set out to do: "return to the things themselves . . . all of them" (*Being Given*, 4). Therefore, in his article "Metaphysics and Phenomenology: A Summary for Theologians," Marion will gloss Husserl's "principle of principles" thus: "It is forbidden to forbid" (*The Postmodern God*, 289).

8. Marion discusses Kant's statement of the crucial interdependence of intuition and concept as the constitutive elements of all cognition: "Without sensibility no object would be given to us, and without understanding none would be thought. Thoughts without content are empty, intuitions without concepts are blind" (Immanuel Kant, *The Critique of Pure Reason*, trans. and ed. Paul Guyer and Allen W. Wood, *The Cambridge Edition of the Works of Immanuel Kant* [Cambridge: Cambridge University Press, 1998], A51/B75, 193–94). Marion argues that both Kant and Husserl recognize the primacy of intuition as that which initially gives rise to cognition. The concept comes after the fact of intuition in order to organize it. However, counter-intuitively (forgive the pun), both reverse this priority: because concepts control and set up the horizon of that which we can cognize, they adjudicate what can and cannot become phenomenal.

9. Marion, "The Saturated Phenomenon," 195.

10. Ibid., 194.

11. Ibid., 212.

12. Ibid., 214. Marion plays between two etymologies here: *voir,* "to see" is placed in contrast with "to look at" from the French, *"re-garder,"* which Marion reads literally from its Latin roots (*in-tueri*), meaning "to guard or to keep." Thus, *regarder* (to look at) is taken in the sense of "to keep an eye on, to watch out of the corner of one's eye, to keep in sight." The two are juxtaposed thus: "In order to see, it is not as necessary to perceive by the sense of sight (or any other sense) as it is to receive what shows *itself* on its own because it gives *itself* in visibility by its own initiative. . . . On the other hand, gazing, *re-garder,* is about being able to keep the visible thus seen under the control of the seer, exerting this control by

guarding the visible in visibility, as much as possible without letting it have the initiative in appearing (or disappearing)" (214).

13. Ibid., 215.

14. For an extended treatment of the difference between *visable* and *visible*, see *God Without Being*, 9–22. Marion coins the term *"invisable"* from the verb *viser:* "to aim at."

15. Marion, "The Saturated Phenomenon," 192.

16. Marion, *Being Given*, 220.

17. Marion, "The Saturated Phenomenon," 212–13, emphasis added.

18. See Horner, *A Theo-logical Introduction*, 114–15.

19. Marion, *Being Given*, 115.

20. Ibid., 323. Marion is clearly drawing on the work of Emmanuel Levinas here, but with a crucial shift from an "accused subjectivity" to a "summoned" one.

21. Ibid., 322.

22. Jean Grondin, "La tension de la donation ultime et de la pensée herméneutique de l'application chez Jean-Luc Marion," *Dialogue* 38.3 (1999), 555 (my translation).

23. Ibid., 556.

24. Marion, *In Excess*, 50.

25. Richard Kearney and Jean-Luc Marion, "A Dialogue with Jean Luc Marion," ed. John P. Manoussakis, *Philosophy Today* (Spring 2004): 12.

26. The addition of "judgment" to "interpretation" raises, as Kearney is determined to, an ethical question. How does one tell the difference between a benevolent and malevolent saturated phenomenon if both defy interpretation? This is an important consideration that I hope to explore elsewhere.

27. Kearney and Marion, "A Dialogue," 12.

28. Both Greisch and Grondin disagree with Marion's appraisal of Heidegger and the original "hermeneutical turn" in phenomenology. Indeed, this is Greisch's main critique. See Jean Greisch, "L'herméneutique dans la 'phénoménologie comme telle'" in *Revue de metaphysique et de morale* 96.1 (1991): 44–57. Grondin, similarly disgruntled with Marion's treatment of Heidegger, also has a strong critique of his phenomenology in itself. He points to the same tension that I have been articulating in the last two chapters: the tension between founding a rigorous science and acknowledging the profound limitations of our finitude— between Husserl and Heidegger, in other words. He argues: "If Marion looks to open, by this inaugurating reflection, a new future to phenomenology, he remains, nevertheless, in a very precise sense, the heir of his two big 'predecessors' . . . One can, in effect, show, and this will be our only proposal here, that Marion inherits from Husserl a Cartesian sense of the ultimate foundation (in his case, it is a question of an ultimate givenness [*donation*]), a Cartesianism which may not be surprising for such a prestigious specialist of Descartes, but who also takes from Heidegger a sharp and probably more powerful sense of the finitude, of the dispossession, of the decentering and of the dereliction which justly bewilders the

Cartesianism of the foundation and of the ultimate certitude. It may be, then, and this will be our thesis, that these two thoughts, which are disputing [with one another] throughout Marion's book, are shown to be finally irreconcilable." See Jean Grondin, "La tension de la donation ultime et de la pensée herméneutique," 549 (my translation).

Grondin thinks this same friction also dominates the structure of *Being Given:* Books 1 and II are taken up with the former reflex—"to establish the essential primacy, absolutely indubitable and incontestable, of the idea of givenness above all the others"—while Books III to V, with their attention to the saturated phenomenon and the "devoted" subject, provide "the best refutation of the idea of ultimate givenness pursued heroically in the first two sections" (553). In the latter books one finds that "in all the occurrences of phenomenality or of 'givenness,' that which fascinates Marion, is manifestly the inconstitutable, unavailable, unforeseeable, indeed, intolerable character of the phenomena (*ED*, p. 224), the fact that they arrive, and that they arrive at *me* always without reason and without cause" (554). See also Grondin's essay in "La phénoménologie sans herméneutique," in *L'horizon herméneutique de la pensée contemporaine* (Paris: J. Vrin, 1993).

29. Kearney and Marion, "A Dialogue," 12.

30. Ibid.

31. Ibid., 13.

32. Shane Mackinlay, "Eyes Wide Shut: A Response to Jean-Luc Marion's Account of the Journey to Emmaus," in *Modern Theology* 20.3 (2004): 543. See also, idem, *Interpreting Excess: Jean-Luc Marion, Saturated Phenomena, and Hermeneutics.* Cf. Horner, *A Theo-logical Introduction*, 117–18.

33. Interestingly, Mackinlay directs a parallel critique of Marion's depiction of faith as derivative rather than ontological. The disagreement takes place over divergent readings of the Lukan text of Christ's resurrected appearance to his followers (Luke 24: 13–35), which Marion interprets in the article "They Recognized Him; and He Became Invisible to Them" (*Modern Theology* 18.2, 2002). Marion reads Christ as the instance of saturated phenomena par excellence. He analyzes the event of the resurrected Christ walking along the road to Emmaus with the distressed disciples. Although no intuition or sense perception of the man they had walked with countless times was lacking, still the disciples do not recognize Christ. While "every intuition gives itself to them . . . their concepts catch nothing of this" (146).

Mackinlay takes exception to Marion's definition of faith in this article as a compensation for a "lack" of conceptual apparatus as opposed to a lack of intuition. Accordingly, Marion posits a "derivative sense of faith" that comes only in response, after the fact. This derivative sense of faith parallels Marion's derivative hermeneutic, which demands response and interpretation after the fact of givenness. Mackinlay argues that this is a misinterpretation of Heidegger's (and Christian theology's) "fundamental or ontological sense of hermeneutics" ("Eyes Wide Shut," 447). He defines faith differently: "Primarily, faith is an acceptance that opens a hermeneutic space of meaning, in which a phenomenon can first be recognized as revelatory; faith is an existential commitment that makes it possible for revelation to be made manifest. Revelation does not simply impose itself on us; rather, it must be actively received and recognized in the meaning-filled world of a recipient's faith" (448). According to Mackinlay, Marion overlooks this—both in general, and in particular in his reading of the journey to Emmaus. I would defend Marion here, by saying that if his understanding of faith is "derivative," as Mackinlay charges, this in itself is not a unique (or illicit!) view of faith within the Christian tradition. Indeed, the debate between whether faith "prepares" for the grace of God or is itself, as a response, only made possible by the previous gift of grace is one that has raged in Western Christianity from Augustine onward. Indeed, it is question Marion tackles head-on in relation to Augustine in *Au lieu de soi*.

34. *Being Given*, 236.

35. Ibid., 239.

36. Kearney and Marion, "A Dialogue," 15–16.

37. Ibid., 16.

38. Ibid., 14. Sarah Coakley discusses the interplay between a "boundary" and diverse interpretation in relation to the etymology of the Chalcedonian definition as "*horos*." See Sarah Coakley, "What Does Chalcedon Solve and What Does it Not? Some Reflections on the Status and Meaning of the Chalcedonian 'Definition,'" in *The Incarnation*, ed. Stephen T. Davis, Daniel Kendall SJ, and Gerald O'Collins SJ (Oxford: Oxford University Press, 2002), 143–63.

Marion comments that the different interpretations and questions are bound together because they are "always raised within the common structures of human experience" (Kearney and Marion, "A Dialogue," 14). The unspoken assumption of a Kantian universality of the categories of experience inflected at this point of the discussion is fascinating. One can only assume that Marion is being careless, since he is not arguing about the universality of the given here but of the receptivity to it. In other words, Marion slides back into a philosophical dogmatism while trying to evade the charge of theological dogmatism. Surprisingly, Kearney does not challenge him on this point but continues, instead, to challenge him on the question of religious exclusivity.

39. Ibid., 15.

40. It is precisely this openness to an infinite range of revelatory possibilities that Marion seems to deny in his most recent work on Augustine, *Au lieu de soi*, and even more explicitly in his essay "Faith and Reason" (in *The Visible and the Revealed*, trans. Christina M. Gschwandtner [New York: Fordham University Press, 2008]). Whether this turn represents a true change of heart or whether he has always covertly believed this to be the case is not clear. That he contradicts his response to Kearney here is undeniable. It is also noteworthy that the shift in rhetoric is accompanied by a shift from Gregory of Nyssa to Augustine as his primary patristic inspiration.

41. Gregory of Nyssa, *v. Mos.* 2.163 (95).

42. I will follow the translation by Stuart George Hall in *Gregory of Nyssa: Contra Eunomium II: An English version with Commentary and Supporting Studies. Proceedings of the Tenth International Colloquium on Gregory of Nyssa (Olomouc, 15–18 September, 2004)*, ed. Lenka Karfíková, Scot Douglass, and Johannes Zachhuber (Leiden: Brill, 2006). Hall separates the text into paragraphs. I will cite the paragraph followed by the page number.

43. Gregory of Nyssa, *CE* II 67, 74 (GNO 1, 245).

44. *CE* II 290–91, 124 (GNO 1, 312).

45. Balthasar, *Presence and Thought,* 27. Balthasar also states that for Gregory the "first essential characteristic of the creature is therefore negative. It consists of the very fact that the creature is not God" (ibid.).

46. "That he transcends every effort of thought, and is found to be beyond the reach of naming, stands as a testimony to mankind of his ineffable majesty." *CE* II 587, 192 (GNO 1, 397).

47. See *CE* II 418, 153 (GNO 1, 347).

48. See Sarah Coakley, "Does Kenosis Rest on a Mistake? Three Kenotic Models in Patristic Exegesis," in *Exploring Kenotic Christology,* ed. C. Stephen Evans (Oxford: Oxford University Press, 2006), 246–64.

49. See Ari Ojell, "Service or Mastery? 'Theology' in Gregory of Nyssa's *Contra Eunomium* II," in *Gregory of Nyssa: Contra Eunomium II,* 479.

50. *CE* II 261, 117 (my emphasis) (GNO 1, 302).

51. *CE* II 85, 78 (GNO 1, 251).

52. *CE* II 88, 79 (GNO 1, 252): "It was also a sure guide towards his goal, that in thinking about God he was not led to an understanding by anything material, nor did his thought ever get stuck in anything comprehensible and desist from the journey towards things beyond knowing."

53. *CE* II 89, 79 (GNO 1, 252).

54. As Morwenna Ludlow has demonstrated, this journey is not yet cast in the fully eschatological schema of his later works, but remains an example of the faithful life. See "Divine Infinity and Eschatology: The Limits and Dynamics of Human Knowledge, according to Gregory of Nyssa (*CE* II, 67–170)," in *Gregory of Nyssa: Contra Eunomium II,* 234.

55. See *In Cant.,* Prologue (GNO 6, 5). It should be observed that Gregory's understanding of "usefulness" as a hermeneutical standard does not reflect anything like we might think of in terms of a "utilitarian" or "pragmatist" measure of the value of scripture. Rather, borrowing from Origen's argument in Book IV of *De Principiis,* Gregory assumes that scripture is anagogic: its purpose is for the uplifting of the soul. The interpretation of any particular passage, then, must be evaluated insofar as it might be of use in training one in the life of virtue or in bringing one closer to God. In this way, Gregory also inherits Origen's understanding of the pedagogical and spiritual function of interpreting scripture. See Origen, *On First Principles,* trans. G. W. Butterworth (Gloucester, Mass.: Peter Smith, 1973), 4.1.6 (265) and 4.2.9 (285–86).

56. *CE* II 91, 80 (GNO 1, 253).

57. *CE* II 93, 80 (GNO 1, 254).

58. In this reading I am somewhat less sanguine than Tina Dolidze about the capacity of faith to "neutralize in some degree the unbridgeable cognitive gap faced by dimensional human reasoning." See Dolidze, "The Cognitive Function of *Epinoia* in *CE* II and Its Meaning for Gregory of Nyssa's Theory of Theological Language," in *Gregory of Nyssa: Contra Eunomium II*, 447.

59. *CE* II 95–96, 80–81 (my emphasis) (GNO 1, 254).

60. *CE* II 105, 83 (GNO 1, 257).

61. Joseph S. O'Leary, "Divine Simplicity and the Plurality of Attributes (*CE* II, 359–386; 445–560)," in *Gregory of Nyssa: Contra Eunomium II*, 337. See also O'Leary, *Questioning Back: The Overcoming of Metaphysics in Christian Tradition* (Minneapolis: Winston Press, 1985).

62. *Horos* means both "boundary, limit, or frontier" and "rule, standard, limit." Hence the Nicene Creed is a *horos*—a rule that marks the boundaries or horizon of Christian belief within which, however, multiple interpretations and divergences live.

63. Language of "subjectivity" is a little anachronistic here, yet it is clear that Gregory has a notion of practices that shape and form the "self" for or against the good.

64. Gregory of Nyssa, *In Cant.* 6, 130 (GNO 6, 181).

65. *In Cant.* 6, 131 (my emphasis) (GNO 6, 183).

66. Ibid., 5, 119 (GNO 6, 158).

67. Ibid., 5, 118 (GNO 6, 157).

68. Ibid., 6, 130 (GNO 6, 180).

69. Ibid., 1, 51 (GNO 6, 32).

70. Ibid., 1, 47 (GNO 6, 22).

71. Again, Gregory demonstrates his indebtedness to Origen on this point. See note 54 above.

72. *In Cant.* 1, 48 (GNO 6, 25).

73. One might note that this is precisely the vision of intellectual and ecclesial symmetry that Marion harks back to with his comments about the bishop as true theologian in *God Without Being.*

74. *In Cant.,* 3, 75 (GNO 6, 71).

75. Ibid., 11, 208 (GNO 6, 338).

76. Ibid., 13, 233 (GNO 6, 381).

77. Ibid., 12, 220 (GNO 6, 358).

78. Kearney and Marion, "A Dialogue," 21.

5. The Apparent in the Darkness

1. For this reason, Thomas A. Carlson calls Marion a "liberation theologian." See "Blindness and the Decision to See: On Revelation and Reception in Jean-Luc Marion," in *Counter-Experiences: Reading Jean-Luc Marion,* ed. Kevin Hart (Notre Dame, Ind.: Notre Dame University Press, 2007), 153.

202 · NOTES TO PAGES 132–136

2. Marion, *Le phénomène érotique* (Paris, Éditions Grasset & Fasquelle, 2003); English translation by Stephen E. Lewis (Chicago: University of Chicago Press, 2007). Unless otherwise noted, I will cite the French pagination and use my own translation.

3. Marion, *Le phénomène érotique*, 24.

4. Ibid., 11.

5. Ibid., 12.

6. Here, Marion returns to his debates with Derrida and Milbank on the question of the gift—its definition and possibility.

7. Ibid., 16.

8. Ibid.

9. Ibid., 22.

10. Ibid., 8.

11. See ibid., 19: "The human is not defined by *logos* nor by the being [*être*] in him, but by this alone, that he loves (or hates), whether he wants to or not."

12. See Claude Romano, "Love in Its Concept: Jean-Luc Marion's *The Erotic Phenomenon*," in *Counter-Experiences.*

13. Romano, "Love in Its Concept," 330.

14. Marion, *Le phénomène érotique*, 15.

15. Ibid., 22–23.

16. Kevin Hart, introduction to *Counter-Experiences*, 42. See also Romano, "Love in Its Concept": "[O]n the one hand, Marion wants to conserve the reduction, which is to say a method that is transcendental or inspired by transcendental philosophy. . . . But on the other hand, Marion's entire fundamental project consists in moving beyond a phenomenology of the transcendental style, and thus in thinking of phenomenality as a giving freed of every prior condition of possibility" (331).

17. See Pierre Hadot, *Philosophy as a Way of Life*, ed. Arnold Davidson, trans. Michael Chase (Oxford: Blackwell, 1995).

18. Robyn Horner, introduction to *In Excess*, xiii.

19. See Marion, *Being Given*, 4.

20. Marion, *Le phénomène érotique*, 17.

21. See Marion, *God Without Being*, xx: "No doubt, God can and must in the end also be; but does his relation to Being determine him as radically as the relation to his Being defines all other beings? . . . I am attempting to bring out the absolute freedom of God with regard to all determinations, including, first of all, the basic condition that renders all other conditions possible and even necessary—for us, humans—the fact of Being."

22. Remembering the commonsense definition of ontology that I have employed in this study, ontology refers to the "worlds" or "whole realities" assumed, implied, or necessitated in one's system of thought.

23. See, for instance, Marion, "Metaphysics and Phenomenology: A Summary for Theologians": "Phenomenology goes beyond metaphysics insofar as it

renounces the transcendental project, to allow an ultimately radical empiricism to unfold—ultimately radical, because it no longer limits itself to sensible intuition, but admits all intuition that is primarily donative" (288).

24. See *Being Given*, 139, 138.

25. Marion, *Cartesian Questions: Method and Metaphysics* (Chicago: University of Chicago Press, 1999), 138.

26. See, Dionysius, *DN* 11.4 (123); *CH* 6.1 (160).

27. Dionysius, *CH* 7.2 (162).

28. Dionysius, *DN* 1.7 (56). Andrew Louth comments on this paradoxical balance of transcendence and immanence in Dionysius in the following way: While, for Dionysius, God is unknowable and ultimately transcendent, "there is a deep awareness of the immanence of God in creation, for each created being depends immediately on God for its very being: 'Everything and any part of anything participates in the One, and on the existence of the One everything depends for its existence' (*DN* XIII. 2: 977 C). This assertion of the immanence of God underlies the doctrine of the divine names" (Louth, *Origins*, 177–78).

29. Dionysius, *DN* 2.4 (61); *MT* 5 (141).

30. Dionysius, *DN* 1.6 (54).

31. Marion, *God Without Being*, 173.

32. Marion, *Idol and Distance.*

33. Marion, *In Excess*, 156.

34. For a discussion of the relatively recent shift in scholarly reception of Gregory, see Sarah Coakley's introduction to her *Rethinking Gregory of Nyssa* (Oxford: Blackwell, 2003).

35. One must note that this is not the case at all within Eastern Christianity, and part of the renewed interest in Gregory's "mystical writings" in the West might be an effect of greater ecumenical discourse between the various Eastern and Western traditions of Christianity. Representative of the earlier trend in scholarship, Bernard McGinn's comprehensive history of Western mysticism, *The Foundations of Mysticism*, vol. 1, *The Presence of God: A History of Western Christian Mysticism* (New York: Crossroad, 1991), both recognizes Gregory as developing "the first systematic negative theology in Christian history" and then justifies allotting a mere three pages to a discussion of Gregory by referring to his "lack of direct influence in the West" (141, 142). Jean Daniélou's influential work on Gregory, *Platonisme et théologie mystique: essai sur la doctrine spirituelle de Saint Grégoire de Nysse* (Paris: Aubier, 1953), is a remarkable exception to this trend.

36. Even whilst observing this trend, Turner propagates it. In a work that takes its beginnings from the remarkable synthesis of Plato's allegory of the cave and the exodus narrative of Moses' ascent on Mount Sinai, Turner only twice mentions Gregory—the one who first accomplishes the synthesis—before directing his attention to Dionysius and other figures in the Western mystical canon (Augustine, Eckhart, *The Cloud of Unknowing*, John of the Cross). See Denys Turner, *The Darkness of God: Negativity in Christian Mysticism* (Cambridge: Cambridge University Press, 1995), 12, 17.

37. See Gregory of Nyssa, *CE* II 80, 77 (GNO 1, 250): "Often, when a sunbeam streams in upon them through a window, they are delighted by its beauty and pounce on what they see, and try to take the sunbeam in their hand, and compete with each other, and grasp the light, catching the ray, as they suppose, in clasped fingers; but when the clasped fingers are opened, the handful of sunbeam makes the children laugh and clap because it has slipped from their hands."

38. Ibid. See also, *Contra Eunomium* II 81, 77 (GNO 1, 250): The "children of our generation . . . see the divine power illuminating their minds through the works of providence and the wonders of creation . . . , yet rather than marvelling at the divine generosity, and revering the one thereby made known, they overstep the mind's limitations and clutch with logical tricks at the intangible to catch it."

39. Balthasar, *Presence and Thought*, 93.

40. Marion repeats the main substance of the argument found here in *Au lieu de soi*, again citing Gregory of Nyssa at the crucial juncture of his argument; see p. 351.

41. Marion, "*Mihi magna quaestio factus sum:* The Privilege of Unknowing," *Journal of Religion* 85.1 (2005): 14.

42. Ibid., 16–17. Marion cites Gregory of Nyssa, "On the Making of Man," in *Gregory of Nyssa: Dogmatic Treatises*, trans. William Moore and Henry Austin Wilson in *Nicene and Post-Nicene Fathers*, series 2, 5, 396–97. He has modified the translation slightly, however.

43. Ibid., 18.

44. Balthasar, *Presence and Thought*, 94.

45. Marion, "The Privilege of Unknowing," 21.

46. Alden A. Mosshammer, "Disclosing but not Disclosed: Gregory of Nyssa as Deconstructionist," in *Studien zu Gregor von Nyssa und der Christlichen Spätantike*, ed. Hubertus R. Drobner and Christoph Klock (Leiden: Brill, 1990), 102.

47. Ekkehard Mühlenberg, *Die Unendlichkeit Gottes bei Gregor von Nyssa* (Göttingen: Vandenhoek and Ruprecht, 1966).

48. Mariette Canévet, *Grégoire de Nysse et l'herméneutique biblique. Étude des rapports entre le langage et la connaissance de Dieu* (Paris: Études Augustiniennes, 1983). See also Morwenna Ludlow, "Divine Infinity and Eschatology: The Limits and Dynamics of Human Knowledge according to Gregory of Nyssa (*CE* II, 67–170)."

49. Mosshammer, "Disclosing but not Disclosed," 104.

50. On this crucial term in Gregory's corpus, see Paul Verghese, "Διάστημα and διάστασι in Gregory of Nyssa: Introduction to a Concept and the Posing of a Problem," in *Gregor von Nyssa und die Philosophie. Zweites Internationale Kolloquium über Gregor von Nyssa*, ed. Heinrich Dörrie, Margarete Altenburger, and Uta Schramm (Leiden: Brill, 1976), 243–60.

51. See Verghese, "Διάστημα and διάστασι in Gregory of Nyssa," 250, for a discussion of the role of the term αδιάστατον in Trinitarian debates: there can be no διάστημα within the Godhead.

52. See *CE*, I 176; 366; 636; 668; 690; *CE* II 578.

53. Mosshammer, "Disclosing but not Disclosed," 107.

54. See Verghese, "Διάστημα and διάστασι in Gregory of Nyssa," 248. See also Gregory of Nyssa, *CE* II 69, 74 (GNO 1, 246): "The barrier which separates uncreated nature from created being is great and impenetrable."

55. Mosshammer, "Disclosing but not Disclosed," 106.

56. Ibid.

57. Ibid., 113.

58. See Marion, "The Banality of Saturation," in *Counter-Experiences*, 383–418. When Marion makes this argument, he seems, at times, to assume that saturation depends on our *mode of reception* rather than the phenomenon that we receive. Only a difference in mode of reception explains why one and the same thing can be both a "common phenomenon" and a saturated one (see especially 391–97). Such an argument, however, runs directly counter to his entire attempt to allow the phenomena to determine themselves unless he is saying that every single phenomenon is, at least potentially, saturated.

59. See Marion, *Being Given*, 199–241.

60. Kathryn Tanner has made a similar critical observation in "Theology at the Limits of Phenomenology," *Counter-Experiences*, 203.

61. Gregory of Nyssa, *In Eccles.* 7.1.729 C: "Creation is nothing other than diastema."

62. Mosshammer, "Disclosing but not Disclosed," 118–19. See also *In Eccles.* 1.

63. Gregory of Nyssa, *In Cant.* 5, 113 (GNO 6, 145); see also 5, 109 (GNO 6, 137): "The *Song of Songs* now leads us to desire a contemplation of the transcendent good."

64. Again, this "distance" should not be understood spatially, but as ontological difference.

65. *In Cant.* 5, 110 (GNO 6, 139).

66. Ibid.

67. *In Cant.* 5, 113 (GNO 6, 147).

68. *In Cant.* 5, 119 (GNO 6, 157).

69. Mosshammer, "Disclosing but not Disclosed," 109.

70. Ibid., 110.

71. See *In Cant.*, "Prologue," 39 (GNO 6, 13).

72. I argued that the seeming contradiction between Marion's insistence on the pure givenness of the saturated phenomena and their infinite hermeneutic could only be resolved if one understood the latter, the interpretation, to be subsequent to the givenness. In the passage from givenness to phenomena, which occurs through "counter-experience," the particular resistance of *l'adonné*, interpretation begins and "follows after" the phenomena ever after in a "search for adequate concepts" to define that which forever eludes conceptualization. Gregory has already provided a perfect typology of this with his analysis of Moses, who, having requested to see God "face to face" is instead granted a vision

of God's "back" and summoned to "follow after" God ever more. See Gregory of Nyssa, *v. Mos.* 2. 232–42 (115–17) and *v. Mos.* 2. 249–55 (119–20).

73. Marion, "The Unspoken: Apophasis and the Discourse of Love," trans. Arianne Conty, *American Catholic Philosophical Association Proceedings* 76 (2002): 39–56.

74. See Marion, *God, the Gift, and Postmodernism*, 20–78.

75. See Marion, "The Unspoken," 39: "The primary thesis of this paper is that we should reject 'negative theology' as a descriptor and replace it, following the *nomenclature of the Dionysian corpus*, with 'mystical theology.' In doing this, we will come to realize that 'mystical theology' no longer has the ambition to make constative use of language; its ambition is rather to be freed from such use. Thus, we move from a constative (and predicative) use of language toward a strictly pragmatic usage. This movement has yet to be proved, and what follows is an attempt to do just that."

76. Ibid., 44–45.

77. Ibid., 44.

78. Ibid., 47. Marion is not precisely correct in setting "perlocutionary" statements over against "performative" in J. L. Austin. For Austin to speak of the "perlocutionary" force of a statement is to speak of the "effect it has on an other." Thus perlocutionary statements can also be performative, and performative language, by definition, is also perlocutionary. See J. L. Austin, *How to Do Things with Words* (Oxford: Clarendon Press, 1975).

79. Marion, "The Unspoken," 52 (my emphasis).

80. Robyn Horner, "The Weight of Love," in *Counter-Experiences*, 237.

81. Marion, *In Excess*, 115.

82. Ibid., 126.

83. See Derrida, "How to Avoid Speaking: Denials," 111.

84. Marion, "The Banality of Saturation," 404.

85. Ibid., 404–405 (my emphasis).

86. This is the language Marion uses in his interpretation of Augustine in *Au lieu de soi*, 163.

87. To be sure, I am not suggesting here that the move to Augustine necessitates such a narrowing of theological possibility—an audacious (and erroneous) claim to make so casually! Rather, I am making an observation about the way these respective retrievals *function* in Marion's thought.

88. See Jean Grondin, "Au lieu de la metaphysique? Les meditations augustiniennes de Jean-Luc Marion" (www.laviedesidees.fr/Au-lieu-de-la -metaphysique.html), and J. Schrijvers, "In (the) Place of the Self: A Critical Study of Jean-Luc Marion's 'Au lieu de soi. L'approche de Saint Augustin.'" Unfortunately, this marks a loss of the very complex fecundity of Marion's work on the margins of these two disciplines that made his work so intriguing and satisfying to enter into.

89. See Marion, "Evidence and Bedazzlement," in *Prolegomena to Charity*, trans. Stephen Lewis (New York: Fordham University Press, 2002), 53–70.

90. Love, Marion tells us, "Opens the eyes: not in the way violence opens the eyes of the disabused, but as a child opens his eyes to the world, or a sleeper opens his eyes to the morning" (ibid., 69).

Conclusion

1. Marion, "The Banality of Saturation," 403.

2. Marion's closest model of such an apologetic retrieval, Hans Urs von Balthasar, came under similar critical fire. Balthasar faced criticisms that his reading of the Fathers was too influenced by contemporary questions, an influence that leads to both an "eclecticism" in his choice of thinkers to retrieve and a certain "ahistoricism" to his approach: he was labeled "audaciously creative" and "transgressive" of normal bounds of scholarship. See Brian Daley, "Balthasar's Reading of the Church Fathers," in *The Cambridge Companion to Hans Urs von Balthasar*, ed. Edward T. Oakes, S.J., and David Moss (Cambridge: Cambridge University Press, 2004), 202. The latter and sharper accusations are made by Dom Polycarp Sherwood and cited by Daley (187, 188).

3. To give but one example, Maximus the Confessor's scholia on Dionysius are not mere replication but are a renegotiation of passages that have become "difficult," given the "shift in interpretative framework" (that is, given the emergent Monoenergist and Monothelite controversies of the seventh century), despite Maximus's disavowal of any sort of innovation of tradition.

4. It should be noted that Marion is, of course, by no means unique in his return to premodern Christian and Jewish sources. Such a return, as a strategy for critiquing modernity, is in abundant evidence in recent Continental philosophy.

5. I must also answer this charge myself: by arguing that a retrieval of Gregory of Nyssa and Dionysius imports two distinct apophatic strategies that emerge from their different ontological emphases, am I not simply reintroducing a premodern Christian metaphysic into Marion's phenomenology as though by fiat? My defense is simply that, if I reintroduce ontology in Marion's thought, it is not an uninvited guest there. In his early writings explicitly (and throughout his thought in a more implicit way), Marion places his understanding of Dionysian apophasis within a liturgical world that necessitates certain ontological assumptions.

6. Marion, *In Excess,* 128, 134.

7. Merold Westphal, "Vision and Voice: Phenomenology and Theology in the Work of Jean-Luc Marion," *International Journal of Philosophy and Religion* 60 (2006): 117.

SELECT BIBLIOGRAPHY

Primary Sources

Dionysius the Areopagite

Pseudo-Dionysius the Areopagite. *De Divinis Nominibus.* In *Corpus Dionsyiacum* I, ed. Beate Regina Suchla. Berlin: Walter de Gruyter, 1990.

———. *De coelesti hierarchia.* In *Corpus Dionsyiacum* II, ed. G. Heil and A. M. Ritter. Berlin: Walter de Gruyter, 1991.

———. *De ecclesiastica hierarchia.* In *Corpus Dionsyiacum* II, ed. G. Heil and A. M. Ritter. Berlin: Walter de Gruyter, 1991.

———. *De mystica theologia.* In *Corpus Dionsyiacum* II, ed. G. Heil and A. M. Ritter. Berlin: Walter de Gruyter, 1991.

———. *Epistulae.* In *Corpus Dionysiacum* II, ed. G. Heil and A. M. Ritter. Berlin: Walter de Gruyter, 1991.

———. *The Celestial and Ecclesiastical Hierarchy.* Translated by John H. Parker. London: Skeffington and Son, 1897.

———. *The Works of Dionysius the Areopagite.* Translated by John H. Parker. London: Skeffington and Son, 1897.

———. *Pseudo-Dionysius: The Complete Works.* Translated by Colm Luibheid. New York: Paulist Press, 1987.

Gregory of Nyssa

Gregory of Nyssa. *Commentary on the Inscriptions of the Psalms.* Translated by Casimir McCambley. Brookline, Mass.: Hellenic College Press, 1997.

———. *Contra Eunomium.* In *Gregorii Nysseni Opera,* vol. 1.2, ed. Werner Jaeger. Leiden: Brill, 1960. Translated by William Moore and H. A. Wilson as *Against Eunomius.* In *Nicene Post-Nicene Fathers,* series 2, 5. *CE* II translated by Stuart George Hall as *Gregory of Nyssa: Contra Eunomium II: An English Version with Supporting Studies. Proceedings of the 10th International Colloquium on Gregory of Nyssa (Olomouc, September 15–18, 2004),* ed. Lenka Karfíková, Scot Douglass, Johannes Zachhuber, and Stuart George Hall. Leiden: Brill, 2007.

———. *De anima et resurrectione.* In *Patrologia Graeca,* 46.12–160, ed. J. P. Migne. Translated by Catharine P. Roth. *On the Soul and the Resurrection.* Crestwood, N.Y.: St. Vladimir's Seminary Press, 2002.

———. *De beatitudinibus.* In *Gregorii Nysseni Opera,* vol. 7.2, ed. J. F. Callahan. Leiden: Brill, 1992. Translated by Hubertus Drobner and Alberto Viciano.

Gregory of Nyssa, Homilies on the Beatitudes: An English Version with Commentary and Supporting Studies. Proceedings of the Eighth International Colloquium on Gregory of Nyssa (Paderborn, 14–18 September 1998). Leiden: Brill, 2000.

———. *De opificio hominis.* In *Patrologia Graeca,* 44, ed. J. P. Migne. Translated by H. A. Wilson. *On the Making of the Human Person.* In *Nicene Post-Nicene Fathers,* series 2, 5.

———. *De perfectione.* In *Gregorii Nysseni Opera,* vol. 8.1, ed. Werner Jaeger. Leiden: Brill, 1952. Translated by Virginia Woods Callahan. *Saint Gregory of Nyssa; Ascetical Works.* Washington, D.C.: Catholic University of America Press, 1967.

———. *De Vita Moysis.* In *Gregorii Nysseni Opera,* vol. 7.1, ed. Herbert Musurillo. Leiden: Brill, 1964. Translated by A. J. Malherbe and E. Ferguson. *Gregory of Nyssa: The Life of Moses.* New York: Paulist Press, 1978.

———. *From Glory to Glory: Texts from Gregory of Nyssa's Mystical Writings,* ed. Jean Daniélou. Translated by Herbert Musurillo. Crestwood, N.Y.: St. Vladimir's Seminary Press, 1979.

———. *In Canticum canticorum.* In *Gregorii Nysseni Opera,* vol. 6, ed. H. Langerbeck. Leiden: Brill, 1986. Translated by Casimir McCambley. *Saint Gregory of Nyssa: Commentary on the Song of Songs.* Brookline, Mass.: Hellenic College Press, 1987.

———. *In Ecclesiastes.* In *Patrologia Graeca,* 44, ed. J. P. Migne.

Jean-Luc Marion (French)

Marion, Jean-Luc. "Distance et beatitude: sur le mot capacitas chez Saint Augustin." *Résurrection* 29 (1968): 58–80.

———. "Ce mystère qui juge celui qui le juge." *Résurrection* 32 (1969): 54–78.

———. "Penser juste ou trahir le mystère: Notes sur l'elaboration patristique du dogme de l'incarnation." *Résurrection* 30 (1969): 68–93.

———. "Le splendeur de la contemplation eucharistique." *Résurrection* 31 (1969): 84–88.

———. "Amour de Dieu, amour des hommes." *Résurrection* 34 (1970): 89–96.

———. "Distance et louange: Du concept de Réquisit (aitia) au statut trinitaire de langage théologique selon Denys le mystique." *Résurrection* 38 (1971): 89–118.

———. "Les deux volontés du Christ selon saint Maxime le Confesseur." *Résurrection* 41 (1972): 48–66.

———. "Presence et distance: Remarque sur l'implication reciproque de la contemplation eucharistique et de la presence reelle." *Revue Résurrection* 43–44 (1974): 31–58.

———. *Sur l'ontologie grise de Descartes: Science cartésienne et savoir aristotélicien dans les Regulae.* Paris: J. Vrin, 1975.

———. *L'idole et la distance: Cinq études.* Paris: Grasset, 1977.

———. *Sur le théologie blanche de Descartes: Analogie, creation des vérités éternelle et fondement.* Paris: Presses universitaires de France, 1981.

———. *Dieu sans l'être: Hors-texte.* Paris: Fayard, 1982.

———. "De la 'mort de Dieu' aux noms divins: L'itinéraire théologique de la métaphysique." *Laval théologique et philosophique* (1985/1).

———. "La fin de la 'fin de la métaphysique'." *Laval théologique et philosophique* (1986/1).

———. *Prolégomènes à la charité.* Paris: Éditions de la Différence, 1986.

———. *Sur le prisme métaphysique de Descartes: Constitution et limites de l'onto-théo-logie dans la pensée Cartésienne.* Paris: Presses universitaires de France, 1986.

———. "Générosité et phénoménologie: Remarques sur l'interprétation de *cogito* cartésian par Michel Henry." *Les Études philosophiques* (1988/1).

———. *Réduction et donation. Recherches sur Husserl, Heidegger et la phénoménologie.* Paris: Presses universitaires de France, 1989.

———. *La croisée du visible.* Paris: Éditions de la Différence, 1991.

———. *Questions Cartésiennes.* Paris: Presses universitaires de France, 1991.

———. "Réponses à quelques questions." *Revue de métaphysique et de morale* (1991).

———. "Le sujet en dernier appel." *Revue de métaphysique et de morale* (1991/1).

———. "Le phénomène saturé." In *Phénoménologie et théologie,* ed. Jean-François Courtine. Paris: Critérion, 1992.

———. "Note sur l'indifférence ontologique." In *Emmanuel Lévinas: L'Ethique comme philosophie première,* ed. J. Greisch and J. Rolland. Paris: Le Cerf, 1993.

———. "Saint Thomas d'Aquin et l'onto-théo-logie." *Revue Thomiste* 95 (1995).

———. *Étant Donné: Essai d'une phénoménologie de la donation.* 2. éd. Paris: Presses universitaires de France, 1997.

———. *De surcroît. etudes sur les phénomènes saturés.* Paris: Presses universitaires de France, 2001.

———. *Le phénomène érotique: Six méditations.* Paris: Grasset, 2003.

———. *Le visible et le révélé.* Paris: Éditions de CERF, 2005.

———. *Au lieu de soi: L'approche de Saint Augustin.* Paris: Presses universitaires de France, 2008.

Jean-Luc Marion (English)

Marion, Jean-Luc. *God Without Being.* Translated by Thomas A. Carlson. Chicago: University of Chicago Press, 1991.

———. "Generosity and Phenomenology: Remarks on Michel Henry's Interpretation of the Cartesian *cogito*." In *Essays on the Philosophy and Science of René Descartes,* ed. S. Voss. New York: Oxford University Press, 1993.

———. "The Final Appeal of the Subject." Translated by Simon Critchley. In *Deconstructive Subjectivities,* ed. Simon Critchley and Peter Dews. Albany: SUNY Press, 1996.

———. "Nothing and Nothing Else." In *The Ancients and the Moderns,* ed. Reginald Lilly, 183–95. Bloomington: Indiana University Press, 1996.

———. "Metaphysics and Phenomenology: A Summary for Theologians." In *The Postmodern God,* ed. Graham Ward. Oxford: Blackwell, 1997.

———. "The Idea of God." Translated by Thomas A. Carlson. In *The Cambridge History of Seventeenth-Century Philosophy,* ed. Daniel Garber and Michael Ayers. Vol. 1. Cambridge: Cambridge University Press, 1998.

———. *Reduction and Givenness: Investigations of Husserl, Heidegger, and Phenomenology.* Translated by Thomas A. Carlson. Evanston, Ill.: Northwestern University Press, 1998.

———. *Cartesian Questions: Method and Metaphysics.* Translated by Jeffrey L. Kosky. Chicago: University of Chicago Press, 1999.

———. "The Other First Philosophy and the Question of Givenness." *Critical Inquiry* 25.4 (1999).

———. *On Descartes' Metaphysical Prism: The Constitution and the Limits of Onto-Theo-Logy in Cartesian Thought.* Chicago: University of Chicago Press, 1999.

———. "Sketch of Phenomenological Concept of the Gift." In *Postmodern Philosophy and Christian Thought,* ed. J. Conley and D. Poe. Bloomington: Indiana University Press, 1999.

———. "The Saturated Phenomenon." Translated by Jeffrey L. Kosky. In *Phenomenology and the 'Theological Turn': The French Debate.* New York: Fordham University Press, 2000.

———. *The Idol and Distance: Five Studies.* Translated by Thomas A. Carlson. New York: Fordham University Press, 2001.

———. *Prolegomena to Charity.* Translated by Stephen Lewis. New York: Fordham University Press, 2002.

———. "They Recognized Him and He Became Invisible to Them." *Modern Theology* 18.2 (2002).

———. *Being Given: Toward a Phenomenology of Givenness.* Translated by Jeffrey L. Kosky. Stanford, Calif.: Stanford University Press, 2002.

———. *In Excess: Studies of Saturated Phenomena.* Translated by Robyn Horner and Vincent Berraud. New York: Fordham University Press, 2002.

———. "The Unspoken: Apophasis and the Discourse of Love." Translated by Arianne Conty. *Proceedings of the American Catholic Philosophical Association* 76 (2002).

———. "Thomas Aquinas and Onto-theo-logy." Translated by B. Gendreau, R. Rethy, and M. Sweeney. In *Mystics: Presence and Aporia,* ed. Michael Kessler and Christian Sheppard. Chicago: University of Chicago Press, 2003.

———. *The Crossing of the Visible.* Translated by James K. A. Smith. Stanford, Calif.: Stanford University Press, 2004.

———. *Descartes' Grey Ontology: Cartesian Science and Aristotelean Thought in the* Regulae. Translated by S. Donohue. South Bend, Ind.: St. Augustine's Press, 2004.

———. "God and the Gift: A Continental Perspective." Interview in *God's Advocates: Christian Thinkers in Conversation*, ed. Rupert Shortt. Grand Rapids, Mich.: Eerdmans, 2005.

———. "*Mihi magna quaestio factus sum:* The Privilege of Unknowing." *Journal of Religion* 85.1 (2005).

———. *The Erotic Phenomenon.* Translated by Stephen Lewis. Chicago: University of Chicago Press, 2006.

———. "The Banality of Saturation." In *Counter-Experiences: Reading Jean-Luc Marion*, ed. Kevin Hart. Notre Dame, Ind.: Notre Dame University Press, 2007.

———. *The Visible and the Revealed.* Translated by Christina M. Gschwandtner. New York: Fordham University Press, 2008.

Jean Luc Marion, Jacques Derrida, and Richard Kearney. "On the Gift: A Discussion between Jacques Derrida and Jean-Luc Marion." In *God, the Gift, and Postmodernism.* Bloomington: Indiana University Press, 1999.

Secondary Sources

Ahn, Taekyun. "The Gift and the Understanding of God: Iconic Theology of J-L. Marion." Ph.D. diss., Drew University, 2003.

Almond, Ian. "How Not to Deconstruct a Dominican: Derrida on God and 'Hypertruth.'" *Journal of the American Academy of Religion* 68.2 (2000): 329–44.

Alweiss, Lilian. "I am, I exist." In *Givenness and God: Questions of Jean-Luc Marion.* New York: Fordham University Press, 2005.

Ameriks, Karl. "Husserl's Realism." *Philosophical Review* 86 (1977): 498–519.

Armstrong, Arthur Hilary. "Platonic Elements in St. Gregory of Nyssa's Doctrine of Man." *Dominican Studies* 1 (1948).

———. "The Nature of Man in St. Gregory of Nyssa." *Eastern Churches Quarterly* 8.3 (1949).

———. "God's Transcendence and Infinity." In *Christian Faith and Greek Philosophy*, ed. A. H. Armstrong and R. A. Markus. New York: Sheed and Ward, 1960.

———. "Negative Theology." *Downside Review* 95.320 (1977).

———. "On Not Knowing Too Much about God." In *Philosophy, supplement 25: Philosophy in Christianity.* Cambridge: Cambridge University Press, 1989.

Austin, J. L. *How to Do Things with Words.* Oxford: Clarendon Press, 1975.

Balas, David L. "*Metousia Theou:* Man's Participation in God's Perfections According to St. Gregory of Nyssa." *Studia Anselmiana* 55 (1966).

———. "Eternity and Time in Gregory of Nyssa's *Contra Eunomium*." In *Gregor von Nyssa und die Philosophie: Zweites internationales Kolloquium über Gregor von Nyssa*, ed. Heinrich Dörrie, Margarete Allenburger, and Uta Schramm. Leiden: Brill, 1976.

Balthasar, Hans Urs von. "The Problem of Evil." *Internationale Katholische Zeitschrift "Communio"* 8 (1979): 193–250.

———. "Denys." In *Glory of the Lord: Theological Aesthetics*, vol. 2, *Studies in Theological Styles: Clerical Styles*. Translated by Andrew Louth, Francis McDonagh, and Brian McNeil C.R.V., ed. John Riches. San Francisco: Ignatius Press, 1984.

———. *Presence and Thought: An Essay on the Religious Philosophy of Gregory of Nyssa*. Translated by Mark Sebanc. San Francisco: Ignatius Press, 1995.

Benoist, Jocelyn. "Le tournant théologique." In *L'Idée de phenomenology*. Paris: Beauchesne, 2001.

———. "L'écart plutôt que l'excédent." *Philosophie: Jean-Luc Marion* 78. Paris: Minuit, 2003.

Benson, Bruce Ellis. *Graven Ideologies: Nietzsche, Derrida and Marion on Modern Idolatry*. Westmont, Ill.: InterVarsity Press, 2002.

———. "Love is a Given: Jean-Luc Marion Tests the Limits of Logic." *Christian Century* 120.3 (2003): 22–25.

———. "Jean-Luc Marion: A Theo-Logical Introduction." *Worship* 80.4 (2006): 383–84.

Benson, Bruce Ellis, and Norman Wirzba. *The Phenomenology of Prayer*. New York: Fordham University Press, 2005.

Blans, Bert. "Cloud of Unknowing: An Orientation in Negative Theology from Dionysius the Areopagite, Eckhart, and John of the Cross to Modernity." In *Flight of the Gods: Philosophical Perspectives on Negative Theology*. New York: Fordham University Press, 2000.

Bloechl, Jeffrey. "Dialectical Approaches to Retrieving God after Heidegger: Premises and Consequences (Lacoste and Marion)." *Pacifica: Journal of the Melbourne College of Divinity* 13 (2000).

Blowers, Paul. "Maximus the Confessor, Gregory of Nyssa and the Concept of 'Perpetual Progress.'" *Vigiliae Christianae* (1992).

Boeve, Lieven, Yves de Maeseneer, and Stijn van den Bossche. *Religious Experience and Contemporary Theological Epistemology*. Leuven: Peeters, 2005.

Bossche, Stijn van den. "From the Other's Point of View: The Challenge of Jean-Luc Marion's Phenomenology to Theology." In *Religious Experience and Contemporary Theological Epistemology*. Leuven: Leuven University Press; Peeters, 2005.

———. "God Does Appear in Immanence After All: Jean-Luc Marion's Phenomenology as a New First Philosophy for Theology." In *Sacramental Presence in a Postmodern Context*, 325–46. Leuven: Peeters, 2001.

Bouget, J. R. "Le vocabulaire de l'union et du rapport des natures chez saint Grégoire de Nysse." *Revue Thomiste* 68 (1968).

Bourdieu, Pierre. *Homo Academicus*. Translated by Peter Collier. Cambridge: Polity Press, 1988.

Bouyer, Louis. *L'Eglise de Dieu*. Paris: Cerf, 1970.

Bradley, Arthur. "God *Sans* Being: Derrida and Marion and a Paradoxical Writing of the Word *Without*." *Literature and Theology* 14.3 (2000).

———. "Without Negative Theology: Deconstruction and the Politics of Negative Theology." *Heythrop Journal* 42.2 (2001): 133.

———. *Negative Theology and Modern French Philosophy.* London: Routledge, 2004.

Breton, Stanislas. *The Word and The Cross.* Translated by Jacquelyn Porter. New York: Fordham University Press, 2002.

Brightman, Robert. "Apophatic Theology and Divine Infinity in St. Gregory of Nyssa." *Greek Orthodox Theological Review* 18 (1973).

Bulhof, Isle, and Laurens ten Kate, eds. *Flight of the Gods: Philosophical Perspectives on Negative Theology.* New York: Fordham University Press, 2000.

Bulzan, Daniel. "Apophaticism, Postmodernism and Language: Two Similar Cases of Theological Imbalance." *Scottish Journal of Theology* 50.3 (1997): 261–87.

Burrell, David. "Reflections on 'Negative Theology' in the Light of a Recent Venture to Speak of 'God Without Being.'" In *Postmodernism and Christian Philosophy,* ed. R. T. Ciapolo. Washington, D.C.: Catholic University of America Press, 1997.

Callahan, John F. "Greek Philosophy and the Cappadocian Cosmology." *Dumbarton Oaks Papers* 12 (1958).

Canévet, Mariette. *Grégoire de Nysse et l'herméneutique biblique: Étude des rapport entre le langage et la connaissance de Dieu.* Paris: Études Augustiniennes, 1983.

Caputo, John D. *The Prayers and Tears of Jacques Derrida: Religion without Religion.* Bloomington: Indiana University Press, 1997.

———. "Apostles of the Impossible." In *God, the Gift and Postmodernism,* ed. John Caputo and Michael Scanlon. Bloomington: Indiana University Press, 1999.

———. *Questioning God.* Bloomington: Indiana University Press, 2001.

———. "The Hyperbolization of Phenomenology: Two Possibilities for Religion in Recent Continental Philosophy." In *Counter-Experiences: Reading Jean-Luc Marion,* ed. Kevin Hart. Notre Dame, Ind.: Notre Dame University Press, 2007.

Caputo, John D., and Michael J. Scanlon, eds. *God, the Gift, and Postmodernism.* Bloomington: Indiana University Press, 1999.

Carabine, Deirdre. *The Unknown God. Negative Theology in the Platonic Tradition: Plato to Eriugena.* Leuven: Peeters, 1995.

Carlson, Thomas A. *Indiscretion, Finitude and the Naming of God.* Chicago: University of Chicago Press, 1999.

———. "Consuming Desire's Deferral: A Theological Shadow in the Culture of Image." *Parralax* 5.1 (1999).

———. "Postmetaphysical Theology." In *Cambridge Companion to Postmodern Theology,* 58–75. Cambridge: Cambridge University Press, 2003.

———. "Blindness and the Decision to See: On Revelation and Reception in Jean-Luc Marion." In *Counter-Experiences: Reading Jean-Luc Marion,* ed. Kevin Hart. Notre Dame, Ind.: Notre Dame University Press, 2007.

Carrol, W. J. "Unity, Participation and Wholes in a Key Text of Pseudo-Dionysius the Areopagite's *Divine Names.*" *New Scholasticism* 57 (1983).

———. "Participation and Infinity in Dionysius the Areopagite." *Patristic and Byzantine Review* 2 (1983).

Coakley, Sarah. "What Does Chalcedon Solve and What Does it Not? Some Reflections on the Status and Meaning of the Chalcedonian 'Definition.'" In *The Incarnation,* ed. Stephen T. Davis, Daniel Kendall SJ, and Gerald O'Collins SJ. Oxford: Oxford University Press, 2002.

———. Introduction to *Rethinking Gregory of Nyssa,* ed. Sarah Coakley. Oxford: Blackwell, 2003.

———. "Does Kenosis Rest on a Mistake? Three Kenotic Models in Patristic Exegesis." In *Exploring Kenotic Christology,* ed. C. Stephen Evans. Oxford: Oxford University Press, 2006.

Cooke, Alexander. "What Saturates?" *Philosophy Today* 48.2 (2000).

Collins, J. J. "The Primacy of Love in St. Gregory of Nyssa's Theology." *Diakonia* 14 (1979).

Corbin, Michel. "Négation et transcendence dans l'oeuvre de Denys." *Revue des sciences philosophiques et théologiques* 69 (1985): 41–76.

Corrigan, Kevin. "'Solitary' Mysticism in Plotinus, Proclus, Gregory of Nyssa and Pseudo-Dionysius." *Journal of Religion* 76 (1996).

Corsini, Eugenio. "Plérôme humaine et plérôme cosmique chez Grégoire de Nysse." In *Écriture et culture philosophique dans la pensée de Grégoire de Nysse,* ed. Marguerite Harl. Leiden: Brill, 1971.

Daley, Brian. "Divine Transcendence and Human Transformation: Gregory of Nyssa's Anti-Apollinarian Christology." *Studia Patristica* 31 (1997).

———. "Balthasar's Reading of the Church Fathers." In *The Cambridge Companion to Hans Urs von Balthasar,* ed. Edward T. Oakes, SJ, and David Moss. Cambridge: Cambridge University Press, 2004.

Damian, Theodore. "The Doctrine of Creation: In Pseudo-Dionysius Areopagite's Theology." *Patristic and Byzantine Review,* nos. 1–6 (1998): 49–67.

Daniélou, Jean. *Platonisme et théologie mystique: Essai sur la doctrine spirituelle de saint Grégoire de Nysse,* rev. ed. Paris: Aubier, 1953.

———. "Eunome l'Arien et l'exégèse neo-platonicienne du Cratyle." *Revue des Études Grecques* 69 (1956).

———. "Akolouthia chez Grégoire de Nysse." *Recherches de science religieuse* (1966).

———. *L'être et le temps chez Grégoire de Nysse.* Leiden: Brill, 1970.

———, ed. *From Glory to Glory: Texts from Gregory of Nyssa's Mystical Writings.* Translated by Herbert Musurillo, SJ. New York: St. Vladimir's Seminary Press, 1995.

Davies, Oliver, and Denys Turner, eds. *Silence and The Word: Negative Theology and Incarnation.* Cambridge: Cambridge University Press, 2002.

Dehart, Paul. "The Ambiguous Infinite: Jüngel, Marion and the God of Descartes." *Journal of Religion* 82.1 (2002).

Derrida, Jacques. *Speech and Phenomena and Other Essays on Husserl's Theory of Signs.* Translated by David B. Allison. Evanston, Ill.: Northwestern University Press, 1967.

———. *Writing and Difference.* Translated by Alan Bass. Chicago: University of Chicago Press, 1978.

———. "*Différance.*" In *Margins of Philosophy.* Translated by Alan Bass. Chicago: University of Chicago Press, 1982.

———. *Donner le temps: I. La fausse monnaie.* Paris: Éditions Galilée, 1991. Translated into English by Peggy Kamuf. *Given Time: I. Counterfeit Money.* Chicago: University of Chicago Press, 1992.

———. "How to Avoid Speaking: Denials." In *Derrida and Negative Theology,* ed. Harold Coward and Toby Foshay. Albany: SUNY Press, 1992.

———. "Sauf le nom (post-scriptum)." In *On the Name,* ed. Thomas Dutoit. Stanford, Calif.: Stanford University Press, 1995.

———. *Of Grammatology.* Translated by Gayatri Chakravorty Spivak. Baltimore, Md.: Johns Hopkins University Press, 1997.

Dolidze, Tina. "The Cognitive Function of *Epinoia* in CE II and Its Meaning for Gregory of Nyssa's Theory of Theological Language." In *Gregory of Nyssa: Contra Eunomium II,* ed. Lenka Karfíková, Scot Douglass, Johannes Zachhuber, and Stuart George Hall. Leiden: Brill, 2007.

Dooley, Mark. "Marion's Ambition of Transcendence." In *Givenness and God: Questions of Jean-Luc Marion,* ed. Eoin Cassidy and Ian Leask. New York: Fordham University Press, 2004.

Douglass, Scot. "A Critical Analysis of Gregory's Philosophy of Language: The Linguistic Reconstitution of Metadiastemic Intrusions." In *Gregory of Nyssa: Homilies on the Beatitudes,* ed. Hubertus R. Drobner and Alberto Viciano. Leiden: Brill, 2000.

———. *Theology of the Gap: Cappadocian Language Theory and the Trinitarian Controversy.* New York: Peter Lang, 2005.

Drabinski, J. E. "Sense and Icon: The Problem of *Sinngebung* in Levinas and Marion." *Philosophy Today* 42 (1998).

Duclow, Donald F. "Gregory of Nyssa and Nicholas of Cusa: Infinity, Anthropology, and the Via Negativa." *Downside Review* 92 (1974).

Elliott, Brian. "Reduced Phenomena and Unreserved Debts in Marion's Reading of Heidegger." In *Givenness and God: Questions of Jean-Luc Marion,* ed. Eoin Cassidy and Ian Leask. New York: Fordham University Press, 2005.

English, Adam C. "Structure, Mystery, Power: The Christian Ontology of Maurice Blondel (John Milbank, Henri de Lubac, Karl Rahner, Jean-Luc Marion)." Ph.D. diss., Baylor University, 2003.

Eunomius. *Apology for the Apology in Eunomius: The Extant Works,* ed. R. P. Vaggione. Oxford: Clarendon Press, 1987.

Ewbank, Michael B. "Of Idols, Icons, and Aquinas's Esse: Reflections on Jean-Luc Marion." *International Philosophical Quarterly* 42.2 (2002).

Farley, Wendy. *The Wounding and Healing of Desire: Weaving Heaven and Earth.* Louisville, Ky.: Westminster John Knox Press, 2005.

——. *Eros for the Other: Retaining Truth in a Pluralistic World.* University Park: Pennsylvania State University Press, 1996.

Faulconer, James E. *Transcendence in Philosophy and Religion.* Bloomington: Indiana University Press, 2003.

Ferguson, Everett. "God's Infinity and Man's Mutability: Perpetual Progress According to Gregory of Nyssa." *Greek Orthodox Theological Review* 18 (1979).

Ferretter, Luke. "How to Avoid Speaking of the Other: Derrida, Dionysius and the Problematic of Negative Theology." *Paragraph* 24.1 (2001).

Fischer, Jeffrey. "The Theology of Dis/similarity: Negation in Pseudo-Dionysius." *Journal of Religion* 81.4 (2001).

Gadamer, Hans-Georg. *Truth and Method.* Translated by Joel Weinsheimer and Donald G. Marshall. New York: Continuum, 2004.

Gersh, Stephen. *From Iamblichus to Eriugena: An Investigation of the Prehistory and Evolution of the Pseudo-Dionysian Tradition.* Leiden: Brill, 1978.

Gilbert, P. "Substance et présence: Derrida et Marion critiques de Husserl." *Gregorianum* 75 (1994).

Godzieba, Anthony J. "Ontotheology to Excess: Imagining God Without Being." *Theological Studies* 56.1 (1995).

Golitzin, Alexander. *Et Introibo ad Altare Dei: The Mystagogy of Dionysius Areopagita, with special reference to its predecessors in the Eastern Christian Tradition.* Analecta Vlatadon 59. Thessaloniki: Alexander Golitzin, 1994.

——. "Hierarchy versus Anarchy? Dionysius Areopagita, Symeon the New Theologian, and Nicetas Stethatos." In *New Perspectives on Historical Theology: Essays in Memory of John Meyendorff,* ed. Bradley Nassif. Grand Rapids, Mich.: Eerdmans, 1996.

——. "Liturgy and Mysticism: The Experience of God in Orthodox Christianity." *Pro Ecclesia* 8.2 (1999).

——. "Revisiting the 'Sudden': Epistle III in the *Corpus Dionysiacum*." *Studia Patristica* 37 (2001).

——. "'Suddenly, Christ': The Place of Negative Theology in the Mystagogy of Dionysius Areopagites." In *Mystics: Presence and Aporia,* ed. Michael Kessler and Christian Sheppard, 8–37. Chicago: University of Chicago Press, 2003.

——. "Dionysius Areopagita: A Christian Mysticism?" *Pro Ecclesia* 12.2 (2003).

Greisch, Jean. "L'herméneutique dans la 'phénoménologie comme telle': Trois questions à propos de *Réduction et Donation*." *Revue de Métaphysique et de Morale* 96.1 (1991).

——. *Le cogito herméneutique: L'herméneutique philosophique et l'heritage cartésian.* Paris: Vrin, 2000.

Griffiths, Paul J. "More than a Bargain." *Commonweal* 134 (2007): 24–26.

Grondin, Jean. "La phénoménologie sans herméneutique": *L' herméneutique de la pensée contemporaine.* Paris: J. Vrin, 1993.

———. "La tension de la donation ultime et de la pensée herméneutique de l'application chez Jean-Luc Marion." *Dialogue* 38.3 (1999).

———. "Au lieu de la metaphysique? Les meditations augustiniennes de Jean-Luc Marion." www.laviedesidees.fr/Au-lieu-de-la-metaphysique.html (accessed Dec. 4, 2009).

Gschwandtner, Christina M. "A New 'Apologia': The Relationship between Theology and Philosophy in the Work of Jean-Luc Marion." *Heythrop Journal* 46 (2005): 299–313.

———. *Reading Jean-Luc Marion: Exceeding Metaphysics.* Bloomington: Indiana University Press, 2007.

Hadot, Pierre. *Philosophy as a Way of Life: Spiritual Exercises Socrates to Foucault.* Translated by Michael Chase. Oxford: Blackwell, 1995.

Hankey, Wayne. "Theoria Versus Poesis: Neoplatonism and Trinitarian Difference in Aquinas, John Milbank, Jean-Luc Marion and John Zizioulas." *Modern Theology* 15 (1999): 387–415.

Hanson, J. A. "Jean-Luc Marion and the Possibility of a Post-Modern Theology." *Mars Hill Review,* no. 12 (1998): 93–104.

Harrison, Verna. *Grace and Human Freedom According to St. Gregory of Nyssa.* Studies in the Bible and Early Christianity 30. Lewiston: Edwin Mellen, 1992.

Hart, David Bentley. *The Beauty of the Infinite: The Aesthetics of Christian Truth.* Grand Rapids, Mich.: Eerdmans, 2003.

Hart, Kevin. *The Trespass of the Sign: Deconstruction, Theology and Philosophy.* New York: Fordham University Press, 2000.

———, ed. *Counter-Experiences: Reading Jean-Luc Marion.* Notre Dame, Ind.: Notre Dame University Press, 2007.

Heidegger, Martin. *Being and Time.* Translated by John Macquarrie and Edward Robinson. San Francisco: Harper, 1962.

———. *The Basic Problems of Philosophy.* Bloomington: Indiana University Press, 1982.

———. "Letter on 'Humanism'." In *Pathmarks,* ed. William McNeill. Cambridge: Cambridge University Press, 1998.

———. Introduction to "What Is Metaphysics?" In *Pathmarks,* ed. William McNeill. Cambridge: Cambridge University Press, 1998.

———. "Phenomenology and Theology." In *The Religious,* ed. John Caputo. Oxford: Blackwell, 2002.

———. "The Onto-theo-logical Constitution of Metaphysics." In *Identity and Difference.* Translated by Joan Stambauch. Chicago: University of Chicago Press, 2002.

———. *The Phenomenology of Religious Life.* Translated by Matthias Fritsch and Jennifer Anna Gosetti-Ferencei. Bloomington: Indiana University Press, 2004.

Heine, Ronald. *Perfection in the Virtuous Life: A Study of the Relationship between Edification and Polemical Theology in Gregory of Nyssa's De*

Vita Moysis. Cambridge, Mass.: Philadelphia Patristics Foundation, 1975.

———. "Gregory of Nyssa's Apology for Allegory." *Vigiliae Christianae* 38 (1984).

Hemming, Laurence. "Reading Heidegger: Is God without Being? Jean-Luc Marion's Reading of Martin Heidegger in *God Without Being.*" *New Blackfriars* 76 (1995).

Henry, Michel. "Quatre principes de la phénoménologie." *Revue de métaphysique et de morale* 96.1 (1991).

Horner, Robyn. *Rethinking God as Gift: Marion, Derrida, and the Limits of Phenomenology.* New York: Fordham University Press, 2001.

———. "Aporia or Excess: Two Strategies for Thinking r/Revelation." In *Other Testaments: Derrida and Religion,* ed. Kevin Hart and Yvonne Sherwood. London: Routledge, 2004.

———. *Jean-Luc Marion: A Theo-Logical Introduction.* Burlington, Vt.: Ashgate Publications, 2005.

Husserl, Edmund. *Ideen zu Einer Reinen Phänomenologie und Phänomenologischen Philosophie, Erstes Buch* in *Husserliana III.* The Hague: Martinus Nijhoff, 1950.

———. *Cartesian Meditations: An Introduction to Phenomenology.* Translated by Dorion Cairns. The Hague: Martinus Nijhoff, 1960.

———. *Ideas Pertaining to a Pure Phenomenology and to a Phenomenological Philosophy.* Translated by F. Kersten. The Hague: Kluwer Academic Publishers Group, 1983.

———. *Logical Investigations, Volume One.* Translated by J. N. Findlay. London: Routledge and Kegan Paul.

———. *The Idea of Phenomenology.* Translated by William P. Alston and George Nakhnikian. The Hague: Kluwer Academic Publishers Group, 1990.

Irigaray, Luce. *Speculum of the Other Women.* Translated by Gillian C. Gill. Ithaca, N.Y.: Cornell University Press, 1985.

———. *Sexes and Genealogies.* Translated by Gillian C. Gill. New York: Columbia University Press, 1993.

Janicaud, Dominique. *Le tournant théologique de la phénoménologie française.* Combas: Éditions de l'Éclat, 1991. Translated by Bernard Prusak as "The Theological Turn of French Phenomenology" in *Phenomenology and the "Theological Turn": The French Debate.* New York: Fordham University Press, 2000.

———. *La phénoménologie éclatée.* Combas: Éditions de l'Éclat, 1998.

Jones, John D. "The Character of the Negative (Mystical) Theology for the Pseudo-Dionysius Areopagite." *Ethical Wisdom* (1977): 66–74.

Jones Farmer, Tamsin. "Revealing the Invisible: Gregory of Nyssa on the Gift of Revelation." *Modern Theology* 21 (2005): 67–84.

Jones, Tamsin. "Dionysius in Hans Urs von Balthasar and Jean-Luc Marion." In *Re-Thinking Dionysius the Areopagite,* ed. Sarah Coakley and Charles M. Stang. Oxford: Wiley-Blackwell, 2009.

Kal, Victor. "Being Unable to Speak, Seen as a Period: Difference and Distance in Jean-Luc Marion." In *Flight of the Gods: Philosophical Perspectives on Negative Theology,* ed. Isle Bulhof and Laurens ten Kate. New York: Fordham University Press, 2000.

Kant, Immanuel. *Critique of Pure Reason.* Translated by Paul Guyer and Allen Wood in *The Cambridge Edition of the Works of Immanuel Kant.* Cambridge: Cambridge University Press, 1998.

———. *Critique of Practical Reason.* Translated by Mary Gregor as *Practical Philosophy* in *The Cambridge Edition of the Works of Immanuel Kant.* Cambridge: Cambridge University Press, 1996.

Katz, Steven. *Mysticism and Language.* New York: Oxford University Press, 1992.

Kearney, Richard. *The God Who May Be: A Hermeneutics of Religion.* Bloomington: Indiana University Press, 2001.

———. *Strangers, Gods and Monsters: Interpreting Otherness.* London: Routledge, 2003.

Keenan, Mary Emily. "*De professione christiana* and *De perfectione:* A Study of the Ascetical Doctrine of St. Gregory of Nyssa." *Dumbarton Oaks Papers* 5 (1950).

Kerr, Fergus. "Aquinas after Marion." *New Blackfriars* 76 (1995).

———. "Balthasar and Metaphysics." In *The Cambridge Companion to Hans Urs Von Balthasar,* 224–38. Cambridge: Cambridge University Press, 2004.

Kessler, Michael, and Christian Sheppard, eds. *Mystics: Presence and Aporia.* Chicago: University of Chicago Press, 2003.

Klemm, David E. "Open Secrets: Derrida and Negative Theology." In *Derrida and Negative Theology,* ed. Robert Scharlemann. Charlottesville: University Press of Virginia, 1992.

Kobusch, Theo. "Die Epinoia—Das menschliche Bewusstsein in der antiken Philosophie." In *Gregory of Nyssa: Contra Eunomium II,* ed. Lenka Karfíková, Scot Douglass, and Johannes Zachhuber. Leiden: Brill, 2007.

Kovacs, George. *The Question of God in Heidegger's Phenomenology.* Evanston, Ill.: Northwestern University Press, 1990.

Kraftson-Hogue, Mike. "Predication Turning to Praise: Marion and Augustine on God and Hermeneutics (Giver, Giving, Gift, Giving)." *Literature and Theology: An International Journal of Theory, Criticism and Culture* 14.4 (2000).

Kristeva, Julia. *In the Beginning Was Love: Psychoanalysis and Faith.* Translated by Arthur Goldhammer. New York: Columbia University Press, 1987.

———. *Tales of Love.* Translated by Leon S. Roudiez. New York: Columbia University Press, 1987.

———. *Black Son: Depression and Melancholia.* Translated by Leon S. Roudiez. New York: Columbia University Press, 1989.

———. *New Maladies of the Soul.* Translated by Ross Guberman. New York: Columbia University Press, 1995.

Kühn, R. "'Sättinung' als absolutes Phänomen: Zur Kritik der klassische Phänomenalität (Kant, Husserl) bei Jean-Luc Marion." *Mesotes. Zeitschrift für
philosophischen Ost-West-Dialog* 3 (1995).

Laird, Martin. "By Faith Alone: A Technical Term in Gregory of Nyssa." *Vigiliae
Christianae* 54 (2000).

———. "Whereof We Speak: Gregory of Nyssa, Jean-Luc Marion and the Current
Apophatic Rage." *The Heythrop Journal* 42.1 (2001).

———. *Gregory of Nyssa and the Grasp of Faith: Union, Knowledge and the Divine
Presence.* Oxford: Oxford University Press, 2004.

Lanzetta, Beverly. *Radical Wisdom: A Feminist Mystical Theology.* Minneapolis:
Fortress Press, 2005.

Leask, Ian Graham. "The Dative Subject (and the 'Principle of Principles')." In
Givenness and God: Questions of Jean-Luc Marion, ed. Eoin Cassidy and Ian
Leask. New York: Fordham University Press, 2005.

Leask, Ian Graham, and Eoin G. Cassidy, eds. *Givenness and God: Questions of
Jean-Luc Marion.* New York: Fordham University Press, 2005.

Lees, Rosemary Ann. *The Negative Language of the Dionysian School of Mystical
Theology: An Approach to the* Cloud of Unknowing. Salzburg, Austria:
Institut für Anglistik und Amerikanistik, Universität Salzburg, 1983.

Levinas, Emmanuel. "Ethics as First Philosophy." In *The Levinas Reader,* ed. Sean
Hand. Oxford: Blackwell, 1989.

———. *Totality and Infinity: An Essay on Exteriority.* Translated by Alphonso
Lingis. Pittsburgh: Duquesne University Press, 1996.

———. *Of God Who Comes to Mind.* Translated by Bettina Bergo. Stanford, Calif.:
Stanford University Press, 1998.

———. *Otherwise than Being, or Beyond Essence.* Translated by Alphonso Lingis.
Pittsburgh: Duquesne University Press, 1998.

Lock, Charles. "Against Being: An Introduction to the Thought of Jean-Luc
Marion." *St. Vladimir's Theological Quarterly* 37.4 (1993).

Lossky, Vladimir. *The Vision of God.* Translated by Asheleigh Moorhouse.
London: Faith Press, 1963.

———. *The Mystical Theology of the Eastern Church.* New York: St. Vladimir's
Seminary Press, 1976.

———. "Darkness and Light in the Knowledge of God." In *In the Image and
Likeness of God.* New York: St. Vladimir's Seminary Press, 1974.

———. "La théologie négative dans la doctrine de Denys l'Aréopagite." *Revue des
sciences philosophique et théologique* 28 (1939).

Louth, Andrew. *The Origins of the Christian Mystical Tradition: From Plato to
Denys.* Oxford: Clarendon Press, 1981.

———. *Denys the Areopagite.* New York: Continuum, 1989.

Ludlow, Morwenna. *Universal Salvation: Eschatology in the Thought of Gregory of
Nyssa and Karl Rahner.* Oxford: Oxford University Press, 2000.

———. "Divine Infinity and Eschatology: The Limits and Dynamics of Human
Knowledge, according to Gregory of Nyssa (CE II, 67–170)." In *Gregory of*

Nyssa: Contra Eunomium II, ed. Lenka Karfíková, Scot Douglass, Johannes Zachhuber, and Stuart George Hall. Leiden: Brill, 2007.

———. *Gregory of Nyssa: Ancient and (Post) Modern.* Oxford: Oxford University Press, 2007.

Mackinlay, Shane. "Eyes Wide Shut: A Response to Jean-Luc Marion's Account of the Journey to Emmaus." *Modern Theology* 20.3 (2004): 447–56.

———. "Phenomenality in the Middle: Marion, Romano, and the Hermeneutics of the Event." In *Givenness and God: Questions of Jean-Luc Marion.* New York: Fordham University Press, 2005.

———. *Interpreting Excess: Jean-Luc Marion, Saturated Phenomena, and Hermeneutics.* New York: Fordham University Press, 2009.

Macleod, C. W. "Allegory and Mysticism in Origen and Gregory of Nyssa." *Journal of Theological Studies* 22 (1971).

Manoussakis, John P. "Thinking at the Limits: Jacques Derrida and Jean-Luc Marion in Dialogue with Richard Kearney." In *Philosophy Today* 48.1 (2004).

———. "The Phenomenon of God: From Husserl to Marion." *American Catholic Philosophical Quarterly* 78.1 (2004).

———. *God After Metaphysics: A Theological Aesthetic.* Bloomington: Indiana University Press, 2007.

McGinn, Bernard. *The Foundations of Mysticism,* vol. 1, *The Presence of God: A History of Western Christian Mysticism.* New York: Crossroad, 1991.

———. "God as Eros: Metaphysical Foundations of Christian Mysticism." In *New Perspectives on Historical Theology,* ed. Bradley Nassif. Grand Rapids, Mich.: Eerdmans, 1996.

McGinn, Bernard, and Patricia Ferris McGinn. *Early Christian Mystics: The Divine Vision of the Spiritual Masters.* New York: Crossroad, 2003.

Meredith, Anthony. *Gregory of Nyssa.* New York: Routledge, 1999.

———. *The Cappadocians.* Scarsdale, N.Y.: St. Vladimir's Seminary Press, 1995.

Meyendorff, John. *Christ in Eastern Christian Thought.* New York: St. Vladimir's Seminary Press, 1987.

Milbank, John. "Can a Gift Be Given? Prolegomena to a Future Trinitarian Metaphysic." In *Rethinking Metaphysics,* ed. L. Gregory Jones and Stephen E. Fowl. Oxford: Blackwell, 1995.

———. "Only Theology Overcomes Metaphysics." *New Blackfriars* 76 (1995).

———. *Being Reconciled: Ontology and Pardon.* London: Routledge, 2003.

———. "Gregory of Nyssa: The Force of Identity." In *Christian Origins: Theology, Rhetoric and Community,* ed. Lewis Ayres and Gareth Jones. London: Routledge, 1997.

Mooney, Timothy. "Hubris and Humility: Husserl's Reduction and Givenness." In *Givenness and God: Questions of Jean-Luc Marion.* New York: Fordham University Press, 2005.

Morrow, Derek J. "The Love 'without being' that Opens (to) Distance Part One: Exploring the Givenness of the Erotic Phenomenon with J-L. Marion." *Heythrop Journal* 46 (2005): 281–98.

———. "The Conceptual Idolatry of Descartes' Gray Ontology: An Epistemology 'Without Being.'" In *Givenness and God: Questions of Jean-Luc Marion.* New York: Fordham University Press, 2005.

Mortley, Raoul. *From Word to Silence: The Way of Negation, Christian and Greek.* Bonn: Peter Hanstein Verlag, 1986.

Moss, David. "Costly Giving: On Jean-Luc Marion's Theology of the Gift." *New Blackfriars* 74 (1993).

Mosshammer, Alden. "Disclosing but not Disclosed: Gregory of Nyssa as Deconstructionist." In *Studien zu Gregor von Nyssa und der christlichen Spätanike,* ed. H. R. Drobner and C. Klock. Leiden: Brill, 1990.

Mühlenberg, Ekkehard. *Die Unendlichkeit Gottes bei Gregor von Nyssa: Gregors Kritik am Gottesbegriff der klassischen Metaphysik.* Göttingen: Vandenhoeck and Ruprecht, 1966.

———. "Synergism in Gregory of Nyssa." *Zeitschrift für die neutestamentliche Wissenschaft* 68 (1977).

Noble, Ivana. "The Apophatic Way in Gregory of Nyssa." In *Philosophical Hermeneutics and Biblical Exegesis,* ed. Petr Pokorny and Jan Roskovec. Tübingen: Mohr Siebeck, 2002.

Ojell, Ari. "Service or Mastery? 'Theology' in Gregory of Nyssa's *Contra Eunomium* II." In *Gregory of Nyssa: Contra Eunomium II,* ed. Lenka Karfíková, Scot Douglass, Johannes Zachhuber, and Stuart George Hall. Leiden: Brill, 2007.

O'Leary, Joseph. *Questioning Back: The Overcoming of Metaphysics in Christian Tradition.* Minneapolis: Winston Press, 1985.

———. *Religious Pluralism and Christian Truth.* Edinburgh: Edinburgh University Press, 1996.

———. "Divine Simplicity and the Plurality of Attributes (*CE* II, 359–86; 445–560)." In *Gregory of Nyssa: Contra Eunomium II,* ed. Lenka Karfíková, Scot Douglass, Johannes Zachhuber, and Stuart George Hall. Leiden: Brill, 2007.

O'Meara, Dominic, ed. *Neoplatonism and Christian Thought.* Albany: SUNY Press, 1982.

O'Regan, Cyril. "Von Balthasar and Thick Retrieval: Post-Chalcedonian Symphonic Theology." *Gregorianum* 77.2 (1996): 227–60.

Origen. *On First Principles.* Translated by G. W. Butterworth. Gloucester, Mass.: Peter Smith, 1973.

O'Rourke, Fran. *Pseudo-Dionysius and the Metaphysics of Aquinas.* Leiden: Brill, 1992.

Otis, Brooks. "Cappadocian Thought as a Coherent System." *Dumbarton Oaks Papers* 12 (1958).

———. "Nicene Orthodoxy and Fourth-Century Mysticism." *Actes du XIIe Congrès International des Études Byzantines* 2 (1964).

Overton, John. "See(k)ing God through the Icon: A Semiotic Analysis of Jean-Luc Marion's *Dieu sans l'Etre.*" *Semiotica: Journal of the International Association for Semiotic Studies* 110 (1996).

Perl, Eric. "Symbol, Sacrament and Hierarchy in St. Dionysius the Areopagite." *Greek Orthodox Theological Review* 39 (1994).

———. "The Metaphysics of Love in Dionysius the Areopagite." *Journal of Neoplatonic Studies* 6.1 (1997).

———. "Signifying Nothing: Being as Sign in Neoplatonism and Derrida." In *Neoplatonism and Contemporary Thought*, ed. R. Baine Harris. Albany, N.Y.: SUNY Press, 2002.

Philipse, Hermann. "Transcendental Idealism." In *The Cambridge Companion to Husserl*, ed. Barry Smith and David W. Smith. Cambridge: Cambridge University Press, 1995.

Pokorný, Petr, and Jan Roskovec. *Philosophical Hermeneutics and Biblical Exegesis*. Tübingen: Mohr Siebeck, 2002.

Proclus. *The Elements of Theology*. Translated by E. R. Dodds. Oxford: Clarendon, 1963.

Puech, Henri-Charles. "La Ténebre mystique chez le Pseudo-Denys l'Aréopagite et dans la tradition patristique." In *En Quete de la Gnose: La Gnose et le temps et autres essais*. Paris: Gallimard, 1978.

Ricard, Marie-Andrée. "La question de la donation chez Jean-Luc Marion." *Laval théologique et philosophique* 57.1 (2001).

Ricoeur, Paul. *Figuring the Sacred: Religion, Narrative and Imagination*. Translated by David Pellauer. Minneapolis: Fortress Press, 1995.

Robbins, Jeffrey W. "The Problem of Ontotheology: Complicating the Divide between Philosophy and Theology." *Heythrop Journal* 43.2 (2002).

Robinette, Brian. "A Gift to Theology? Jean-Luc Marion's 'Saturated Phenomenon' in Christological Perspective." *Heythrop Journal* 48 (2007): 86–108.

Rogers, Annie G. *The Unsayable: The Hidden Language of Trauma*. New York: Random House, 2006.

Romano, Claude. "Love in Its Concept: Jean-Luc Marion's *The Erotic Phenomenon*." In *Counter-Experiences: Reading Jean-Luc Marion*. Notre Dame, Ind.: Notre Dame University Press, 2007.

Rorem, Paul. *Biblical and Liturgical Symbols within the Pseudo-Dionysian Synthesis*. Toronto: Pontifical Institute of Medieval Studies, 1984.

———. *Pseudo-Dionysius: A Commentary on the Texts and an Introduction to their Influence*. New York: Oxford University Press, 1993.

Rorem, Paul, and John C. Lamoreaux. *John of Scythopolis and the Dionysian Corpus: Annotating the Areopagite*. Oxford: Clarendon Press, 1998.

Roques, René. *L'univers Dionysien: Structure hiérarchique du monde selon le pseudo-Denys*. Paris: Aubier, 1954.

Roth, Catherine. "Platonic and Pauline Elements in the Ascent of the Soul in Gregory of Nyssa's *Dialogue on the Soul and the Resurrection*." *Vigiliae Christianae* 46 (1992).

Rubenstein, Mary-Jane. "Unknow Thyself: Apophaticism, Deconstruction and Theology after Ontotheology." *Modern Theology* 19.3 (2003).

Shanley, Brian. "Saint Thomas, Onto-theology, and Marion." *The Thomist* 60.4 (1996).

Schindler, David L. "The Theology of Henri De Lubac, Communio at Twenty Years." *Communio* 19 (1992): 332–509.

Schrijvers, Joeri. "Ontotheological Turnings? Marion, Lacoste and Levinas on the Decentering of Modern Subjectivity." *Modern Theology* 22 (2006): 221–53.

———. "In (the) Place of the Self: A Critical Study of Jean-Luc Marion's 'Au lieu de soi. L'approche de Saint Augustin.'" *Modern Theology* 25 (2009): 661–86.

Sells, Michael Anthony. *Mystical Languages of Unsaying.* Chicago: University of Chicago Press, 1994.

Sherry, Patrick. "The Art of Theology: Hans Urs Von Balthasar's Theological Aesthetics and the Foundations of Faith." *Ars Disputandi* 5 (2005).

Sigurdson, Ola. "Contemporary French Theology and Philosophy. 2." *Svensk Teologisk Kvartalskrift* 79.4 (2003): 170–99.

Smit, Peter-Ben. "The Bishop and His/Her Eucharistic Community: A Critique of Jean-Luc Marion's Eucharistic Hermeneutic." *Modern Theology* 19.1 (2003): 29–40.

Smith, James K. A. "Respect and Donation: A Critique of Marion's Critique of Husserl." *American Catholic Philosophical Quarterly* 71.4 (1997).

———. "Liberating Religion from Theology: Marion and Heidegger on the Possibility of a Phenomenology of Religion." In *International Journal for Philosophy of Religion* 46.1 (1999).

———. *Speech and Theology: Language and the Logic of the Incarnation.* London: Routledge, 2002.

Stead, G. C. "Ontology and Terminology in Gregory of Nyssa." In *Gregor von Nyssa und die Philosophie: Zweites internationales Kolloquium über Gregor von Nyssa,* ed. Heinrich Dörrie, Margarete Allenburger, and Uta Schramm. Leiden: Brill, 1976.

———. "Logic and the Application of Names to God." In *El 'Contra Eunomium I' en la Produccion Literaria de Gregorio de Nisa,* VI Coloquio Internacional sobre Gregorio de Nisa. Pamplona: Ediciones Universidad de Navarra, 1988.

Steinbock, A. "Saturated Intentionality." In *Rereading Merleau-Ponty: Essays Across the Continental-Analytic Divide,* ed. L. Hass and D. Olkowski. Amherst, N.Y.: Humanities Press, 1995.

Svenungsson, Jayne. "God's Return: A Study of the Concept of God in Postmodern Philosophy (Jacques Derrida and Jean-Luc Marion)." Ph.D. diss., Lunds Universitet, 2002.

Sweeny, Leo. "Gregory of Nyssa on God as Infinite Being." In *Divine Infinity in Greek and Medieval Thought.* New York: Peter Lang, 1992.

———. "Deconstruction and Neoplatonism: Jacques Derrida and Dionysius the Areopagite." In *Neoplatonism and Contemporary Thought,* ed. R. Baine Harris. Albany: SUNY Press, 2002.

Tanner, Kathryn. "Theology at the Limits of Phenomenology." In *Counter-Experiences: Reading Jean-Luc Marion.* Notre Dame, Ind.: Notre Dame University Press, 2007.

Tavard, George H. *The Inner Life: Foundations of Christian Mysticism.* New York: Paulist Press, 1976.

Taylor, Mark C. *Erring: A Postmodern A/Theology.* Chicago: University of Chicago Press, 1984.

———. *Altarity.* Chicago: University of Chicago Press, 1987.

———. *nOts.* Chicago: University of Chicago Press, 1993.

———. "nO nOt nO." In *Derrida and Negative Theology*, ed. Robert Scharlemann. Charlottesville: University Press of Virginia, 1992.

Turner, Denys. *The Darkness of God: Negativity in Christian Mysticism.* Cambridge: Cambridge University Press, 1995.

———. "Atheism, Apophaticism and 'Différance.'" In *Theology and Conversation: Towards a Relational Theology.* Leuven: Leuven University Press, 2003.

Vase Frandsen, Henrik. "Distance as Abundance: The Thought of Jean-Luc Marion." *Svensk Teologisk Kvartalskrift* 79.4 (2003): 177–86.

Verghese, T. P. "Diastema and Diastasis in Gregory of Nyssa." In *Gregor von Nyssa und die Philosophie: Zweites internationales Kolloquium über Gregor von Nyssa*, ed. Heinrich Dörrie, Margarete Allenburger, and Uta Schramm. Leiden: Brill, 1976.

Vogel, Arthur A. "Reduction and Givenness: Investigations of Husserl, Heidegger, and Phenomenology." *Anglican Theological Review* 82.4 (2000).

Völker, W. *Gregor von Nyssa als Mystiker.* Wiesbaden: F. Steiner, 1955.

———. *Kontemplation und Ekstase bei ps.-Dionysius Areopagita.* Wiesbaden: F. Steiner, 1958.

Vries, Hent de. *Philosophy and the Turn to Religion.* Baltimore, Md.: Johns Hopkins University Press, 1999.

———. "The Theology of the Sign and the Sign of Theology: The Apophatics of Deconstruction." In *Flight of the Gods: Philosophical Perspectives on Negative Theology.* New York: Fordham, 2000.

Ward, Graham. "Between Postmodernism and Postmodernity: The Theology of Jean-Luc Marion." In *Postmodernity, Sociology and Religion*, ed. Kieran Flanagan. New York: St. Martin's Press, 1996.

———. "The Theological Project of Jean-Luc Marion." In *Post-Secular Philosophy: Between Philosophy and Theology*, ed. Phillip Blond. London: Routledge, 1998.

Ware, Owen. "Rudolph Otto's Idea of the Holy: A Reappraisal." *Heythrop Journal* 48 (2007): 48–60.

Weiswurm, A. A. *The Nature of Human Knowledge according to Gregory of Nyssa.* Washington, D.C.: Catholic University Press, 1952.

Welten, Ruud. "Saturation and Disappointment: Marion according to Husserl." *Bijdragen* 65.1 (2004).

Westphal, Merold. *Overcoming Onto-Theology: Towards a Postmodern Christian Faith.* New York: Fordham University Press, 2001.

———. "The Importance of Overcoming Metaphysics for the Life of Faith." *Modern Theology* 23 (2007): 253–78.

———. "Vision and Voice: Phenomenology and Theology in the Work of Jean-Luc Marion." *International Journal for Philosophy of Religion* 60.1 (2006): 117–37.

Williams, J. P. *Denying Divinity: Apophasis in the Patristic Christian and Soto Zen Buddhist Traditions.* Oxford: Oxford University Press, 2000.

Williams, Rowan. *The Wound of Knowledge: Christian Spirituality from the New Testament to Saint John of the Cross.* Cambridge, Mass.: Cowley Publications, 1979.

Yannaras, C. *De l'absence et de l'inconnaissance de Dieu d'après les écrits aréopagites et Martin Heidegger.* Paris: Cerf, 1971.

Young, Frances. "The God of the Greeks and the Nature of Religious Language." In *Early Christian Literature and the Classical Intellectual Tradition,* ed. W. R. Schoedel and R. L. Wilken. Paris: Editions Beauschesne, 1979.

Zhang, Ellen Y. "Icon without Logos, Theology without Ontology." *Cross Currents* 43.2 (1993).

Ziarek, Krzysztof. "The Language of Praise: Levinas and Marion." *Religion and Literature* 22.2–3 (1990).

INDEX

Tamsin Jones is Director of Undergraduate Studies and Lecturer on Religion for the Committee on the Study of Religion at Harvard University.

Printed and bound by CPI Group (UK) Ltd, Croydon, CR0 4YY

13/04/2025

14656550-0001